Conversations with Boulez: Thoughts on Conducting

Pierre Boulez at seventy, at the time of his appointment as principal guest conductor of the Chicago Symphony Orchestra in April 1995. *Photo by Cheri Eisenberg, courtesy the Chicago Symphony Orchestra.*

Conversations with Boulez
Thoughts on Conducting

by
JEAN VERMEIL

Translated from the French by
Camille Naish

AMADEUS PRESS
Reinhard G. Pauly, General Editor
Portland, Oregon

"Body Language" reprinted by permission; © 1993 Paul Griffiths.
Originally in *The New Yorker*.

Selection of Programs Conducted by Boulez and Discography compiled
by Paul Griffiths; © 1996 Paul Griffiths.

Amadeus Press is grateful to Pierre Boulez for providing corrections to
the original French edition, to Astrid Schirmer of IRCAM for her generous assistance, to Marc-Olivier Dupin of the Conservatoire National
Supérieur in Paris for contributing the foreword, and to Paul Griffiths for
compiling the list of concerts and the discography for this edition.

Whenever possible, works originally written in English are quoted
from the original; however, when the original could not be located, a
retranslation into English is provided.

Photographs courtesy Peter Hastings, Cleveland, Ohio; Cheri Eisenberg,
Chicago Symphony Orchestra; the New York Philharmonic; and the
BBC Symphony Orchestra.

Printed in Singapore

AMADEUS PRESS
The Haseltine Building
133 S.W. Second Avenue, Suite 450
Portland, Oregon 97204, U.S.A.

Library of Congress Cataloging-in-Publication Data

Boulez, Pierre, 1925–
    [Conversations de Pierre Boulez sur la direction d'orchestre avec
Jean Vermeil. English]
    Conversations with Boulez : thoughts on conducting / by Jean
Vermeil; translated from the French by Camille Naish.
        p.   cm.
    Translation of: Conversations de Pierre Boulez sur la direction
d'orchestre avec Jean Vermeil.
    "Selection of concerts conducted by Boulez": p.
    Discography: p.
    Includes index.
    ISBN 1-57467-007-7
    1. Conducting. 2. Boulez, Pierre, 1925–   —Interviews. 3.
Conductors (Music)—France—Interviews. I. Vermeil, Jean. II. Title
ML458.B6813   1996
784.2′145—dc20   95-20952
                                                            CIP
                                                            MN

Contents

Contents

Body Language
137
by Paul Griffiths

Acknowledgments

Liduine and Hans Citroen, The Hague; Pr. Kostios, Athens; Jean-Jacques Chantreuil, Institut National de l'Audiovisuel, Paris; Jacqueline Gachet, Jean-Michel Court, University of Toulouse-Le-Mirail, Toulouse; Dr. Alden Dittmann, Ibero-Amerikanisches Institut Preussischer Kulturbesitz, Berlin; Lukas Handschin, Paul Sacher Foundation, Basel; José Bergher, Venezuelan Symphony Orchestra, Caracas; Service de Documentation du Commissariat Général du Plan, Paris; Charles Vial, *Le Monde*, Paris; Henri Zuber, Archives Diplomatiques, Paris; Pascal Even, Archives Diplomatiques, Nantes; Elizabeth Williams, Nicola Gould, BBC Symphony Orchestra, London; Monique Herzog, Isabelle Masset, Opéra du Rhin, Strasbourg; Carole Roset-Claridge, European Broadcasting Union, Geneva; Martin Stroheker, Ulm; Françoise Granges, Pierre Chalve, Bibliothèque Nationale, Paris; Christophe Huss, Béatrice Fischer, *Répertoire* Magazine, Paris; Detlef Kieffer, Studio 111, Strasbourg; Erika Kralik, Renaud-Barrault Company, Paris; Odile Roux, Orchestre National de France, Paris; Brigitte Geais, Orchestre Philharmonique de Radio France, Paris; Elfie Wittwer, Musica Viva, Bavarian Radio, Munich; Josef Häusler, Southwest German Radio, Baden-Baden; Truus de Leur, Marius Flothuis, Concertgebouw Orchestra, Amsterdam; Gary Hanson, The Cleveland Orchestra; Dr. Marion Kazemi, Archives of the Max Planck Gesellschaft, Berlin; Bibliothèque Jean Vilar, Avignon; Hervé Péjaudier, Paris; Marie-Hélène Arbour, IRCAM (Institute for Research and Coordination in Acoustics and Music), Paris; Martine Lévy, Nicolas Dagan, Ensemble InterContemporain, Paris; Catherine Laulhère, Jacques-François Marchandise, Éditions Plume, Paris; and, of course, Astrid and Nancy.

Foreword

Pierre Boulez, who was a student at the Conservatoire, has contributed in many ways to the development of the institution, notably by creating the concept of the Cité de la Musique and by occasionally conducting the student orchestras.

Working with Boulez is always a privilege, for he has much to give his students. Indeed, analyses of techniques of composing or conducting can lead an artist to higher levels of understanding. For the conductor, such understanding may engender an economy of means, of gesture, which will ultimately become second nature.

In the realm of composition, Boulez's lectures given at the Collège de France (published as *Jalons: Dix ans d'enseignement au Collège de France, 1979–1988*) are both audacious and lucid descriptions of the compositional process. The present book, based on informal interviews, approaches conducting more casually. Yet we learn much about many aspects of the conductor's work, from planning a program to rehearsing and to the actual concert performance.

Reading these observations one comes away with the feeling that, for Boulez, orchestral conducting is above all a kind of language ("before I conducted fluently . . . ") that facilitates artistic expression, especially for contemporary music. Here the relationship between conducting and composition is striking, and Boulez's remarks can lead to a greater understanding and awareness of both crafts. Paradoxically, the views of a self-taught conductor prove to be rich in insights for conducting students and for all who are fascinated by Boulez.

Marc-Olivier Dupin
Director, Conservatoire National Supérieur de
Musique et de Danse de Paris
March 1995

For Jean Batigne: "To the Czar!"

I raced up the Strasbourg autoroute in my ramshackle military jalopy and entered the discreet luxury of Baden-Baden, turning off at the old station and climbing past the network of villas until I reached the forest with its autumnal hues. Before me loomed the large fake renaissance house. I was early; I was nervous. One last time I sorted my index cards, representing three months' work, into a probable order. Lace curtains fluttered beneath the trees. The German police were already there, and the officer, too young for his ugly green kepi, courteously reassured himself that my canvas-covered truck was merely incongruous in this isolated fringe of wood. "I've come to see the composer." This formula put to rest the unspoken questions that exceeded his authority.

At three o'clock I rang the bell by the long industrial-type railings. No reply. Tucked beneath my arm were the thousand or so pages of *Goethe's Conversations with Eckermann*, an instruction manual, product of the inflated nerve of a minor writer who nonetheless managed to monopolize the attention of the genius in that century of geniuses. It was my secret medicine too: cure one ill with another. At least he was faithful in his reports, the preface was assuring me, when suddenly a luxurious car interrupted my reading. An elegant sexagenarian opened the gate, showing no surprise at my presence. "Isn't he there?" he inquired in his Rhine accent. He puffed himself up: "I'm Maestro Boulez's Master Gardener." No sign of interest in who I was, but perhaps he knew all along. At the end of the driveway he rang the bell at the top of the front steps. No reply, of course. He pointed to the steps and I sat down, plunging back into my reading. The gardener took a rake from behind a tree trunk and gave a finishing touch to the impeccable expanse of gravel. He disappeared. I heard a rustling from next door, and then the gardener re-

13

appeared through a hole in the railings: even greatness has its little tricks. And perhaps his domain is not subject to the limits placed on us, since he surpasses us with his flowers, as the other surpasses us with his music. We walked around the sandstone footing but saw no one upstairs in the checkered kitchen and no one downstairs in the bachelor's dwelling, which was stuffed with cookbooks. The German car with its Parisian license number 75 was there. "Then they've gone off for a walk."

He spoke in the dialect of Baden-Baden, and I dared to reply in the same patois, the Alsatian that had once been forbidden us. My speech was uneven but had the quick, stabbing rhythm of old women watching over a deathbed. The gardener stopped in midsentence, staring at me, his blue eyes meeting mine. His professional glance confirmed that I was not poisonous. Pierre Boulez had summed me up with the same quick, powerful stare at IRCAM (Institute for Research and Coordination in Acoustics and Music) when he said yes. And so the gardener began to talk; he had to talk, the Master Gardener. We were destined to meet. He talked about the musician, about the trees he'd had planted, the trees he admired every day. I contemplated their leaves, so delicate against the disturbing backdrop of pine. Goethe, the waiting, this intensity. The wheel turns, and here I was in the perfect garden of the *Elective Affinities*, where beauty permits everything, where the son of the legitimate marriage will look just like the lover. The accented voice recounted the visits they received here, the work they did, the pleasures of going shopping. I heard pathetic little secrets, men's secrets; I heard about happiness in Germany—

I left a page from a notebook with a note that I'd return next day. Next day Pierre Boulez was there. No apologies, the trees had said it all. He ushered me through the house, through the rooms he'd gradually won over to his style, in much the same way as the map of France is slowly filled out in school books. Everything was modern, in a style that was fashionable some fifteen years before. I paid little attention to Miró and Kandinsky, preferring the geometric style of the Bauhaus artist Joseph Albers. This pleased Boulez. The sun was shining so we went out to the terrace. I set up the tape recorder, took out my index cards. We did a voice test. Boulez glanced at the beginning of the tape and started to speak as soon as the cue mark appeared. It all went very quickly, and even his introductory tirade—the "Here's what I would like to say" coughed up by every interviewee—was concise. The agreement that we both had to respect was that we would discuss only conducting, not composing, except when the one impinged upon the other, as in the case of Mahler, Maderna, or Boulez himself. I was beginning a book; Boulez was turning over a page. Certainly his creativity had regained the upper hand, but he was still tempted to suppress and, if we read between the lines, was still waiting to exorcise an American malaise. We would avoid the legendary ten years spent in glorious and barren exile, far from France and musical composition. Others had already dealt with that. Boulez's compositions from that time, although not numerous, count among the most serious, solid, or bewitching of his works: *Éclat/Multiples, Domaines, Livre pour cordes, cummings ist der Dichter, . . . explosante-fixe . . .* , and *Rituel in memoriam Maderna*.

My index cards filed past us. I thought of what had been said already but perhaps had changed; I asked new questions, set him traps. Boulez replied amiably, rarely taking advantage of the numerous moments when he could have reduced me to confusion. Only when I hammered away at the small number of works he conducts by young composers did we engage in an impassioned altercation. The facts are harsh. That evening, he showed me to my truck in his elegant shoes, holding aloft an enormous umbrella as the rain came sheeting down.

But why should I be tactful, when he himself lashed out so strongly against those who mistook the postwar period for an artistic truce? His courtiers can deal in tact. For a few hours I was the unruly nephew in this comfortable interior, resuscitating the major battles fought by Boulez who, in 1958, when he was my age, wrote in one of his elegant programs:

> It has come to my knowledge [that a composer] violently criticized the concerts given by the Domaine Musical, declaring that only duchesses, snobs, and people from Saint-Germain-des-Prés enjoy going to them. . . . Then he added that he would be delighted if these concerts were banned by the Paris police. . . . Since he should be named, the composer in question is André Jolivet. . . . Even if the particular kindness of this uninteresting small potato brings us to the benevolent attention of police headquarters at least a hundred times, we shall never submit him to the insult of serving the listening pleasures of duchesses, etc., etc.; rather, because of our proper deference for this pale and empty vegetable, we shall preserve his virtue.

Boulez and I talked on the balcony, before the wind whistling through the trees drove us inside. Beneath the white roof we heard only a distant rustling sound, doubtless caused by branches, or possibly the gardener. The telephone would ring, and Boulez would disappear. A few snatches of conversation would filter through the intervening pane of glass: a concert in Japan, the uncertain future of the Bastille Opera House, a new musical director. These splinters of Parisian intrigue seemed quite absurd amid the scent of waxed parquet floors and the round, appliquéd forms of German-American design. Boulez would return in a cheerful mood, affectionately associating me with his distant conversations as if I must have listened to them. "The multipurpose hall must be kept— that's important, isn't it?" Or "Enough of all these journalists and failed composers, we need a good administrator at the ministry!" And the multi-purpose hall was kept, and an administrator joined the ministry.

Everything seems simple with Boulez. I questioned him at length about his lucidity, his essential Frenchness, his sophistication, and his false objectivity, but I did not expect to fall victim to these qualities myself. When Boulez talks to you, he's all voice, hands, mouth, eyes, and body, like anyone else, of course, except that these elements—parameters—combine so subtly that the absence of any one of them alters the impression of the whole. Listening to the tape afterward I fully expected to lose his gestures and his gaze, but would at least still have the characteristic intonations and rhythm of his speech. But when I transcribed the spoken text onto paper, I found I had lost everything, or almost everything. Boulez speaks in an impoverished language, as is the privilege of powerful thinkers—he uses words like *thing* and *do* very often and incessantly needs to terminate a phrase with adverbs such as *obviously* or *naturally*. He repeats emphatic words but without offering them further support. His voice, on the contrary, gets thinner, becomes shrill, slows down slightly. His French is full of foreign words picked up in the Babel of his international rehearsals: words such as *conduire* (to drive) instead of *diriger* (to conduct), for example; and neologisms, like *détrimental*; and titles of works—other people's precious works—as well as grammatical constructions that are risky but expressive. These are in quotation marks or italic in the text. (In translation, "c'est qu'il y a toujours un *feedback* entre direction et composition" becomes "there's always some *feedback* between conducting and composing.")

Pierre Boulez pursues a rhythm, and the words have to adapt to it. His sentences move forward in repeated segments, each new segment canceling the previous one, as in popular ritornellos, biblical litanies, or the prosody of Thomas Bernhard. Perhaps the German soil on which we conversed—the soil raked by the gardener—inspired our phrases with the heavy, *gemütlich* mechanisms of the language of those parts. Certain syntactic structures recall the popular speech of Belgium or Switzerland, countries close to Germany.

I have tried to render as faithfully as possible this vocal style that so closely parallels the compositional style of *Éclat* or *Répons*. I removed wasted words and afterthoughts that led nowhere, but retained significant self-corrections like "I, that is, we decided. . . ." The litanies have been preserved just as I heard them, with no apologies for the obsession with repetition that we have inherited from Bossuet. Whenever a word was inappropriate and Boulez skipped over it—as one tries to forget wrong notes when sightreading a score—I replaced it with the most Boulezian word possible: a neutral word, fluid but still fleshy, with no exotic vowels or Greco-intellectual brutality.

The articulation of a sentence best renders its rhythm, better than the choice or repetition of a word. My rendering in the original French edition follows the rhythm of Boulez's breathing, an old-fashioned method that does not debone a sentence as is the habit now. For example, Boulez has a highly individual way of whispering, almost with embarrassment, words he could pronounce more forcefully—*very, very, very*—usually repeating them. One should really take the time—as in Saint Augustine's day—to read these conversations aloud, to savor their sensual elements.

Was this process important? I discovered its richness and its necessity as I transcribed, without having any previous opinion on the matter. A banal, conventional transcription would have stifled all the emotional content, betraying Boulez's speech. One might as well betray it in style. After all, Henry Miller's French manuscripts have been published with a scrupulous reproduction of his amazing mixture of normal French expressions, literary turns of phrase, anglicisms, and mad creations of his own. I therefore reaffirm the subjective nature of this transcription, which is in no way scientific but adopts a translator's intuitive rigor, flirting with the impossible to convey the spirit of a language or of a particular world within that language.

Readers may well find literary echoes in these conversations. One thinks of Céline, Thomas Bernhard, Marguerite Duras, or Peter Handke, all of them writers or dramatists. I was also greatly helped by Jean Tardieu's play *Conversation-sinfonietta*. Musicians will recall the strange transcriptions of *parlar-cantando*, of melodrama, of *Sprechgesang*. The system of speech notation developed by Georges Aperghis also proved most helpful. This attempt to impose one authorship upon another, to make music with words, exposes me to all manner of criticisms. I shall be happy if, like Eckermann, I have at least been sufficiently mediocre not to have betrayed Boulez. "At least he was faithful to Goethe in his accounts of their conversations."

The notes that complete the text compensate in their thoroughness for my occasional liberties. Everything I state in them has been checked, nor have I stated anything I was unable to verify. I have corrected certain erroneous statements that appear in the best books on Boulez. The journalistic part of my inquiry led me to Caracas; the scholarly part, to consult the scores he "reworked." I welcome any further information that could enrich or improve this work. (Corrections by Boulez have been incorporated into the English edition of this volume.) Even the notes, however, could not remain entirely neutral. In them I complete what Boulez did not say, either for want of time or from a wish to conform to his own legend. In them I add what I already knew but had omitted from the conversations, so that he would make the conventional response. The notes also contain everything I discovered subsequently, in the course of my systematic verifications, and this information provides retrospective responses—positive or negative—to statements made by Boulez. Thus text and notes form a highly fugal dialogue, with themes passing from one staff to another.

On the penultimate afternoon in Baden-Baden, the wind dropped. The sky was still overcast. I missed the sounds that had cheered me as I confronted the composer, the creaking of branches mixed with the slightly shrill noise of the gardener's rake. The tape recorder had never managed to pick up these signs of recognition, of a complicity already grown old. Boulez answered my unspoken question: "The gardener's not well; he's had to stay in his room. He does too much." He, too, was thinking of him—of his contemporary.

Next day, Jean Batigne came to join us with his young, pretty wife. In the course of the conversation with "Pierre," the founder of the Strasbourg Percussion Group recalled their signal of mutual recognition, "To the Czar!" The wind did not bring me ours, the gardener's and mine; the branches of the pine trees remained obstinately still, mute debris gathered by giant rakes. I listened to a conversation between the old friends, the kind of conversation that leaves you feeling excluded. But I discovered a different Boulez, a Boulez asking about the health of a musician in the Strasbourg orchestra, about another player's children, a Boulez who knew everyone by name and reacted to each person's news with sadness or with joy, showing all the concern of a pastor for his flock. To bring me back into the circle he even murmured, "I'm worried about the gardener; he isn't getting better." And for my benefit he reviewed the more familiar topics: problems with the new Opéra orchestra (this was before the Barenboim affair), a series of individual cases to be treated with great care. He would, he guaranteed, avoid a crisis.

I was the first to leave. Standing alone on the front steps, his cheeks flushed with friendship, Boulez waved until my truck disappeared. Behind him, the trees still called to me, "Don't forget!"

That very evening, the gardener died.

Jean Vermeil
Baden-Baden, September 1988
Strasbourg, July 1989

A Journey

BOULEZ: Conducting now occupies a minimal position in my work. It has followed a bell curve. It started as an extremely minor activity, reached a level of such intensity that at one time it interfered with all my other work, and now has fallen back to its initial low level.

The immediate explanation for this curve is that conducting used to be a vital necessity: I needed to earn a living, and I needed to promote organizations that didn't receive much general support at first. And then there was a secondary need—getting to know the instrumental milieu that had never been a part of my conservatory education.

These two reasons are intimately linked, but the former was the stronger, the one that asserted itself first. In fact I began my career in 1945–46 by playing incidental music for the Jean-Louis Barrault Company, simply to earn a living. I started one day by playing the Ondes Martenot for Barrault.[1] Then I got into conducting when the pantomime of *Les enfants du paradis* went on tour. Joseph Kosma was the conductor, but he didn't want to go on tour so I took his place.[2] By 1947 they were giving me things to conduct, just little things at first. I took it on gradually. Playing incidental music put me in touch with a completely different expressive medium—the theater—with very distinguished actors, and with the directors of one of the most important companies of that time.

It taught me certain professional skills. Above all it led to the creation of the Domaine Musical, a group founded to perform contemporary music and some from the preceding era that hadn't yet been played in

---

These conversations between Pierre Boulez and Jean Vermeil took place during 1988. They are here translated into English for the first time.

Paris.[3] At the Domaine I was immediately faced with budgetary problems—performance problems, too, because those very first performances, those scores that no one knew, had to be rehearsed. There weren't too many people in France capable of conducting them, once Desormière had disappeared from public life for health reasons. Rosbaud and Scherchen were still active in Germany, and there were a few younger ones. But I didn't have enough money at my disposal to invite Rosbaud and Scherchen every time. I invited Scherchen once or twice, and Bour too.[4]

So then I began to think, "Why not do it myself? After all, the players are all pals of mine. I know them well, and I was the one who hired them to play incidental music for Barrault." They were willing to give up their time for the project. So we formed a group, a very small group but an extremely homogeneous one. I conducted as the need arose, and that's really how I got started. I didn't begin conducting the Domaine Musical myself until around 1954–55 because I wasn't sure I should do it.[5] I had so many other things to do—things like setting up music stands, collecting tickets and checks. In fact I did just about everything in that outfit!

I started out gradually, occasionally conducting one or two works in a concert, then steadily increasing the load. I told myself that those few persons I did engage—not the big names, but the others—really weren't any better at it than I was, all things considered.[6]

VERMEIL: *You've admitted you were rather inept.*

Very inept. Exceedingly inept. I had no talent—I felt I had no talent for it at all. To tell you the truth, I never really aspired to become a conductor. But by the time I arrived here in Baden-Baden in 1958–59, replacing Rosbaud, who was ill, my ineptitude had slowly disappeared.[7] By that time I was thirty-three or thirty-four and not really a beginner anymore. Even so, I was far from certain I could carry out such tasks successfully. It was only at that juncture that I really flung myself seriously into conducting. I think I'd conducted a large orchestra for the first time only a short while before, in 1957.[8]

Without any previous instruction?

That's right, I was purely self taught. I do believe that it's possible to tell young would-be conductors why the various gestures are necessary, what functions they perform. But all that is useless unless they themselves conduct a group—any group, whatever group they can.

In the absence of training, did you at least have role models?

Oh yes, some. But role models are rather distant figures, all the same. I'd seen the three major conductors at work—major in the field of contemporary music, I mean—Desormière, Rosbaud, and Scherchen. Those were the three I particularly admired. But they weren't the only ones I'd seen. I'd mostly seen conductors of the standard repertoire. Among the great ones of the past—well, there was Furtwängler, and I also saw Kletzki, who's not of Furtwängler's stature, and the conductors who passed through Paris. But I can't say that this really taught me anything, because it all had to do with a repertoire I had no thought of actually conducting myself.

I don't include among them Ansermet, whose repertoire was basically quite limited. I never saw him conduct anything beyond Stravinsky or Frank Martin. Never any Schoenberg or Webern.

Your transition from being a contemporary militant to a major figure in orchestral institutions was pretty abrupt.

Yes, I was catapulted into large orchestras. The first opportunity came in 1957 when Scherchen wanted to conduct my *Visage nuptial*, which he'd included in a program of contemporary music in Cologne.[9] It was obvious he hadn't prepared it, that he wasn't ready for such a thing. But I had already been conducting the chorus for a week, and so they asked, "Would you like to conduct it?" I replied, "If Scherchen told you to ask me, then yes, I would. But it's a bit like taking a bath in boiling water." Indeed, it wasn't easy at all, because I had practically no experience in that area, and the score was far from simple. However, I got through it as best I could, though with no great glory. When I came here in 1958, to write *Poésie pour pouvoir*, I started conducting again, but only little by little. Strobel,[10] who was the Southwest German Radio's musical director, entrusted me with small orchestral groups. This was very sensible. I worked on chamber music, especially my own *Mallarmé* improvisations, Stockhausen's *Kontrapunkte*, and even Stravinsky's Symphonies of Wind Instruments, because this piece interested me. These were works I could have conducted at the Domaine Musical, where, as it happened, I'd just done Webern's Cantatas.

Then, during this process of advancement, fate struck its second blow, and Rosbaud fell ill. I really had to plunge in at that point. It's always the same story: Bernstein got his chance when Bruno Walter, I think it was, fell ill, or maybe it was somebody else. When someone's ill, there's no going back; it's beyond anyone's control, everything bows to necessity. The organizers can't be cautious anymore, and neither can you. It happened in 1959 at Donaueschingen, I remember clearly.[11] I did all the programs, since the Domaine Musical, my group, was also giving a concert there. Strobel said, "You'll have to conduct everything else," and I told him, "I'm going to have to, I can see." I got through it far better than the previous time, really. After all, two whole years had gone by!

It was at that point that *this* career, my career in conducting, really began—rather against my will, actually. I don't mean that I had to force myself, but I felt pushed into it. I see it very clearly now, whenever the same situation crops up—whenever some young person shows a certain talent, he's immediately absorbed by the market. There aren't too many of them around, and promoters are always waiting to pounce. Sometimes it works out, as was indeed the case with me, but it may just as easily not work out. Three or four years later people realize it was a mistake, that the initial promise hasn't been fulfilled. I was pushed ahead that way, but I might have fallen flat on my face a few years later.

At that point I really became a sort of ersatz Rosbaud—for example, at the Festival of Aix, that July, as soon as Rosbaud knew he was going to have an operation.[12] He was very, very nice at the start of my career. I was lucky enough to meet two or three conductors—including, much later, George Szell—who were probably more perspicacious even than I was in regard to my work. After Rosbaud's illness took hold, I took his place more often. On his death in 1962, I was invited to conduct everywhere, especially by the Concertgebouw.[13] The enterprising artistic director of the Residencie Orchestra of The Hague had previously called upon my services, it's true, but he still envisaged only a small number of concerts, to expose his orchestra to current works.[14] But when I took over from Rosbaud at the Concertgebouw, I had, of course, to perform some classical works. You can't plan a subscription series that consists entirely of contemporary premieres. So it was then that I began getting more and more involved with the standard repertoire.

After that, my path was very simple. I did Berg's *Wozzeck* in Paris, at the request of Georges Auric.[15] *Wozzeck* led to Bayreuth and my collaboration with Wieland Wagner.[16] Besides that I hopped across the English Channel and went to London. Sir William Glock had heard of me, and asked me to come.[17] We got on extremely well right away. I remained perfectly in sync with the BBC Symphony Orchestra—I went to London *often*. And London, like Amsterdam, is a springboard for the United States. George Szell had heard about me in Amsterdam, where he conducted regularly, and he was responsible for originally bringing me to Cleveland. I did several seasons there as guest conductor.[18] In fact, Szell asked me to become their principal guest conductor, presumably with a view to my succeeding him.[19] At this point, however, I received the offer from New York.[20] And then the record companies chipped in, since record companies are mainly based in London and New York.

So that's how it all came about. One thing led to another without my having to lift a finger—except to conduct, of course.[21]

This career as a conductor was rather like a blank space I began filling in. People knew what I would choose, knew perfectly well I would include things in my programs that many other conductors wouldn't do. I operated not so much through compromise as by establishing a different ratio between the standard repertoire and more adventurous programs. If you consider every concert season I did, contemporary music was either the focal point of our activity or one of its major elements. I always held firmly to that policy, whatever the polemics, resistance, or outright hostility I encountered because of it. I think on that I never yielded.

You're expunging your famous "strike" from this hagiography.

I could see that nothing in particular was happening in France, and that the future was blocked up like a sink. Along with Baisini at the Ministry of Culture, I'd thought a lot about the situation of music in France, at the request of Gaëtan Picon. When Malraux abandoned his project, which was really an important one, it seemed to me that the situation was hopeless. Everything had collapsed into conventionality; there was no hope of reform.[22] At Jean Vilar's request I did nonetheless take part in an attempt to reform the Paris Opéra in 1967.[23] The attempt was aborted in May 1968.

Even here in Baden-Baden, a plan sponsored by the Max Planck Gesellschaft to set up an institute for musical research had collapsed earlier.[24] Neither France nor Germany was offering me much financial help, so in 1968 I decided to settle in London, then the following year in New York. I said farewell to France with no intention of coming back. I turned to England and the United States because, especially at that time, that was where one found the highest conceivable degree of professionalism—there and in Germany, with the Berlin Philharmonic.

Then you owe "this" career, the conducting, to your struggles with Landowski?

It wasn't due to Landowski, not at all. As I said already, I'd begun conducting seriously around 1957–58, long before this storm arose. And I'd immediately come across the problem, because even back then one had to think hard about the situation. I'd conducted *Wozzeck* twice at the Opéra, and an evening of ballets. I was communicating with Holland and Germany of course, and I was starting to be in touch with England too. Thus I had every reason to know that paradoxically the situation was easier to resolve in France than in other countries, because the institutions in

France were much weaker—many of them in fact were helplessly adrift. Reforms were desperately needed.

What exasperated me in 1966 wasn't so much Landowski himself—he's no more than a mediocre figure.[25] What infuriated me was that all hope of reform had been thwarted for many years to come. I remember that when the Orchestre de Paris was founded, the press clippings were full of things like "Wow! The Berlin Philharmonic had better look to its laurels. This is the most prestigious orchestra now."[26] It was pure stupidity in lieu of reform—the path that seemed the simplest was in reality the least productive.[27]

"People knew what I would choose, knew perfectly well I would include things in my programs that many other conductors wouldn't do."

Boulez conducting the New York Philharmonic, where he was music director from 1971 to 1977. Photo courtesy New York Philharmonic.

It wasn't until Barenboim arrived and devoted a lot of time to the new orchestra that it acquired a different image. What Barenboim and I managed to accomplish together—a blend of contemporary and classical music—all came about despite the institutions, rather than because of them. All these programs and exchanges saw the light of day only because Barenboim and I were personal friends.[28]

It's perfectly apparent that changes were always in the wind, and these changes eventually came about. Didn't Gilbert Amy, deservedly, get Radio France's New Philharmonic Orchestra to agree to become something I'd proposed back in 1966: an orchestra he describes as having "variable geometry"?[29] In other words, an orchestra that can be split up and turned into a suppler and more flexible body, one that is more interesting for the musicians. It isn't always easy to manage, but orchestral reform could have been explored sooner, and things arranged so that chamber music was included, contemporary music performed correctly, and classical music studied properly.

I had also recommended that the Paris Opéra orchestra give concerts, and that symphony orchestras include opera in their repertoire. Since then, Barenboim has done his Mozart series with the Orchestre de Paris.[30] Then when Liebermann came, the Opéra gave a series of concerts. All that was foreseeable. There's even a document to prove that I foresaw it—the beginning of my discussion with Biasini, published in the *Journal de l'Artiste Musicien*, the official newsletter of the musicians' union in Paris, of which I was the honorary president.[31]

If due thought had been given to these matters, they could have begun reforming everything, and in a big way. There would have been three poles of activity in Paris: an orchestra for the city, an orchestra for the state, and an orchestra for the radio. That would have been ample.

What strikes me is that all these ideas were in fact realized, but later. Michel Guy actually carried them out by founding first the Ensemble InterContemporain, then IRCAM.[32] That created some momentum. Initially, the people we asked to patronize our concerts—even those we gave at the Théâtre de la Ville—did not have much faith in them. Contemporary music had fallen completely out of favor by then because it had never been in the hands of true professionals.

You wanted to be the Trojan horse of modernity in the stronghold of tradition. Didn't you end up getting nabbed by the establishment?

Oh no! I never let myself get nabbed. In the first place, I had already begun thinking about IRCAM in 1971, when my career in conducting was at its height.[33] At that time I had London and Cleveland and I was just starting in New York, where they already wanted to extend my contract for three additional seasons—and that's a lot. For a whole year Pompidou had been suggesting that I return to France, and was talking about a cultural center there. I drafted my first proposal during a Cleveland Orchestra tour, and sent it to him. So you can see, I was determined not to let myself be swamped by my conducting. In June 1972 the first plans were discussed. That tells you that even then I wasn't expecting to be still in New York in 1977.

All that sounds very organized, but what happens is that things just occur one after another. When Pompidou sent me that signal, I realized he was serious and that I wasn't going to continue conducting for very long. That's why I gradually gave it up. I extended only one contract—the one with the BBC—and that only by one year, until 1975. I didn't want three occupations at once. In 1977 it was all over in New York.

In 1976, right after a concert that had been announced as "Boulez's first act of reconciliation with a French orchestra"—the Orchestre de Paris in fact—a popular radio station managed to evince this confidential pronouncement, which is worthy of an athlete after a hard match:

> While I was a conductor, I let myself get dragged along by a kind of machine, which took me much further than I originally expected. I began conducting simply as an attempt to establish ways of performing my own works, our own works, the works composed by my generation and the people who followed. And then in the end I realized that if those works were going to be included in programs, the world of music would have to be transformed completely, and that you can transform it only if you're at the head of a specific body with a more general task. At the same time, I realized that you really can't do it if you're out in the wilderness—if you want to bring about reforms like that, you absolutely have to be at the head of the best musical organizations, among the very top people in the profession. All those considerations eventually generate a machine that has all manner of consequences, and this machine dragged me a long way. When I saw how far it was taking me, I said, "No thank you,"—it's as simple as that. Because what truly interests me most, as an activity, is not disseminating musical ideas, but creating them.[34]

That's right, that's still exactly what I think. If you're not at the heart of some big institution, you haven't any power. Or else you can do only two or three contemporary programs per year, which doesn't exactly define the musical landscape. I've always got on very well while working for people who would never have engaged me if there were any dissent over our goals. Here in Baden-Baden I had a great intellectual rapport with Strobel. Then there was Sir William Glock, with whom I also got along very well. Glock was, and is—he's still alive, thank God—a remarkable man with very sound intentions. In New York, Carlos Moseley booked me on the basis of the programs I had done in Cleveland, which was certainly thanks to George Szell's influence.[35] In my case conducting did, indeed, take me a long way. But to do well at it you have to take over the whole field, and that presupposes a level of activity that, when I began, I had no idea would prove so time-consuming. Not only does one have the burden of being the artistic director, but one must also plan the programs, recruit the members of the orchestra, contact soloists, and deal with all the problems that crop up in rehearsals. Naturally there are people who attend to the details, and very well too, but all the important things, especially the recruiting, I did myself, just as I still do for the Ensemble InterContemporain.

What amuses me now is that in London, particularly, but in New York too, people say, "That was a splendid era," endowing my tenure with an imposing aura of activity. But when I think of all the battles it caused!

In his book about the BBC Symphony Orchestra, Nicholas Kenyon ends the chapter on Boulez by remarking, "It was a revolution, but it remained rather a minor one."[36]

That's true, because the economic conditions weren't very—I think that *golden ages*, no matter how much you put the words in italics, last only as long as the people who give rise to them, which means that a certain kind of activity can be bold and adventurous only if a felicitous meeting occurs, as it did between Glock and myself. Otherwise it won't work. Nothing's ever guaranteed, from that point of view.

In New York I was very attached not just to the contemporary music concerts, but also to the nonsubscription Rug Concerts we gave for young audiences. They were discontinued almost as soon as I left, because the auditorium was being remodeled. I'm sorry about that, but I do realize that my own image was partly involved in their success and that people came because they more or less agreed with my ideas and the way I carried them out.[37] Once I've left a place, someone else has to find other ways of doing things. Nothing's passed on or inherited. One is there, one performs for the prescribed time, and that's that. As I've always said, my aim was never to effect a revolution in social mores, but rather to provide a model of my thought, a model that other people could see in action.

The periods when you intervene are always highly intense. You act by means of master strokes. There will suddenly be a Boulez moment, a moment impregnated with Boulez, rather than a sprinkling of you here and there throughout a season.

Yes, because one can fix people's attention on a single point and thus arrange for programs to be thematically linked over a short space of time. If they're spread too far apart, people lose the thread, quite fatally, and the impression the programs make is much weaker. When I had to conduct in London and New York during the same period, I used to leave constant reminders of my presence, if only to keep in touch with the orchestra. You can't just be absent for five months, then come back. That's why I preferred stints of three or four weeks, at intervals of three or four weeks. My contract required me to be physically present for sixteen to eighteen weeks per year, divided either into five periods of three weeks or four periods of four weeks.[38] They were certainly periods of intense activity, and I had a great deal to do when I arrived. In particular, the events that focused on me I always did myself. I conducted all the Rug Concerts, for example, except for one or two.

There's an immersion effect. One could talk about a Boulez Period, the way one talks about the Christmas Sales or Earth Week.

Yes, there may be weeks when you concentrate on a single aspect of a question, then afterward you can detach from it. There are weeks of remission, as it were. (*Boulez laughs.*)

Do you stay faithful to the same few orchestras in order to plough the same furrow better?

Yes. Even now that I conduct only sporadically, I almost always go back to the same orchestras. I've been cured once and for all of continually trying to do the same program in different places. I was cured by my first U.S. tour, which was arranged by a business manager so that I could make contact with the rest of the country, outside Cleveland. It was my own choice, I'm not complaining—it did get me the job in New York, after all. But I conducted rather similar programs in Boston, New York, Los Angeles,[39] and Chicago—I'm thinking of Berg's Three Pieces for Orchestra, Opus 6, which I conducted in most of those cities. Just as I was really getting somewhere with an orchestra, or thought I was, I'd have to leave. I had to attack the same score all over again with another orchestra and correct all the same mistakes, because orchestras tend generally to make pretty similar mistakes. I decided this was a total waste of time. I would rather maintain the level an orchestra has reached than always have to start again from scratch. The pieces by Webern, for example— I managed to reach a high level there, and if I could do them again the following year with the same orchestra, I would gradually build a repertoire. That's what I accomplished in London, especially at the BBC,[40] where there were works we hardly needed to rehearse any more. That's what I still do with the Ensemble InterContemporain. We now have works we know so well they simply need refreshing, a spring cleaning you might say.

So in London I stick to the BBC Symphony Orchestra or the London Symphony Orchestra, in other words, two orchestras, no more. If I go to the States I conduct the Los Angeles Philharmonic, and the Chicago and Cleveland orchestras, and New York once in a while—which really isn't much. In Paris I conduct the Orchestre de Paris or the Ensemble almost exclusively now.

Wherever you go, you find musicians that you trained. What about the ones who came after—does their work show your influence as well?

Since I left New York in 1977—that's quite some time ago now—more than thirty percent of the orchestra has been replaced, thanks to the pyramid effect as members grow older. One can't really say there's a Boulez tradition, an imprint stamped upon them. I think you have to stay with an orchestra much longer than I did if you're going to set your mark on it. The Philadelphia Orchestra, for instance, spent fifteen or twenty years with Stokowski[41] and thirty with Ormandy.[42] That really does leave a mark.

Strangely enough, the New York Philharmonic is one of those orchestras where, on the whole, people stay only a short time. Bernstein stayed with them a bit longer than I did, but not much—eight or nine years, I think. Mehta stayed for ten years, and I was there for six—seven really, if you include the first year when I took over from Szell before I'd even been engaged.[43]

In most orchestras, a conductor generally lasts between eight and ten years, maximum. Especially now, orchestras hate having permanent conductors who monopolize them all the time. It's not just that they get restless: they have a legitimate reason. Orchestral seasons are much longer than they used to be, and musicians expect a certain amount of diversity—they want to get acquainted with different personalities. In the United States the season now lasts practically the whole year, from forty-six to forty-eight weeks. Previously, they lasted only about ten. The same conductors stayed on, and there were rarely any guest conductors because there were so few concerts. But today, the acceptable ratio is pretty much half permanent conductor, half guest conductors.

You do make commitments to Barenboim, and you've even conducted the insipid works of Giuseppe Sinopoli.[44] Are you fascinated by the big brains of the "classical music scene"?

I've got nothing against international monsters, big stars if you will. I'm not fascinated by them, but I don't exclude them either. On the contrary, if you give a concert of contemporary music with Pollini playing the piano, and with, oh, I don't know, Abbado, for example—it attracts more people, and the level of performance will always be higher than it ever would be with equally dedicated musicians who have less talent. There's a bit of reverse snobbery involved—sour grapes, perhaps—in certain contemporary milieus, when people say, *"They're* not for us." Quite the reverse: if people have far-ranging abilities, it's really *detrimental* not to use them.

You say that now, because you've achieved the same stature.

Yes. I wanted to achieve it, not so much in order to have the career I have had, as to rescue contemporary music from its wretchedness. When I was young I saw how badly it was treated. I particularly remember some performances of the Viennese school that were more appalling than anything you can imagine, given by very mediocre players—all dead now, God rest their souls.

Then you've been courting stature as well as quality.

Yes, but stature is achieved through quality. In fact, it's quality that interests me, not stature. And I realized that if contemporary music wasn't reaching a wide enough audience, this was to a great extent because the audience had reservations concerning the poor quality of performance, as well as problems with the music's expressive idioms. What the "spectators" appreciate—I see this very clearly each time I go on tour with the Ensemble—is when new scores are played with the great sense of reliability projected by our players. Under those circumstances people can venture a critical opinion of the works, because they feel they're being given a *document* of the highest quality. That's always been my main concern: to present the closest possible document of a score through literal interpretation, a literal reading that is at the same time transformed by familiarity and ease.

Stature brings star performers closer together—people in high places, too. You once said after a concert, "The president is in the audience, that's a good sign. Unfortunately it doesn't happen nearly enough."

Frankly, I'd rather the president be interested in music than in the French snail harvest! Music is already the poor cousin in our cultural life. Look in your daily newspaper and see what a small amount of print it allots to musical events. In the unacknowledged hierarchy that determines which art form gets the most lines, motion pictures are always first, followed by the theater. Then come music and painting, treated about equally, except that major exhibitions, retrospectives that is—I don't mean the shows of smaller galleries—often receive more space than any concert or announcement of a concert, because they're phenomena that last a long time.

When the president listens, that shows recognition for you as much as for your music.

I don't give a damn. I don't need a president of the republic or a prime minister to tell me how much recognition my work gets.[45] After all, if I travel to New York or Wellington, New Zealand, now that the Ensemble is beginning to be famous, it's not because the tastes of people over there have been influenced by the French president. No, what gets my attention is when the person in power sets a certain example and people say, "O.K., maybe that's interesting, we ought to see what it's like." For example, Pompidou was very interested in the plastic arts, and that helped develop the French public's taste in furniture. I'm convinced that the success of the Centre Georges Pompidou, quite apart from its own intrinsic qualities, had to do with its being launched by a president. After all, whether he wants to or not, an important figure like that becomes a role model. When someone of that caliber, somebody in that position, I should say, takes an interest in what one is doing—I don't mean in what *I* do, but in what musicians do, or even in what some theater is doing—then that becomes significant.

I'm not opposed to power in particular. I have distinct preferences with regard to certain politicians or political agendas, but that's my personal opinion and shouldn't enter into artistic considerations. What matters to me is when somebody powerful becomes interested in cultural events and acts on that interest. If the person comes to listen simply because it seems necessary, just as a politician might attend a football match in order to win votes, that's obviously not significant. But if a powerful figure can prove to be a "genuine," as they say in England, to have a genuine interest in contemporary music, then I'm all for it.

Conducting to Compose

It seems conducting has also helped you to compose.

(*Boulez takes a deep breath.*) I'm going to indict the education I went through, beginning with the way the composition classes were arranged. I found the people in charge of them extremely dull—there was nothing I could learn from them, after being in Messiaen's class. I didn't even go to the classes. Those composition classes—composition classes in general, since harmony was really what I'd done with Messiaen—were not in any way geared to instrumental development. And the instrumental classes had absolutely nothing to do with the composition classes. At the end of the year one simply produced a piece of work as best one could, under the most unsatisfactory conditions.

So I had to find other ways of learning what I hadn't been taught at the conservatory—on a small scale at first, with incidental theater music, as I said. That gave me direct and daily contact with instrumentalists. And I often had to arrange the music to suit the whims of the director—patch up something, rearrange it, reassign an instrument, or even rewrite the instrumentation.

That's where you learned to connect music with words.

I learned how to watch and follow speech, rather than singing. I learned how music can blend with the spoken word. That's also where I learned the technical aspects of theatrical productions, although the connections between music and the stage were rather rudimentary, except in one or two more developed cases, such as the *Oresteia* I did in 1955.[1] All that has its limits, and besides, I didn't carry the experience any further. There comes a moment when there's nothing more to learn; it's just routine. I left Barrault after being with his company ten years, which I think was quite enough.[2] In the meantime, in 1953 I'd started doing concerts with the Domaine Musical, where I had direct access to the contemporary repertoire and where I learned a great deal.[3]

From conducting your own works?

From conducting everybody's works, those by Pousseur, Stockhausen (I did the first Paris performance of *Zeitmasse*), Berio, Nono, everyone in my generation. My experience broadened very quickly. But I have to admit, I did learn a lot from conducting my own works. It all began when I started conducting *Le marteau sans maître* in 1956.[4] From then on I really conducted a lot of the Domaine concerts—not all, but most.

So the conductor influenced the composer, and vice versa?

There were what you might call informative effects. I gradually discovered what was possible and what was not. As I progressed, I learned how to put this technical improvement into writing things that were both more daring and more realistic. In my opinion, the more realistic one is, the bolder one can be.

Then it's a matter of your "musical yield."

Exactly. That's how I state the connection between boldness and being realistic. When one is realistic, one has the possibility of getting far better returns. Before I conducted much—before I conducted *fluently*— I tried to write things I wasn't sure about, with minimal returns. They were very difficult to play and gave rather unpredictable results. If, even after numerous rehearsals, one has only a thirty or forty percent chance of playing the work as written, it's better to write in a different manner and have a ninety percent—well, that's optimistic, let's say, between eighty and ninety percent—possibility of success. You learn to simplify as you go on. But one also has to guard against acting too cautiously, to guard against the temptation to simplify one's thought too much. You have to preserve that inner vision that leads you on, and worry later about whether it's feasible or not. So, in terms of actual performance, you either cast the problem differently, or go about it in such a way that the very elements of conducting become a springboard rather than a set of chains.[5]

Can you really say, as a composer, that you don't get caught in the trap of worrying about the effect?

Absolutely. A young composer said to me recently, "I would love to know how you conduct your own pieces, then I'd know how to do mine." I told him, "That's not the point, not as far as you're concerned, anyway. If I were you, I'd draw conclusions from conducting my own work and use them to write something else, and then draw further conclusions from that." What I appreciate, after practicing the various techniques of conducting and doing it rather well, what I appreciate is that there's always some *feedback* between conducting and composing. It sets up a circle, which has nothing to do with virtuosity. Obviously conducting has its virtuoso side, but in a positive sense. Virtuosity should serve the music's content rather than conceal it.

This dual role of composer and conductor has weighed on your mind—you've even seemed afraid of it. In your funeral orations for Scherchen, Rosbaud, and Maderna, and in speaking about Mahler, you raised the question of the balance each established between the two constituent activities, and the question of which activity destroyed the other. You suggested that with Scherchen and Rosbaud, the conductor killed off the composer; that Maderna perhaps went as far as one can in both directions.

It's a real problem, this question of balance. If there hadn't come a point when I decided to start refusing invitations and firmly saying no, it's obvious the composer in me would have been reduced to shreds, because as I told you, I could have conducted all year long if I'd wanted to. Even now, I still refuse more often than I accept.

And as for Gustav Mahler, you wrote that he did "too much conducting, not enough composing."

That's true of a certain period, when he accepted all engagements. I looked at his schedules in Vienna and saw that he really had only two or three months of calm in which to compose. The rest of the time he just worked on orchestration, which isn't really mechanical—some inventiveness is involved, but certainly not at the same level. He, too, got out of it after a while, but he didn't live much longer. He was trying to free himself from onerous activities.

One has to realize that as an administrator, whether operatic or orchestral, one is preoccupied by many things that tend to prove completely absorbing. Keeping the institution going requires such close attention from a conscientious person that even when not much is going on, one's mind is still taken up with it.

We're back to the Trojan horse. Through becoming a conductor, you found better ways to create.

I didn't think of it like that—

Without New York, there wouldn't have been IRCAM.

Of that I'm sure. But things don't always follow logically in real life. One seizes opportunities, and certain consequences result. When I accepted New York, I couldn't foresee that there would be IRCAM. Granted, I'd always thought it would be necessary to have an institute. And I certainly would not have been brought back to France with full administrative powers if I hadn't already demonstrated some administrative ability. Of course, there are people who find that kind of position enviable. But if I was given that to do it wasn't on account of my pretty face, as they say, but because I'd held some important jobs and done them in a relatively satisfactory way, I think. You don't entrust just anyone with a budget the size of IRCAM's—it gets very expensive. If the experiment fails, there are people who will be held accountable, you know. Yes, New York and London led to IRCAM, in a way, but only because my time there had proved I was competent.

Brahms was never willing or able to return to Hamburg, the hometown that had rejected him. Béjart's wanderings always keep him just outside France. Wasn't it hard for you to come back?

No. Things like that don't bother me.[6] I'm neither a Francophile nor a Francophobe—I don't much care about nationality.[7] If I'd been offered similar working conditions in Munich, Los Angeles, or heaven knows where, I would have gone to live there. But I'm not trying to shirk responsibility. When they asked me to go back to Paris to carry out what I'd shown I could do, I agreed. There was no reason not to.[8] I could have had a job in Freiburg, yes, but the conditions were less interesting than those offered to me in Paris. Freiburg is a small town, after all, with a studio that can't be enlarged beyond a certain point, and its budgetary resources can't be compared to those that support IRCAM. I wouldn't have chosen Germany simply to be in Germany; I wouldn't have leaned toward some smaller place because it was German. I simply chose the place with the most seductive working conditions, that's all.[9]

Choosing the Works

Before you even start to conduct, you have to choose the works.

Yes, I've always loved making up the programs, because what interests me is precisely that they should have some meaning.[1] I hate those programs that look like baskets in a supermarket, with everything thrown in together. Completely incoherent programs, really.

You used to call them "plastic lunch."

Exactly. One includes this or that, and there you are, the program is ready. As far as I'm concerned, a program should bear a deeper relation to something. Of course, one can't always be didactic about it; didacticism gets very tedious after a while. I think the works one brings together in a program should correspond in some way—either correspond or clash. They can't remain totally indifferent to each other. That's why I used to make sure my concert seasons had some guiding threads running through them, or threads of continuity. They weren't too constricting, but they were firmly enough indicated to permit comparisons among quite a lot of works. The works didn't even have to be concomitant— they could be quite far apart.[2]

One of these connecting threads is mythology. For example, when I was in New York I did the Faust myth as it occurs in music. This wasn't really a demonstration, but during the year people heard Liszt's "Faust" Symphony, Schumann's *Faust Scenes*, and Mahler's Eighth Symphony. I wanted to do Busoni's *Faust*, too, but then I couldn't.[3]

What about Gounod's Faust?

Gounod's *Faust*, no, no, that scarcely needs help. But Busoni's *Faust* is seldom played, and it's a fascinating piece. That's why it was so interesting to do *Faust* with Goethe's text set directly to music in a different way every time—in the three works we played, in any case. The Schumann concludes with a part of the text that Mahler uses. And the end of the Liszt symphony also contains the text by Goethe which Mahler uses at the end of his Eighth Symphony. It's interesting to make the connection, to show the literary inspiration and the way it's translated into music from the same text.

There were other guiding threads like that, or else we'd emphasize a single composer: we'd do the complete works of Berg, for example, in one season. That's not very original, you'll say, but it does enable people to hear all Berg's work within a single year. Which is possible with Berg—you wouldn't hear all of Mozart played in the same season, that's for sure. But you could feature his piano concertos in the solo literature, for instance. I think it's interesting to establish a link between the different programs, without stressing it too much.

When I did the Rug Concerts for young people—a far less cautious and more adventurous audience than the regular subscribers—I dreamed up programs with a great many contrasts, programs beginning, say, with Bach's *Brandenburg Concertos* and ending with Ligeti's *Aventures et nouvelles aventures*. I chose programs that went from one extreme to another, full of deliberate contrasts, like a shower that runs hot and cold.

Something for everyone, then.

It all depends upon one's goal. If the activity you have in mind has a very distinct focus, then you can do programs consisting almost entirely of original premieres, one after another. But if you're planning a series for a much wider audience, then you have to present a sort of panoramic view, a very broad view, and there'll be room for only one new work.

I once did a concert that included four new works, before a very large audience in London. I no longer conduct the general repertoire—I take part only in what you might call meticulous operations, though even in these, one can take risks. First I played a work by Benjamin, a young English composer born in 1960,[4] then Messiaen's *Chronochromie*. I began the second half with my own *Visage nuptial*, and ended with Schoenberg's Variations. So I deliberately juxtaposed works from different generations. There was a pyramid effect of ages, too, and it was interesting to see the contrast among vocal works, works for orchestra, works for various types of orchestra. But for the Proms I plan to do

Mahler's Tenth, *Erwartung* with Jessye Norman, and *The Miraculous Mandarin*—a program going from romanticism to the reaction against romanticism, to oversimplify a bit. That's the kind of program I can schedule, with a main attraction and a big star. One does Mahler, and one slips in *Erwartung* at the same time.[5] You have to push the customers into listening to things they've never heard before.

Choosing a program is risky in itself. To begin with, there's the perilous problem of having to encompass four or five centuries of repertoire.

That's true, unfortunately—one can't possibly include everything. Things are becoming more and more specialized now, as with doctors, when the one who treats noses doesn't know a thing about knees. Or else you have to surround yourself with experts. I find that if I do music from the sixteenth or even the late seventeenth century, I won't have time to study all the treatises on ornamentation. So I have to ask someone who has worked on the problem to tell me what to do.

All that has changed a lot during the time that I have been conducting—don't forget it was about twenty years ago when I really began conducting in earnest. There were far fewer specialized groups then than there are now. Specialization has become a veritable mania. One of these days somebody will do Brahms with catgut—with instruments strung with catgut—while trying to convince us that it's the only valid way to do Brahms.

The pendulum has swung from one extreme to the other. It was much more interesting when the period piece being performed was actually distorted by the period performing it. At least that implied some creativity, even if it caused a few distortions, whereas specialized reconstruction leads to a total and remote historicism. The more one reconstructs, the further one drives things back into history, resulting in a totally dead contact—the myth of the Golden Age. It's like people who think dinner without candlelight is not a proper dinner. It's as vulgar as that really—rather *nouveau riche*.[6]

This being said, there are still some things one absolutely has to know. The principles of ornamentation, for example, just can't be ignored any more. With Bach, for instance, if you're content to repeat the da capo arias exactly the way you played them the first time, without any ornamentation, it's obvious that they become extremely dull. Literal repetition was not required at the time of composition because there was a certain degree of invention, of ornamental invention in the repeats, even if it was superficial. Musical training needs to move more in that direction, but many interpreters don't have time to devote themselves to the problem. That's why groups now specialize in music of the fifteenth or eighteenth century, or the sixteenth or the seventeenth—there's certainly no dearth of specialists! Is that a good thing? I don't know; it's debatable.

I would really prefer people in large orchestras to specialize, if they have the time, rather than sit by and watch as these completely isolated practices proliferate. At least there would be some exchange of ideas. A musician approaching an eighteenth-century work after playing something from the twentieth would have a much broader view than these eighteenth-century specialists who end up locking themselves in an antique armoire.

What you've called "specialists in nullity"?

I think that about all specialists, including those who specialize in contemporary music. I've seen so many who are not very good, who are in fact awful. They tell themselves, "That'll get by, the audience won't notice." But mediocre performances never get by. I have too many memories of hearing contemporary music atrociously performed by dilettantes who possess neither personality nor artistry, who don't even have talent. It's not a recent phenomenon. To avoid these formidable musicians who specialize in a particular century, I always have candidates for the Ensemble InterContemporain play a classical piece during their auditions. That way I can see how someone focussed on twentieth-century music approaches the general repertoire. I think it's very important to maintain this link with classical literature, with history—I think it's essential.

The other peril in choosing pieces is habit. Even in contemporary music, one can soon fall back on memories of what one has played previously.

That's only too true and I've noticed it. People frequently get bored and eventually lose their sense of curiosity. It's a question of hormones, I think. Up to a certain point the hormones continue to function, and people are still curious. Then they grow weary of rehearsing, of learning, of looking for new insights. I try not to get like that. There is a natural tendency to tell oneself, "Yes, I know that work—it will be a piece of cake." But I'm very vigilant. I keep looking out for new scores and I try to conduct them myself, as soon as the opportunity arises.

A further risk: having to conduct works that once exasperated you. Do you accept them with equanimity now?

One of the things I reacted most violently against when I was young was *Neoklassizismus*. I still detest neoclassicism, but at the same time I've become indifferent to it. I'm not obsessed by it anymore, whereas back then, when neoclassicism actively prevented people from developing, it posed a real problem for me. Now it no longer presents itself in those terms. If someone plays a neoclassical work, I simply hear it and dislike it—it just goes in one ear and out the other. At that stage, especially after certain achievements of one's own, one becomes quite indifferent and impervious to it all.

Indulgent, even?

No, no, not indulgent, absolutely not. Impervious, I would say.

You're speaking of very small fragments of musical history.

Yes. Fragments of history that are going to bring about their own shipwreck. We can see perfectly well which of Stravinsky's works are still floating: certainly not *Apollo*, but *The Rite of Spring* and *Les noces* are. That's becoming ever more apparent. Today, one can view Stravinsky's neoclassical works as mere curiosities, as one tries to grasp how such a man could suddenly get lost in the quicksand.[7] I personally will never find them very exciting, that's for sure.

Maybe it's one's duty to play everything.

But I have conducted works I don't like very much! (*pause*)—although whenever possible, I leave them to the guest conductors. After all, I did have some discretion in the matter. As musical director, I tried to present certain works I felt no affinity with as auditory *documents*. I had my own opinion of them. But for each listener to form a personal judgment—no matter how different it might be from mine—I felt obliged to communicate the musical document, since not everyone can read a score. In that respect I was far more open-minded than is often said, since I conducted a lot of things that were actually quite removed from my own temperament, and which I simply tried to perform as best I could.

Let's keep separate, if you don't mind, orchestral conducting and conducting an ensemble. While I was checking through the main works you've conducted with large orchestras,[8] I was astonished to find that Debussy had been played more than Schoenberg, and Schoenberg more than Webern, whose champion you were. The volume of orchestral works they wrote can't be the sole criterion, because you've conducted Stravinsky, who was so prolific, less than one would expect, and Boulez, whose works are few and far between, rather copiously.

Well yes, naturally, because I'm often asked to conduct my own works. It's true, I've conducted a great deal of Debussy and Ravel, and quite a lot of Berlioz as well, because I was often asked to conduct the French repertoire. When you are French, you are always labeled as French—even a somewhat eccentric Frenchman like me. Perhaps one has a greater affinity for French music, all the same.

Still, you've offered Ravel less often than Debussy.

That's entirely possible, but there aren't too many works by Ravel either. I've often conducted *Daphnis et Chloé* in the complete version, but the other pieces only rather intermittently. Besides, it can't really be said I'm crazy about either *La valse* or *Boléro*. Rather than doing those works, which are essentially postwar, I conducted his earlier pieces: *Daphnis*, *Rapsodie espagnole*, and *Le tombeau de Couperin*.[9]

On the other hand, I've conducted everything by Debussy, even the works I judged less interesting, because I wanted to present an overall view of him. For example, *Images* has some interesting moments, but the *Rondes de printemps*, except for a few passages, is not Debussy's best writing. Nor is *Gigues:* the work has fine musical qualities, but it isn't as good as either *Jeux* or *La mer*. If I've played them nonetheless, it's because *Ibéria* is a very powerful work. I've always played all three parts of *Images* together because they form an ensemble. That's how Debussy conceived them and therefore how they have to be played.

With regard to Images, *you've explained most convincingly that despite the order in which the composer himself may have placed them—a good example of the way you combine scholarship and cunning—*

Yes—(*Boulez smiles.*)

—You say that, despite that order, you prefer to put Ibéria, *the strongest piece, at the end.*

Yes.

And that is indeed how you've usually performed it, except once, with the Concertgebouw in Amsterdam, where you followed the order given in the score. That was just at the time when you were hammering out this explanation, so why—?

Because I tried it that way—

So why did you do that? Were you capitulating to the Batavians?[10]

No, not at all, not at all. I'm never very obstinate, at least, not about things like that. It must have stemmed from a discussion with Flothuis, who was the artistic director then. I wanted to do it my way. He put forward the argument that *Images* had been published as a triptych in three parts, with the main panel in the middle and the two smaller pieces flanking it. He thought that, viewed this way, the triptych seemed entirely logical. I don't think so at all. I probably did it once to try it out, in that order.[11] But ever since, instead of concluding with *Rondes de printemps* (which really doesn't work; it's the weakest of the three parts), I always begin with the *Rondes*, continue with *Gigues*, and end up with *Ibéria*. That way, appearances notwithstanding, the suite remains quite logical: you have panels one and two and then, in the third, three segments that reproduce the overall one–two–three design. You begin with a moderato movement, followed by a slow movement, and then there's the moderato–slow–rapid ensemble. In relation to the content of the music, that's far more logical, in my view. Otherwise, the *Rondes de printemps* sounds like an unwanted encore of *Ibéria*, which, in fact, (*Boulez savors the image*) always falls flat.

I'm amazed to find so great a proportion of dead composers among your twentieth-century classics. Living ones occur rather rarely.

It all depends on the programs. Besides, there's the problem of the meager orchestral repertoire. The highly contemporary composers haven't written much for standard orchestras. For example, the Stockhausen repertoire, such as it was then, consisted of a single work: *Gruppen*. And even *Gruppen* isn't easily performed in the context of a normal concert. I managed to do it twice in London but never in New York, because of the huge expenditures it requires. I would have needed a different auditorium. Such enormous expenses didn't enter into the American subscription format, and we never found enough money to perform it.

I've conducted Berio, because he more or less fits into the normal schema, and Zimmermann too. But Kagel had never written a work for a conventional orchestra at the time when I conducted.[12]

This problem is a threat to the future of large orchestras. Most modern composers either haven't written anything for them or else did so poorly, prescribing a particular number of instruments and an unorthodox seating arrangement. Their works don't last long enough to justify the enormous changes in the seating. You can't play a piece that lasts for fifteen minutes but needs thirty minutes just to shift people around. There are certain programs for which you'd have to have a revolving stage!

"When you are French, you are always labeled as French—even a somewhat eccentric Frenchman like me."

Boulez lived away from France for several different periods in his career, notably during his years with the New York Philharmonic, the BBC Symphony Orchestra, and the Cleveland Symphony. Photo courtesy New York Philharmonic.

You'd have to alter the seating arrangement backstage, move people into view, turn the stage, and then other players would appear.

Do you think those are adequate reasons?

They're imperative reasons. You simply cannot do it.

And you never managed to persuade your contemporaries to compose with those considerations in mind?

Very few of my contemporaries have had any direct contact with large orchestras. They don't realize the difficulties such institutions face when arranging special concerts, especially in the United States, where the management has to arrange for special series. I managed to do that only once. Stockhausen came to New York to conduct his own *Hymnen*. The hall was filled more or less artificially—at least half, maybe two-thirds of the tickets were complimentary. That evening alone cost us as much as two or three weeks of concerts. These financial constraints are very hard to overcome. I was able to take more risks when I was with official bodies like the BBC or Radio France. I was allowed more rehearsal time and I could do special concerts. The programs I did in London for full orchestra were often more adventurous than those in New York.

As for the works you chose, you often delved into the Museum of the old, established repertoire. According to your own words, one can "walk about" inside the Museum[13]—it is not necessary to "keep the door closed."[14]

The two remarks don't contradict each other. They mean, "I'm quite happy to go to the Museum, I'm all in favor of its being well maintained and kept alive, but I don't want to be a prisoner inside it." I don't remember the exact words I used; it all depends on how they were written down. Sometimes I didn't write the words myself.

You uttered them. I consulted the sound archives.

Ah well, if it's on tape, that's different.

You even said you admired the Red Guard for destroying the traditional temples.

Precisely, because that way they avoided getting locked inside. But it wasn't really admiration: there was a strong dose of humor in that notorious German interview.[15] To put it briefly, one should not be held captive by past cultures. A civilization that cannot do without or even demolish certain things in its own past is itself in the process of expiring. In architecture that's obvious. During the transition from Gothic to Renaissance, a lot of buildings got destroyed and other things were built instead. It's always been like that—people take some monument, disfigure it, and then transform it according to the tastes of the time. In music, that went on until the eighteenth century, almost. They would take up something and revise it. Mozart made no bones about modifying Handel, nor Wagner about Gluck. In that respect, I think it's far healthier to live in the

"The quarrel between ancient and modern has always existed, but not this fetishistic attitude toward the past."

Boulez studying scores. Photo courtesy New York Philharmonic.

present. The quarrel between ancient and modern has always existed, but not this fetishistic attitude toward the past. History is there, of course; it made us what we are. It's senseless to ignore it—like breaking down wide-open doors—but that's not to say one has to be imprisoned by it.

This Museum creates a living for a lot of people.

The entire music industry has its foundations in the past: the manufacture of instruments, the stringed-instrument trade, even musical education. That's partly what prompted me to found IRCAM. It's an attempt to create a space where these socio-industrial pressures are less evident, even if they still exist. I've preserved an area for freedom and research that's like yeast, causing the dough to rise. It's an area where art and technique meet, a sort of musical Bauhaus.

So the pillars of the Parthenon are no longer a precursor to skyscrapers?

Hardly at all, in any case. They can serve as a stimulus. An architect's reflections on the Parthenon are certainly quite different from mine. I suppose an architect finds what he seeks in it, something that prods him into clarifying aspects of his own vision. That's entirely possible. But again, it doesn't mean one has to worship the Parthenon. Too much adoration can lead to those monstrosities they tried to bring back into fashion, like the skyscrapers in lower Manhattan, around Wall Street. On top of a fifty-story building, you get a Greek temple.

Johnson's been doing that again, of late.

I know, it's come back into style. Architecture now, whether by Johnson or Bofill, is entirely devoted to slabs. Buildings are suddenly becoming Mussolinian.

When you conduct the classics, are you giving proof of creativity or of filial devotion?

I don't much care. I read the score again, examine it, go back inside the Museum, and that's all. I don't turn it into a political platform or a manifesto, I simply play it as I like to hear it, as I think it should be heard. Which doesn't mean I turn it into something wholly personal. Consider my most ear-splitting intrusion into the Museum: Wagner's *Ring* cycle. Contrary to what's been said, I didn't want to change a thing in it. I read the score very attentively, and decided it was full of details I never heard in most performances. It's not that those performances were bad, but I wanted the satisfaction of actually realizing my inner vision of the score. I think that in Wagner there are more modulations of tempo than one normally hears, and a greater distinction between full orchestra and chamber orchestra, among other things. I felt strongly about it and I was determined to perform it that way, but without turning it into a manifesto against this or that.

When one takes inventory of your Museum—Handel, Mahler, Rameau, Liszt, Purcell, Balakirev, Saint-Saëns, Mendelssohn, Berlioz, Schumann, Wagner, Schubert, Haydn, Mozart, Beethoven, Bach—one is struck by the absence of Italian composers.[16]

It's true. There aren't any Italians because, well, whom can one play? There's always Vivaldi, of course, but then, *The Four Seasons*, I mean, really—I did actually conduct it once in my life in a minor festival in Ulm. Did you have that one in your notes?[17] No, I haven't conducted Italians. One can't play Monteverdi; it has to be done at the Opéra. What else is there? The Verdi *Requiem* or the *Four Sacred Pieces*?[18] Apart from that, there's scarcely anything that constitutes a repertoire. There are the modern Italians, like Petrassi, whom I've played.[19] But throughout the nineteenth century the operatic composers were the dominant ones in Italy, and I've done too little theater to be able to conduct *that*. (*Pause.*)
And in any case, it's a repertoire that frankly doesn't attract me much.

I don't feel you're very attracted to—

No, not at all.

Is it their profusion, their glibness that bother you?

No, it's their vulgarity, more than anything else. That and the lack of depth. I can't get very attached to Puccini because it's so easy to understand, and that's never very interesting, at least not to me. What interests me is to turn back to certain works. I don't mean because one hasn't understood them, I mean because they have such depth that one can return and be enriched each time. That's the difference between Wagner and the rest of the nineteenth century—as far as opera is concerned, that is.

There aren't many Russian composers either, in your programs.

Because there isn't much Russian repertoire, if this is how we're considering things. You know, if I were to consider the repertoire that was held in esteem around the turn of the century (apart from Mussorgsky, and I know they've rediscovered the original version of *A Night on Bald Mountain*, which I had always heard in the Rimsky-Korsakov orchestration),[20] other than *Boris*, what is there for a symphony orchestra? There's *Pictures at an Exhibition*, an admirable piece but now an old warhorse that everybody's heard at least a thousand times. And other than that? I once played a symphony by Borodin, but it doesn't have much substance to it.

What else is there? The big symphonic poems by Rimsky-Korsakov? There again, I can't really say I'm wild about them. I did examine *Le coq d'or*: it has some interesting ideas, but they've been realized a hundred times better by Stravinsky. I'd rather play *The Firebird* than *Le coq d'or*, since we're on the subject of birds. (*Boulez laughs.*) Then there are *Antar* and *Scheherazade*, which have become terribly hard to perform now because they're so dated. Rimsky's worth doing occasionally, like when Cartier produced *Le coq d'or* at the Châtelet theater.[21] I went to see it because it contains some interesting ideas, but it's obviously not music of the highest order.

Russian music is basically Mussorgsky—and he didn't write that much—or else Stravinsky. And Scriabin: I've conducted Scriabin, too, but I don't much care for his orchestral works; I find them badly constructed. There again, certain passages in *The Firebird* are far better than Scriabin's symphonic poems, because the musical thought is more profound. Scriabin is very interesting when he writes for the piano, less so where orchestral literature is concerned.

Is it a question of the works' excesses again?

No, not at all—it's a question of the works' value, that's all. One could still play Balakirev's *Islamey*, for example, which is a piano work and very Lisztian. But there aren't too many pianists who play it because it's very hard. Yes, one can do *Islamey*, but it's still a lesser work.[22]

What about Shostakovich?

He doesn't interest me. We've played a few things by him, but he really doesn't interest me at all. I've done a bit of Prokofiev, such as his early ballets, which I wanted to try out because I had youthful memories of a certain vitality. But Prokofiev is actually quite hollow, with the possible exception of the *Scythian Suite* from *Ala and Lolli*, which is much better than everything else, and also the piano concertos, which are very well written. So if you have an excellent soloist it's fun to watch him raking the keyboard from one end to the other, like this (*Boulez gestures broadly*), but otherwise it's not very exciting.

There's a high proportion of Haydn, Mozart, and Schumann among your selections, but not much Bach. Yet Bach was such an architect—[23]

There are six performable works by Bach: the *Brandenburg Concertos*! And I've done them, the *Brandenburgs*, in my career as a conductor. But even as I was making my way forward, until about 1978, the specialists were simultaneously taking over. They were starting to say, "If they're not played in the true baroque manner, with baroque instruments, it's useless to play them any other way." Then one isn't going to play them at all.

Among the French composers in your Museum, I see a small amount of Saint-Saëns and a great deal of Berlioz.

Yes, a great deal of Berlioz. For obvious reasons. In the first place, the works are superb, and I used to love conducting Berlioz on account of the orchestration. The economy and virtuosity with which he orchestrates are quite exceptional. He's the first great modern orchestrator.

Your tastes have changed over the years. Some composers crop up more frequently during a certain period, then disappear. The case of Webern is a strange one because he figured more at the beginning of your career than he does now. Have you burned your former idol?

I did a lot of Webern early on because he wasn't known.[24] Especially the Six Pieces for Orchestra, Opus 6, and his Passacaglia, Opus 1.[25] But even in Webern there are only four works for a full orchestra; that's the sum total. You can't be constantly performing them, especially with the same orchestra. There are also the Five Movements for String Orchestra, Opus 5—originally a quartet[26]—and then one jumps to the Variations for Orchestra, Opus 30, and even those are for a small orchestra.[27] One can do the symphony, but it's not—As for the Opus 10, it's a chamber work and can be given in another context.[28]

If you consider the Webern repertoire, then, there really isn't much. Same thing with Schoenberg. For a full orchestra, you have his Five Pieces for Orchestra, Opus 16; the Variations for Orchestra, Opus 31; *Pelleas und Melisande*; *Transfigured Night*; the Incidental Music to a Motion Picture Scene, Opus 34; and a few bits and pieces—period. Once you've done those five works, you start to go in circles.[29] So at a certain point you have to turn to other composers. There's *Erwartung*, but one can't always schedule a vocal work. Also *Die glückliche Hand*,[30] but you need a chorus for that. And the concertos. But even there you need a soloist who can play them, and the Schoenberg concertos are rarely part of their repertoire. I have done them with a few good soloists, but they're rather hard to find.[31]

So experience gradually teaches one how important material difficulties are in scheduling programs. Some excellent ideas never get off the ground because a soloist is unavailable or there isn't enough rehearsal time. A program is a mixture of intentions and luck. By luck, I mean that you have to keep track of numerous circumstances that can get in each other's way, but at the same time you mustn't let your intentions get pared down to less than they were to start with.

Let's put aside the small number of suitable pieces written by certain composers. It's still a fact that Webern and Debussy were more frequently played in the beginning, as if they'd once had something to offer—some educational or polemic content that subsequently crumbled—whereas Berg and Stravinsky have clearly received a more constant attention.

That stems from the weariness one feels after playing certain works too often. I've been asked I don't know how many times to conduct *The Rite of Spring*. I conducted it very well and I enjoyed doing so. But after a while one finds oneself branded as the *Rite-of-Spring* conductor, and that's quite intolerable. One can't find anything new in works one's supposed to be helping others to discover, and so one needs a change. For instance, I had often conducted Bartók's *The Miraculous Mandarin*, but just before I wearied of Bartók I finally discovered a correct edition of *The Wooden Prince*. I thought it ought to be performed and I was able to do so frequently thereafter. Similarly, I wore out Berg's Three Pieces for Orchestra, Opus 6, after a certain time. Just imagine, in 1969 I was still giving them their first performance in Boston!

The trickiest choice of all is when Boulez conducts Boulez. Boulez has conducted Boulez in an inverse ratio to the bell curve of his conducting career: a lot in the beginning, not much in the middle, and now extremely often.

It doesn't surprise me to hear that. It's quite understandable. In the beginning, I was invited as a composer, not as a conductor. I essentially came for my own compositions. Later on, when I had the responsibility of being artistic director or principal conductor, I obviously wasn't going to take advantage of my position to play my own work. On the contrary, I had a deliberate policy of playing myself as little as possible, even in a very contemporary atmosphere.

In the concerts given downtown with the New York Philharmonic or at the Round House with the BBC Symphony,[32] I almost always excluded my own works. It was a question of ethics, first, and of freedom of choice. That way I had much more freedom in choosing what composers I would or would not play.[33] If I excluded myself, I could exclude a lot of other people too. In the institutional positions I've held, I struck myself off the list practically without exception. And then, when I stopped conducting regularly, the composer in me naturally resurfaced. I have no scruples now about doing my works along with other composers' works, especially since people usually invite me in the hope that I will. Now that the context has changed, the conditions have changed too.

Let's move on to the repertoire you conduct as head of a twentieth-century chamber ensemble. If we look through the programs of the Ensemble InterContemporain,[34] it's surprising to see the extent to which dead composers predominate over living ones. And Stravinsky's presence is quite overwhelming.

Let me tell you this: your statistics haven't put a stopwatch on the works. The Stravinsky pieces we play are all extremely short, sometimes just two or three minutes long, whereas Schoenberg's Serenade, the way I do it, lasts for half an hour. If you reckon by individual works, for every piece by Schoenberg you'd need ten by Stravinsky. How long a work lasts enters into it a lot.

That doesn't alter the weak proportion of living composers. You conduct your contemporaries in the chronological sense of the term, Berio, Ligeti, Stockhausen, sometimes a little Messiaen, but as for young composers, you virtually ignore them.

True, and I'll tell you why. (*Boulez frowns.*) It's because we divide up the work, Peter Eötvös and I.[35] With the Ensemble, I'm essentially carrying out a pedagogical task, in the sense that I formed it and its repertoire, bit by bit. I've always, that is, we've always given priority to classical composers of the twentieth century because both the players and the outside world expected the Ensemble to have a basic repertoire. Eötvös, it's true, has done a lot more world premieres up to now. But when the opportunity occurs, if I find the works and their composers particularly interesting, then I'm happy to conduct them. For example, I've conducted Dufourt, Murail, Dalbavie.[36]

They don't seem to interest you much. Dufourt appears only five times.

Well, that's practically all he's composed for us. We can't perform things he hasn't written yet.

For young composers, though, your support would represent the seal of approval.

(*Quickly.*) I'm on my guard against that too. If I were to pull out a score at random, then everyone would say, "Aha! Boulez chose this work, he must think very highly of it, therefore—" and so on and so forth. I find that quite a nuisance. If I did more concerts with the Ensemble, I would present a lot more *documents*, as I call them, including scores that may not interest me particularly. So you shouldn't assume a work's been consecrated just because I've played it. I'm very much on my guard, you see, because it's true that people would tend to react that way. But as I told you, I've done Murail, I've done pieces by Dufourt.

Five by Dufourt, five by Murail—[37]

Yeah.

It's amazing, you claim to be interested in new scores and yet I found no sign of this in the—

I choose them myself, you know, I choose them myself. When I'm conducting, especially when we go on tour—and I don't want to do more than I'm already doing—we have to be able to present the basic repertoire. That's why I've conducted those pieces more often than the newer things. But when we go on tour I always take along people who are much younger than I am. I've done so quite recently. (*Pause.*)
It's true that Eötvös conducts younger people a lot more than I do—for the time being. As I said, it's because we divide the work between us.

I'm going to insist on this: the major dead composers come first with you, then your own contemporaries, and, last of all, the young ones.

It's a question of proportion. If you play in Rome without presenting a few classics, hardly anyone comes. That's partly the problem. You need a carrot and a stick—a carrot and a baton, as it were. You have to design the programs so that a few familiar landmarks counterbalance one or two more surprising elements. But I always include a few new things. In my New York programs, which essentially stressed innovation, I did Murail, Donatoni—three or four works like that which were all entirely new to New York. (*Pause.*)
Personally I really like this younger generation. If Manoury were to write something for us, I'd be happy to conduct it. Durville too. We have a lot of composers around in the style of Hurel, too, such as Durrieux and

others.[38] I'm very happy to conduct all those people, even though it's hard to fit them in. You see, I conduct so few of them that they'd have to wait about two years, and I think they would find that impossible.

We do divide up the work. But what I mean is, what I don't do myself, I get other people to do, from time to time, not from lack of interest but because the season has to hang together.

Let's take your orchestral repertoire and your ensemble repertoire, and consider them together. Let's look at the proportion of older works as compared to the contemporary ones. When it comes down to it, there are far fewer contemporary works than one is led to believe.

That's true. I once had a conversation with Maazel about that, in New York. I said, "Supposing you were to do fifty percent contemporary works and fifty percent traditional ones, and that I were to do exactly the same program. In regard to you, everyone would say, 'Aha! He's doing at least fifty percent traditional things.' And in regard to me they'd say, 'Oh my God, he's doing at least fifty percent contemporary pieces.'" It's the old story of the bottle being half full or half empty. When you have tenure in a place like New York, you have to be extremely cautious because the wind isn't behind you. On the contrary, it's driving in your face. And so you have to tack about a lot to get where you want. I always took into account the subscription system, especially in New York. One has to respect it, because one wouldn't be there at all without it.

Even so, I gradually became more ambitious. I don't know how many first performances we did by the time I left—it must have been something like at least eight to ten in the course of the year, which is a lot for an institution of that kind. At the same time, I had instituted a concert series specially for premieres, as a sort of small gallery adjoining the Museum.[39] So there is a strategy one can adopt. One has to consider rehearsal time too. In the United States, rehearsals are limited to four per concert, so one can't indulge in extravagantly difficult programs.

There you have it. Given those terms, under those conditions, the path was very narrow. Certainly, you can't do everything you want, because the institution would fall apart immediately.

Yet they engaged you, knowing full well who you were. Weren't you perhaps chosen by those orchestras precisely because you offered them a guarantee of modernism without turning them completely upside down?

Completely upside down? They were pretty shaken up as it was. You have to understand the limits within which we work.[40] My first programs in Cleveland, when George Szell was still alive, had much more bite to them, that's certain. Szell had clearly summoned me to do a repertoire he either couldn't or didn't want to conduct himself. I corrected a terrible time-lag. As I was telling you, I did the first Cleveland performance of Berg's Three Pieces for Orchestra, Opus 6, in 1967, and the first Boston performance in 1969. Even in the mid-sixties, many twentieth-century classics had never been performed. I was also responsible for the New York premiere of Webern's Opus 30 Variations.

That's the state those huge orchestral institutions were in. The essential core pieces of what we call the twentieth-century classics had maybe been played only once in the last thirty years. When I arrived in New York I had them check back through several decades to see what had been played in the contemporary field and also in the standard repertoire, to find out what had not been played. Generally speaking, they'd always done Schubert's Unfinished or his Ninth Symphony, and had always done Schumann's Third and Fourth Symphonies, but almost never his First or Second Symphonies—and so it went on. In other words, even in the standard repertoire there were enormous gaps.[41]

Again, I wanted to know which works had been played less often than the rest in the nineteenth-century repertoire. Sometimes there are reasons why certain pieces get played less: they're simply not as good, not such masterpieces as the others. All the same, in a good museum you have to have representative paintings of almost every level. That's why I've quite regularly played works written at the same time as the nineteenth-century masterpieces—works which are generally entirely neglected.[42] Twenty years after the event, it's easy to ask, "Couldn't we have done more premieres?" But there was so much ground to make up! And if we hadn't made it up, the twentieth-century repertoire that influenced today's composers would never have been played, or almost never. Not that that's surprising. In Paris, just a short while before, and despite what was being done on the radio—which wasn't particularly innovative, in any case—it was the Domaine Musical that invited the Southwest German Radio Orchestra to do the premiere, I think, of Webern's Six Pieces for Orchestra, Opus 6, and Berg's Three Pieces for Orchestra, Opus 6, too.[43] The Five Pieces for Orchestra, Opus 16, by Schoenberg had not been played in Paris for more than thirty-five years,[44] and the Opus 31 Variations for Orchestra, never. During the fifties and sixties, the tardiness institutional orchestras displayed with regard to a certain repertoire was really alarming. Of Stravinsky, they really played only the three ballets: *The Rite of Spring*, of course, though not very often; *Petrushka*; and *The Firebird*—scarcely ever *Le chant du rossignol* or the Symphonies of Wind Instruments. Bartók's Music for Strings, Percussion, and Celesta was seldom performed, and *The Miraculous Mandarin* hardly at all. Let's not even mention *The Wooden Prince*, whose first complete performance I gave just ten years ago. So you see, if you consider what I did in its overall perspective, you have to recognize the things I rediscovered—things close to being defunct, most of the time.

I have the impression that the pinnacle of your career corresponds to that euphoric period in industrialized civilization when people felt guilty if they didn't assert a certain modernism. That's no longer the case today. The current programs of the orchestras you used to conduct are far less adventurous than they were.

That has a lot to do with the conductor's personality.

Don't you think it was a phenomenon of the time?

No. If there was somebody now like me but younger, at the head of the BBC Symphony, for example, he'd do what I did twenty years ago. (*Pause.*) All the same, I do think the period in question was a little more adventurous, for a whole lot of reasons. But the part of society that gravitates to institutions has never been particularly adventurous in and of itself, even in what you might call more turbulent periods.

I was thinking the same, especially since the countries where you flourished are all Protestant and thus more concerned with modernism, being more inclined to both guilt and prosperity.[45]

No. (*Pause.*) I think England was actually rather behind the Continent in that respect. It was Glock who, at a particular moment, encouraged the step forward. The BBC hadn't been nearly as adventurous as the German radio stations of the immediate postwar period. But then, there's been a conservative ebb in Germany, too, just as there was a brilliant period in England corresponding more or less to the *swinging sixties*, which has settled down a bit now. These things come in waves. Why is Paris considered to be somewhat the capital of contemporary music now? Why do they play more there, and why do more people go to listen? It's because a few vigorous institutions are doing a lot for contemporary music. In ten years it may be Berlin. There's an ebb and flow which is enormously dependent on the dominant personalities in music.

Aren't there determining factors due to the era? If someone attempted to do today what you did thirty years ago, could he succeed?

I think so, yes. Take Los Angeles for example. There you have someone like Ernest Fleischman who feathers his nest and pays his bills with huge concerts at the Hollywood Bowl. Thanks to that, he can arrange some highly contemporary series at the same time.[46] It always depends on individual initiative. See how Sacher's activities in Basel have turned a not particularly large city into a very well-informed center with regard to contemporary music.[47] More so than Zurich, for example, where there's a fine musical organization that's met with less response. Why is that? That's for the sociologists to decide.

After orchestral music and music for a smaller ensemble, you've conducted a third kind of music, and that's opera. Was this by force of circumstance, or was it a strategic choice?

It's always the result of both. Opportunity, they say, makes the thief. I've always chosen according to what was offered to me, especially in the beginning when I had no experience in opera. The first opera I conducted was *Wozzeck*. That suited me well, because nobody in Paris knew the work; everyone was new to it, including the orchestra.[48] That enabled me to beat myself into shape with a work I did know well, having analyzed it in detail when I was a professor in Basel.[49] Thanks to that thorough knowledge and my youthful experience as a conductor, I was able to hold my own against the orchestra, which didn't know the work as well. Then came my contact with Wieland Wagner. He wanted me to do *Tristan*, but I said, "No, that's too difficult, I'd feel more at ease with *Parsifal*"—and I did *Parsifal*. I did *Wozzeck* again with him, but very few things after that.[50] I was asked to do a *Pelléas*—that was also a Wieland Wagner project.[51] Then there was the *Ring* cycle and Berg's *Lulu*—in other words, I've almost always stayed with the same composers.[52]

And then came Rameau's Hippolyte et Aricie.

That wasn't the most beautiful thing I've ever done. Besides, it was just a concert version.

Occasional music?

Yes, it was the fault of the event. It had been arranged through some intermediary or other. I was asked to conduct it and I agreed, to get acquainted with the music. I would have liked it to come off better, but the circumstances weren't right.[53]

Lulu *has proved to be your most contemporary opera. And yet it was only a partial premiere, fifty years after the original incomplete text was written.*[54]

No, no, no, what I did contained no additions to the original text. The third act was composed by Berg absolutely in its entirety, as the photocopy of the manuscript attests. It's in short score, which means it wasn't orchestrated, but the music was composed from start to finish. I saw the document before I made up my mind. If I hadn't seen it, I would never have been able to bring myself to conduct that third act. What Cerha did was to fill in the orchestration.[55]

And you accepted his orchestration as it was, without being tempted to correct it?

Absolutely. No, I didn't change a thing. It's very well done. Cerha studied the orchestration of the first two acts very thoroughly and perceptively, and he's reproduced the spirit of them in the third act. Except for part of the scene in Paris, where there are only a few musical references to the preceding scenes.[56] The beginning of the act had already been orchestrated by Berg, the end of it too. In the middle, well, the scene in London consists almost entirely of recollections or things which have been reworked.[57] So Cerha was able to make a direct comparison against the parts that already existed.

As for the Paris scene, I think he's really done a good job with it. The passages he's written are just passages he's filled in for the ensembles. There were only two ensembles that weren't completely written, but all the major parts were written and all the orchestral parts, too, so it wasn't very hard to write connecting passages.

Orchestral works, works for chamber ensemble, or opera: you make your choice. The conductor's second task is to learn his score thoroughly. After deciding what to play, it's the first step in deciding how to play it. Speaking of how to go about it, Charles Munch set some virtuous guidelines: "One may examine the score and correct physical errors." Then he immediately infringes upon his own rule: "It is obviously beneficial to take a few small liberties." At this stage in the process, do you react to the score as a conductor or as a composer?

On the whole, the scores of great composers don't need any finishing touches. They stand up very well on their own. I would say it's only very rarely that one—well, the only time I've ever added any finishing touches was in Schumann, not to his symphonies but to the *Faust Scenes*. The orchestration is really so boring that at times one wants to do more than correct it. The balance sometimes isn't good at all and so, yes, one does correct that. But it's extremely rare. One never touches either Mendelssohn or Berlioz because their orchestration is perfect.

You added some vowel sounds to Debussy's Sirènes.

I did so because it's rather monotonous otherwise. It's probably one of the extremely rare instances when I actually added something, rather than making corrections. And in fact, it wasn't so much for the actual sounds of the vowels as to make them blend better with the sound of the orchestra, to increase the dynamic effect. As a general rule, people are content to sing "Ah," or to keep their mouths closed. Keeping the mouth closed is quite all right in certain *pianissimo* passages, but it's not at all good in others, because one either can't hear a thing, or else it's too high to resonate properly. So then you have to open your mouth. If one is working with the mouth-closed/mouth-open principle, one may as well take advantage of all the intermediary stages between a fully open mouth—the "Ah" sound—and a completely closed mouth. So one includes the "Oh" and "Ou," but not the "Ee," which doesn't resonate. Basically it's more a matter of dynamic response than instrumental coloring.

To justify this adaptation you wrote, "Since nothing is expressly indi-
cated in the score, I repeat, I don't think an action of this kind contradicts
the musical text."[58] *This subtle blend of scholarship and cunning re-*
mains, and it almost looks as if, once you start reading the score, you try
to conceal your own preferences behind a veil of erudition. Speaking of
the legendary scherzo in your Beethoven's Fifth, you actually uttered
this sovereign pronouncement: "I think a physical error simply slipped
into the first editions."

And so it did. One of my students wrote a two-hundred page thesis on the subject. I don't know what became of it—he studied the orchestral parts, too, from the music they used in Beethoven's time. Those sources prove without a doubt that the repeat in the scherzo is quite wrong. In my opinion my interpretation is entirely justified.

You also rely on direct testimony from the period in question, for exam-
ple, Wagner's entreaty, "No aria, no opera." It's research work, really.

Yes, one has to do research. Take *Parsifal*, for instance. I discussed tempos with Wieland Wagner and told him that the interpretations of my predecessors seemed to me too slow. He told me something he must have learned through family tradition: during a rehearsal of *Parsifal* which Levi had conducted, Wagner kept bellowing, "It should be faster, don't go too slowly, go faster, it's dragging." The publication of Cosima's diaries in 1976, well after Wieland's death, showed we were right. She clearly states that Wagner was irritated by the slow pace of *Parsifal*, and that he did indeed insist on its not dragging. So there was something quite authentic about that.

Some of your corrections to scores look like deliberate rewriting. I have here a score by Ms. Kimi Sato, as performed by the Ensemble Inter-Contemporain—[59]

—So?

—in which the amount of red ink, here, would better suit the authority of the composer.

Kimi Sato? I remember having played it, but I don't recall all that. If I made corrections, it was because in my opinion there were some mistakes, that sort of thing.

Did you go ahead point blank or did you discuss it with the composer?

Let me have a look. Yes, there's a mistake there, an accidental one, that's all. Here it's in unison, there too. And here you can see it's a mistake. As you yourself said, when one examines the score, one corrects any errors. The real specialist in that domain is Ernest Bour. He's much better at it than I am—he spots everything, like a microscope. He examines scores so minutely one can barely see what he's doing.

He showed quite a sense of humor in his criticisms of you.

Yes, exactly. Like Rosbaud, he was always a kindly figure. But above all he had a formidable capacity for analyzing things. His rehearsals were always conducted very peacefully and with a kind of ease.

What about the correction you made in this piece by Schoenberg. Is that a physical error, or are you committing parricide?[60]

It's a physical error, yes.

The publishers are not so sure.[61]

(*Pause.*) Yes, it's a mistake, most likely. Because yes, I remember looking at it, I checked the chords. It comes back with a B-natural at one point, and here, with a B-flat. It was obvious. I had to analyze the sequence, that's all. We must have analyzed the chord sequence and realized that at one point there's a chord which should have a B-natural and not a B-flat. It could be a B-flat but I'd be very surprised; it must be a B-natural.

Was the mistake made by the composer or the publisher?[62]

I don't know, I haven't seen the manuscript. I hesitate, because I haven't checked the original manuscript. I have, however, checked certain mistakes against the manuscripts, especially Debussy's manuscripts, because you can see them at the Bibliothèque Nationale.[63] But at the time when I first did that Schoenberg piece, his manuscripts were not yet available. Now they are, and so one can look. I did recently consult the manuscript of the Serenade, though without comparing anything against it. But that is certainly a mistake, there. Of course, one sometimes has to look extremely carefully.

And here in the Opus 29, look at this mark that's been surreptitiously added.[64]

Yes, that's a D-flat. I remember that one because I did it fairly recently. That line ought to be read like this—it's a printer's error, simply.

Is it? So the conductor can feel free to tamper with it?

You have to make corrections, absolutely. Here, for example, in this bar in 5/8 time, it should really be marked like this, which makes it much easier to play.[65] No, it doesn't bother me at all to do it like that.

When you select a particular version of a work, that's another sign of your power. For Stravinsky's The Firebird, *you prefer the original version, which you've pronounced "indissolubly connected to the musical thought that gave birth to it."*

Absolutely. *The Firebird* was written for a very large orchestra, with three harps and everything else on the same scale. But as it's often been played, especially as a ballet, certain conductors have taken it upon themselves to reduce the score to what becomes almost an arrangement. Stravinsky got so tired of this he preferred to write his own scaled-down version, which was inevitably more intelligent, more artful, and better done. Even though he made the best possible use of this reduced apparatus, however, it's obvious that the full wealth of his ideas can be displayed only through the original orchestration, without any reductions. His arrangement is really very good, but it's still an arrangement. If I had to conduct *The Firebird* in Saint-Quentin, maybe I'd take the scaled-down version too, because with an orchestra of sixty players that's O.K. But when I've had an orchestra of a hundred and ten players at my disposal, I don't see why I should be content with the version written for sixty.

You've also said, "I hope Stravinsky would have allowed me to differ with him on this point. I remain convinced—even where my own work's concerned—that the composer proposes and his listener disposes."[66]

Certainly. When a particular version was originally written with regard to some constricting circumstance—such as having to play in the orchestra pit for a ballet—one's not obliged to go on respecting it for ever. That said, I admit I maintain a very pragmatic attitude on the subject, because I don't systematically advocate returning to the original score either. Sometimes when composers have reworked their original version—and that's what I get paid for knowing—it may well be that their compositional power has improved, and that the later score is better. So if I'm confronted with someone who wants to go back to the original version of *Pelléas and Melisande* in order to avoid the interludes, then I ask to see the original version and I consider whether or not it's really better than the one which has interludes. I could also perform the so-called original version and the definitive version side by side, as happens when two texts are printed side by side in critical editions. In addition to printed critical editions, there could very well be auditory critical editions, to see what works best in a given version.

So the actual work slips completely out of the composer's control?

Completely. Yes, he's still the one who composed it, even if he wrote two versions. One has to consider how much he was obliged to respect the constraints of his time. Gardiner recently presented a supposedly original version of *Pelléas*.[67] Fine. In the subterranean scene, for instance, he prefers the way the chords originally sounded when the double-basses were divided into four. Afterward Debussy split up those four parts between the cellos and the double-basses.

But if Gardiner had visited the pit of the Opéra-Comique as it was when Debussy knew it—and as it was when I saw several productions there in 1944–45, and again in 1966–67[68]—he would know that the double-basses numbered only four in all. Naturally, doing the subterranean scene with four solo double-basses could produce only a very thin, uneven sound. I'm convinced that when Debussy heard those four wretched double-basses all by themselves he decided, "All right, I'll redistribute that among all the cellos and double-basses." And in so doing he obtained a much deeper sound, a more subterranean sound you might say.

That's what's so absurd about this. If you have an orchestra with ten double-basses, as in the United States, you can divide them into four, that's fine. But when you find yourself with only four double-basses, four divided by four, that means you have only one double-bass per part, which isn't going to sound too convincing.

You're still playing detective.

Yes, it's very interesting. Consider the case of Mahler. With his vast professional knowledge of conducting, he reworked his orchestrations so often that one sometimes hesitates as to which is the definitive version of certain of his works. Why is that? You can see why when you play them. In the past, it often happened that the bass clarinet was rather weak, because it was generally palmed off onto a bad clarinetist. But now that's no longer the case: bass clarinetists have a really strong sound and hold up very well against the rest of the orchestra, so there's no point in going back to the original version and replacing the bass clarinet by a bassoon, as they used to. It would be stupid to go back to the original just for the pleasure of doing so. In *Jeux*, for example, Debussy decided on some corrections which were certainly prompted by the performers' irritating lack of experience. He must surely have said to himself, "It's too awful; I'll simply take that out." These are basically corrections that one finds in his working scores and that were never transferred to the manuscript. That must mean he had no intention of retaining them.

So you really reconstruct the composer's intention?

One has to pay serious attention to that, to the material circumstances in which the work was performed, and sometimes to the era in which it was played. I can well imagine that the first bassoonist to play the beginning of *The Rite of Spring* must have felt very apprehensive. But now all the bassoonists have practiced that solo and it's part of their repertoire. They can't quite play it with their hands tied behind their backs, but they do it with far greater ease than before.

That reminds me of something Georges Auric once said. He'd heard the first performance of *The Rite of Spring* and he told me, "I'm very disappointed now each time I hear the beginning of *The Rite*. I always miss the anxiety I felt at the premiere."[69] That's all very well, but one can't try to reconstruct the perplexity felt by a bassoonist in 1913! We're now at the end of the century, and performance literature has changed so much that *The Rite of Spring* may still be a difficult solo, but it's no longer so perilous as to be deemed superhuman.[70] Conditions have altered: that's all one can say. It would be equally silly to look for an old 1913 bassoon and kill yourself trying to play it.

Then the only true criterion is the conductor's personal feeling?

The only true criterion is to see what is possible and proper to do. (*Boulez laughs.*) There are no rigid criteria, ever. You have to consider the contingencies of the period in question and those of today, and then see what works, that's all.

On Gestures

After doing all this research, you have to move to the podium.

And then, well, you have to try not to be surprised when you listen. What you've heard inside your head eventually has to correspond to what you hear played. There's a risk it won't at first, especially with new scores, and even with one's own scores. But after conducting them a certain number of times, one knows exactly what to expect. By then there's a pre-existing auditory model in one's mind, and not just in one's mind but in reality as well. So memory plays a part. And until this ideal auditory model has been attained—until what you hear coincides with the auditory ideal as closely as possible—then you simply have to work at it. Many things are involved: rhythmical accuracy, intonation, balance, good phrasing, and so forth—all those qualities.

You listed the virtues of the ideal conductor in your eulogy for Desormière: restrained gestures, good taste, rhythmical accuracy, open-mindedness, exactness, and respect for the music. Let's discuss gestures first.

Gestures are entirely personal. You can't try to impose them on someone else. They're as personal as a voice: you can't make a baritone sing like a tenor, nor a tenor like a bass. The relationship between music and gesture has a physiological aspect that depends on each individual. Karajan always conducted with very rounded gestures, whereas Solti's are extremely angular. Both obtained the results they wanted, with orchestral sounds particular to them. Each technique has its merits—the resulting interpretation doesn't sound any better or worse because the conductor's gestures are angular or rounded.

I think it's an entirely individual matter. You make your own gestures, and find out as you go along which ones serve you best. I've seen young people trying to conduct like Karajan. It was utterly useless: there was the outward form of his gestures, but not their essence. Of course, there are a few which are absolutely essential, no matter how you do them, as when you give an upbeat or want the orchestra to stop. But there are kinds of gesture which nobody can imitate—those that indicate phrasing, for example. There you have as many types of gesture as you have conductors.

The gestures have a prop. Let's talk about that. In your case it's your hands, not the baton.

The baton, no. I've never been able to conduct with a baton.

Munch found conducting without a baton "stupid." He said so, in writing.

Yes, that's what he's supposed to have said, in any case. I don't know if it's what he really thought. If it is, too bad for him.[1] I once had an argument on the subject with Monteux. He used to conduct with a baton that was at least three feet long. He wanted one like that because he was extremely sparing in his gestures. When he saw me conduct at the Concertgebouw, he asked me why I conducted without a baton. "Because I feel more comfortable that way," I replied. "All right, but you'll come around to it," he fired back. Well, (*Boulez laughs*) I haven't come around to it yet, and I certainly never will.

So, the baton? The more one is inclined toward contemporary music, the less one needs this particular extension. There's a certain technique involved: the accuracy of the gesture resides in a perfect coincidence between arm, hand, and intention—and what one can physically execute, as well. And so, especially for phrasing, both hands are needed.

What was the cause of this absence? A particular model, an idea?

No, nothing. It just happened. I think I didn't encumber myself with a baton because I began by conducting chamber music, music for a very small ensemble. You can't conduct that kind of music with a baton; it's quite useless.[2] And even though I was gradually promoted, as it were, to conducting ever greater numbers of instrumentalists, I still never used one. Though God knows, I've certainly conducted some works that were rhythmically difficult! But I've never experienced any problems with a large orchestra, never.

You watched Desormière's rehearsals avidly.

Yes, Desormière used to conduct with a baton. In fact everybody did. Cluytens was the only one who sometimes conducted without one.[3] He used to put it down during the slow movements and pick it up again for fast ones.

If I conduct without one, it's in no way because I followed some sort of model; it's that I personally never felt the need for one.[4] What's important is for the gesture to be accurate and instructive. If the gesture is precise, there's no need to extend it visually. You know, it's a bit like the evolution of the tail, in animals and humans. It was anatomically indispensable, and then it gradually disappeared as we evolved. I'm convinced a style of conducting will develop that does not require a baton.[5]

"Gestures are entirely personal . . . as personal as a voice."

Boulez conducting the Cleveland Orchestra in Japan—without a baton. Photos by Peter Hastings.

Concerning evolution, have you any heirs who don't use one?

No, I don't think so. Not at the moment in any case.[6] Most of the people I've seen conduct do use a baton. Simon Rattle and Salonen both do, and good luck to them. I don't mind in the slightest whether they obtain the desired result by using one or not. I don't think that defines anything at all.

So the fact of not having founded a school doesn't—

"The accuracy of the gesture resides in a perfect coincidence between arm, hand, and intention. . . . And so, especially for phrasing, both hands are needed."

(*Boulez grows solemn.*) I don't want to found a school, to tell you the truth. The young people observing me now will conduct as they please. There's something about a gesture that can never be transmitted. A gesture can be as personal as the way you walk, the color of your eyes, or the shape of your nose. In other words, it's something that absolutely cannot be transmitted.[7]

Your own gestures are restrained, to say the least. Is that a matter of musical yield *again?*

It's a question of yield, yes. I think useless gestures are superfluous. Obviously that's been said before, but it's exactly what I mean. (*Boulez laughs.*) For me, economical gestures are the fruit of long preparatory labors. During concerts you obviously go at it full blast, as it were, but that doesn't mean you start flailing like a windmill. On the contrary, you have to do all you can to make people feel secure. The more complex a score is in its texture and rhythmic divisions, the more controlled the gestures have to be, so that the players understand them at a glance. When members of the orchestra have played a score a hundred times, they simply use it as a sort of safety-net they rely on occasionally. Above all, they watch the conductor. On the other hand, if the work is difficult and the musicians aren't very sure of themselves, they have to follow the printed text. And so, when they look up at you, they need to be absolutely sure of what you're doing. That's why, on those rare occasions when I've taught conducting, I've always insisted on a geometric system of gestures. First of all, they're an excellent help to one's memory, just as fingering helps pianists or violinists. And the conductor is far less likely to make a mistake if he has this precise geometric design in his head.

You have been dubbed the "semaphore operator" and the "station master," so it caused much laughter recently when you told one of your students that he "looked like a robot."[8]

Well, the gestures have this geometric form, yes, but the influence of the written music turns them into an individualized form of the actual sound. If you content yourself with some sort of mechanical gesture, the sound won't emerge properly. And so you have to make sure that the geometric form and the sound are amalgamated.

An illustrator once pointed out to me that when you're conducting, you keep your right hand hollowed, and your left hand flat.

Ah, I can't tell you whether that's the case or not because I don't do it intentionally. I mean, I don't think about it much—I don't see myself when I conduct.

It's very sensual, watching you knead the sound.

Yes, it probably is, that's why I keep both my hands free, without a baton. I can conduct the rhythm with my left hand and a phrase with my right hand, then change them over at times. In other words, neither hand has a function that's been eternally defined; they can vary. For example, they can both conduct the rhythm when a difficult passage requires that. People would have to watch to see what it is I do. My hands can switch functions, in relation to specific tasks performed by different portions of the orchestra.

One's eyes play a part too. If you're conducting something highly rhythmical with one hand while the rhythmical activity you're directing is taking place over there (*Boulez points in opposite directions*), that obviously isn't going to help them, the musicians, at all if you're conducting over here while something more flexible is going on over there. So, you really have to conduct according to the orchestra's geographical arrangement, according to its topography and the function it serves.

Your personal choreography also contains the swiveling motion, when you pivot from a low center of gravity.

Yes, quite possibly.

You do it from close to the waist, whereas one habitually sees conductors waving expansively around their heads.

Yes. But when I make a sweeping gesture, it's because it really has to trigger many activities. It rather depends on the numbers of people involved. With a small chamber group, it's completely silly to make an enormous gesture if the contact between you and the musicians is assured. You should have seen me conducting in the final chorus of the *Gurrelieder* in 1987, and especially in the male chorus in the middle, which is very fast and very difficult.[9] We were in the Royal Albert Hall with three male choirs, which made things large scale. In a setting like that, you really have to conduct (*Boulez gestures broadly*). Likewise, when I'm conducting *Répons*, the gestures are much grander than usual, simply because it's necessary. Otherwise, people playing fifty feet away don't see you.

Sometimes your hands make contrary gestures, and sometimes they move in parallel.

Yes.

Big horizontal and vertical cross-hatchings.

Yes indeed. It all depends on the musical text. I can't specify any in detail for you, but it depends on the text. If there's a piece of music that calls for a marshalling of forces, as it were, then the gesture becomes really (*Boulez hugs the empty air*)—for instance, at the end of *Éclat*, where everybody plays perfectly synchronized and extremely fast.[10] At that point, you really have to make sure everyone understands you. I could actually do it with one hand, but there I use both, so that everyone feels utterly obliged to keep to this very fast collective rhythm.

Gestures convey a multitude of things, beginning with the tempo.

That's one of the most important aspects. It's funny, I've just been reading with great interest what Wagner thought about conducting. "If one does not find the right tempo"—this is the substance of his words—"or at any rate a tempo that suits the music, then the most important idea is lost."[11] That's precisely my opinion. Until one finds the right speed—not necessarily a constant speed, but one that fits the moment, and can vary with the context—until one finds that tempo, then even in one's own compositions the interpretation remains weak and prevents the music from swelling forth. The right tempo imposes itself all at once, within a precise limit. It's like when you look through a telescope and the object you're aiming at suddenly comes into focus. If you turn the focus a bit too much, the object's blurred, and if you don't turn it enough, it's blurred too. Not in the same way, but blurred all the same. Similarly, the musical text remains blurred until you find the right tempo. Of course it may vary according to personality, temperament, and experience.

The most commonplace example of this physiology of tempo is the extremely slow first movement of your Beethoven's Fifth. It's a symbol of the paradox that constitutes one of your principal strengths: in the middle of a relatively tranquil movement, things go very quickly.

You know, I think a lot about tempos. But it's not a purely theoretical reflection. One thinks as one puts it into practice. I won't take Beethoven's Fifth as an example, since it's perhaps not the best thing I've ever done, but I will always defend the tempo I found for the "March to the Scaffold" in the *Symphonie fantastique*. It's slower than the usual versions, especially the ones you hear in France, where people have been in the habit of racing to the gallows since Munch conducted it. I think that so precipitate a tempo endows the music with an excessively vulgar character. Whereas if one respects the tempo that, after all, Berlioz himself suggested, the "March to the Scaffold" does not become some kind of polka. It has to be played more slowly than is generally the case. I won't give way on that point and if I were to conduct the march again now, I'd do it exactly as before.

In Munch's version, the march does indeed last only four minutes and twenty-three seconds. Cluytens takes four minutes and forty-five seconds, Solti four minutes and fifty-four, Dutoit four minutes and fifty-two, Markevitch four minutes and forty-four. Boulez takes five minutes and fifty-seven seconds. The only one who takes longer is Roger Norrington, at seven minutes and twenty-five seconds.[12] And yet, listening to Norrington, one has the feeling it goes faster than in your version.

I can't say; I haven't compared them. Maybe that's because he uses period instruments and the result sounds much lighter. I'm not saying my recording of the *Symphonie fantastique* is the best I ever did, but the "March to the Scaffold" has always seemed too fast to me. And then it becomes excessively vulgar. Berlioz didn't intend it to sound jolly. So there's a gravity, a kind of severity about it that seem to me essential. No, if I were to conduct the *Symphonie fantastique* now, I don't think I'd conduct it the way I did before, but I certainly would not speed up the "March to the Scaffold." As for Beethoven's Fifth, I probably would take that rather faster. At the time it seemed to me people generally took off like bats out of hell in the first movement, thereby diminishing the movement's substance and weight, despite the dynamics. I probably overcompensated. Certain things set one off—this was more than twenty years ago.[13]

There are a few tempos I've almost never changed my mind about. But I'm certainly far more aware now of the consequences. The hardest thing about being a conductor is not just that you have to provide the necessary impetus, but that you must be able to learn from the result, and make changes accordingly. As an example, I'll compare the two recordings I made, many years apart, of Schoenberg's Chamber Symphony no. 1 in E.[14] One of them is clearly faster, and the other is taken at a more moderate tempo, though without being slow. In the faster version I wanted to provide a very powerful impetus, but the articulation of the musical text suffers from a lack of clarity. The connections between the movements aren't sufficiently clear. I've subsequently discovered that

there are very gentle transitions between these different movements—
no abrupt bumps or cuts. Everything depends on these transitional connections. In my second recording, I think the texture is much clearer and
there's a greater respect for substance.[15] When one plays extremely fast,
there are certain things that cannot be clear. When I conduct now, I still
provide momentum, but at the same time I have a better idea of how fast
I can go while maintaining a comprehensible texture. When one's young,
one can try very hard without really listening. But gradually one learns
how to listen to what's going on, and to rein in one's impulses.[16]

Does it take very long to learn about tempos?

Tempos are extremely flexible. Naturally there are tempos that are
flexible within firm delimitations, and others that, on the contrary, can be
violently disturbed. What matters to me—and I'm not the first to state
this principle—is that expression should not automatically be associated
with dynamics and tempo. Very often there's a tendency to link them automatically. If you play louder and the musical text is more intense, it's
very likely you will automatically play faster.

On the other hand it's very hard to obtain an acceleration with a
diminuendo, that is, with something that quietly disappears. It's a completely unnatural reaction, you see. I'm aware of it because I've written
that particular effect myself, and that's what I intended. To obtain a fast
diminuendo you have to struggle against your natural reflexes. For example, at the end of my *Éclat/Multiples* there's an extremely gradual
ritardando that lasts almost thirty pages. I was very struck by the way
Balinese musicians—I'd invited an authentic group to Paris—perform
accelerandos; moreover, they have no rallentandos. They execute accelerandos over an extremely long period, led by their equivalent of a
conductor—the one who leads the whole group with his drum. Their accelerandos are incredibly impressive. And all of a sudden they'll change,
return to the original tempo, and then set off again.

I did that in *Éclat/Multiples*: I gradually reduced the tempo and later
realized that even though I'd written the work myself and knew what I
wanted, a gradual ritardando was very hard to control. I had to perform it
several times before I managed it correctly. Because in slowing down a
tempo, one becomes *emotional*—an accent escapes, the old tempo re-
verts—and yet one has to uphold a steady deceleration.

I've worked hard at some things because they are so difficult: when
the music suddenly falls away or surges back, when there are breaks in
tempo, or when, as I said, the tempo is subject to violent disturbances. An
extremely supple tempo, as in Debussy, for example, is achieved by simply following the phrasing. But a more turbulent tempo is far harder to

obtain, especially if the musical material that's subject to such disturbances doesn't really indicate them, and they have to be superimposed. In fact I did that in *Le marteau sans maître*, and it's one of the pieces I found hardest to conduct, at first.

And then you have rhythm and attack to consider.

That depends on what you mean by attack. Attack in its simplest form is an ensemble chord. But what is meant by ensemble playing varies from country to country. It depends on the tradition by which each instrument is taught. In France, the attack presents no problem; you simply do this (*Boulez makes a sharp gesture*) and the chord immediately follows. But if you do the same thing in Germany, there's a slight delay before the chord. The advantage is that the German attack is gentler and less choppy; the disadvantage is that you have to pause slightly, and allow for this short break in your rhythm. Once the first chord is behind you, this no longer poses a problem. For these chord attacks, I would say there's a difference between the German method and everyone else's method: even the Anglo-Saxon method doesn't involve that delay. One has to get used to it.

As for rhythm, it's extremely varied! Look at the twentieth-century repertoire. I'll take Stravinsky and Berg as examples, because their cases are the two most diametrically opposed. In Stravinsky, rhythm is absolutely and quantitatively defined by an almost arithmetical relationship with duration. You have to provide a beat, and that beat depends on an arithmetical irregularity that's really the basis of his thinking. You have to be able to master that, otherwise you'll never play Stravinsky well. In Berg the beat is divided up, whereas in Stravinsky it is small, continuous, but varied. It's divided, and therefore far more flexible, and it also depends far more on the phrasing. In other words, if there's an accent or a crescendo, or if you have all these variations in tempo such as accelerando, rubato, and so forth, then the beat has to be far more flexible.

One experiences quite different physical reactions when playing Stravinsky and Berg. I personally benefited greatly from conducting the two. And even in my own compositions, I sometimes include these two types of beat. I may have the very slow continuous beat with many things happening inside it, and I may on the other hand use the very precise beat with its equally precise subdivisions. Then I can also have both at the same time, which is the hardest thing of all to manage. In certain pieces, you have to keep shifting the tempo while simultaneously maintaining a very vigorous beat. That's the hardest thing to do, the one I found most difficult to master.

It's something Berlioz already requires.

Yes, but Berlioz doesn't have this irregularity of beat.

Respect for the text and mastery of tempo—are those the necessary ingredients for your legendary clarity?

Clarity derives from an understanding attained partly through re-flection, partly through experience. As you go along you realize that reflection contributes to experience, since thinking deeply about a given score more or less enables you to foresee what's going to happen when you play it, especially with new scores. But at first one's ideas are natu-rally rather hazy: one reflects, but sometimes the music does not respond as one expected.

Isn't this clarity a way of removing oneself from the musical text, of mak-ing the interpretation more objective?[17]

No, not at all. This question of objective interpretation is in no way particular to my generation. It really belonged to the preceding genera-tion, Ansermet's generation, which was greatly influenced by Stravin-sky and Ravel, and claimed to have an objective view of the text. I know that one can only have a subjective view of it. But that does not preclude a respect for the text.

Then your subjectivity looks very much like objectivity.

Yes, but it's an extremely strong subjectivity. Each time I've tackled a work, especially from the classical repertoire, everybody's groaned about how incredibly subjective my interpretation was.[18] No, objectivity is certainly not my generation's problem.

Maybe it's that people tend to confuse clarity with objectivity.

Yes, objectivity has nothing to do with clarity. It's impossible to be totally objective. Consider the very notions of musical transcription, of musical language. What is *forte*? Can it be defined? Of course not. A *forte* is defined essentially in relation to context and balance. What is intona-tion? Intonation results from the adjustments one makes, among maybe a hundred or so musicians. No matter how acute these questions are, the an-swers to them are purely approximate. The same holds true for rhythm. What is an exact tempo? That depends greatly on the acoustics. If you're in an acoustically dry performance space, you play faster. If you're in a humid one—or, as I was going to say, an environment that reflects the sound—you play a bit more slowly, because it forces you to do so.

No idea is purely objective. The person who came closest to it—and even then not always—was Stravinsky when he wrote *Les noces*. There, yes, you find a certain objectivity of tempo, since the tempo is metronomically given. The music is conceived around that, and so it's very hard to get away from it. But even so, the dynamic relationships are entirely subjective in that they depend strictly on the vocal element, or, as Stravinsky put it, "music that's breathed, music that's struck."[19] So already there are nonobjective elements.

Objectivity is a problem for any generation traumatized by the excessive subjectivity of the generation preceding it. My own generation finds its predecessors' quest for objectivity quite fruitless. Subjectivity no longer bothers us at all. Yet it's not the kind of subjectivity that's content just to ad lib: it's a subjectivity based upon respect for the text, upon those values that can be respected in the text.

Lucid analysis and finesse in execution—aren't those attributes that are typically French?

If I were purely French, I would never have left the Hexagon.[20] My career as a conductor has developed almost entirely abroad—in Holland, Germany, England, and the United States. Some characteristics may be specifically French, but I don't really believe that. When I'm conducting Schoenberg, I'm not aware that some distinctive quality makes me French, because I'm not trying to be French at all. Any music of superior quality, be it Schoenberg or Stravinsky, any music that's achieved a certain prominence completely transcends nationalistic points of view.

So a universal heritage does exist?

One can speak of universality when that level has been reached. It's a universal language. All gifted people can attain that universality if they work hard and if they're drawn to it. Nationalist conductors simply tend to be third-rate. Those who are capable of approaching the entire repertoire are the genuine ones. As I've already said, I mistrust specialists of any kind, whether French, English, or German—I find them too narrow.

There's something astonishing about this all the same. We're now in Germany, where you've had part of your career, you've worked in Northern Europe and in the United States. Did you charm these countries with your Frenchness, or do you possess qualities—rigor, accuracy, the capacity for hard work—that fit in in those countries?[21]

It's not for me to answer that. I can't really say—it would be better pondered by an external observer.[22] I've certainly felt drawn to Germany—at least, to Germanic regions, be they Austrian or German—and to this entire musical tradition, which is so strongly developed and certainly the most continuous and elevated musical tradition since the sixteenth century. Even statistically, the largest number of significant composers to play a major role in music are found within the German tradition.

The other traditions, if one can call them that, are more sporadic. The French tradition limps along, because it has not been properly handed down. The equally lame Russian tradition began tardily and has manifested itself only through individual talent. And those individuals don't constitute peaks in a chain of mountains; I feel they're more like volcanic islands. I have always felt strongly attracted to Germany. Perhaps I was prompted by a reaction typical of my generation: a need to break out of the enclave, after being shut in by the war, to see what was happening elsewhere. There was a lot of curiosity, back then. There was also the strange pre-eminence Stravinsky enjoyed in France immediately after the war, emblematic of a general nostalgia for the prewar period. Several of us, however, felt Stravinsky was completely spent. That's why all of recent Germanic tradition—I'm referring mainly to the three Viennese composers—was fascinating to us. We were all the more attracted to this culture in that it was held in scant esteem in France.

Germanic culture is not very attractive to French people, whether in the domain of literature, philosophy, or the plastic arts. The French have seldom shown much curiosity about the German tradition. Curiosity came later, which explains why the exhibitions on Vienna and Berlin were so successful: they generated a retrospective curiosity about the period. French people suddenly discovered that something had been going on in that part of the world, and they overcame that almost visceral rejection of German culture that harked back to 1870, when the violent nationalist struggles between our countries began.

Isn't your view of Germany a bit idealized? The three Viennese composers scarcely toiled on German soil, and there are other branches of the tradition, such as Hindemith, whom you've hardly ever conducted. Then there was the Nazi era—this lineage you speak of is purely intellectual.

No, I don't believe a German lineage of that kind exists. The Germanic tradition has certainly produced a few minor geniuses, such as Hindemith, who is quite acceptable but not really extraordinary, with his rather heavy music in the style of Max Reger. No, after Wagner and Mahler, the Germanic tradition is surely represented by the three Viennese. In any case, it doesn't much matter whether it's a question of Vienna or Berlin. Besides, Schoenberg spent part of his life teaching in Berlin.[23] I think those three really represent the German tradition at its strongest. Of course there were other creative minds before them, like Richard Strauss, but they didn't achieve such a high level. Another thing that attracted us was precisely this barrier of prejudice that we had to knock down. We had to take something new and introduce it to France, and the introduction was very coldly received at first by the musical establishment. They rejected it because they'd always rejected it and continued to reject it. The polemics of the time were rather rough—not to say violent—from 1945 until around 1952–53, even against the Viennese school.[24]

From the standpoint of conducting, did this intellectual relationship with Germany save you from becoming an island yourself?

No, I felt that my true origins were there and that I would certainly find models, or at least a path, that would help me to assert myself and find what I was looking for.

In entering into this business of quasi-filial adoptions by Scherchen, Rosbaud, and even Bour, who may be considered a Rhinelander,[25] you nonetheless registered yourself with a particular pedigree.

Yes, I belong far more to that pedigree than to the French one. It's probably because I've always been exasperated by the French tendency to say, "Oh yes, French music, the Ile de France, moderation, clarity, and so forth." In my opinion there are some great French geniuses who are neither moderate, lucid, nor whatever. Look at Claudel, who's really the weirdest genius imaginable when compared to the French stereotype. Look at Berlioz, who isn't moderate or harmonious or anything like that. That's always irritated me, this reductive attitude toward French genius— or what's been termed French genius—turning it into something stunted and stark. That's why I've always tended to look elsewhere.

And you found Germany to be the best possible "elsewhere"?

Yes, because in Britain there are no models at all, nor in the United States. There was Varèse over there, who was still a European, even if he grew up overseas. Once a European, always a European, even if you rebel—and Varèse remained one till the end of his days.[26] The most typically American composer was Ives, who wasn't known at all because he'd not been published very much, so people were just vaguely aware of his name. One of the first I met was Cage, and that was out of curiosity.[27] So neither England nor the United States provided sufficiently strong models.

You include Fernand Léger among three examples of French bad taste. Coming from you, the very idea sounds paradoxical.

I find French bad taste entirely necessary. Otherwise there's always this notion, that even foreigners have at the back of their minds, that French artistic expression is a sort of luxury product of the Faubourg Saint-Honoré, like good restaurants. The French are quite happy to go along with this because, unfortunately, it's an image of themselves they like to cultivate and one they're very proud of. I think the most interesting examples of French creativity don't necessarily fit into that mold, though it's true that there is a certain French elegance. But let me take three examples: Mallarmé's poetic language is so elegant it's crazy, and yet it hides unfathomable depths. The better he presents those yawning chasms, the less you realize at first how deep they are. You let yourself get caught and only afterward do you discover the depth of his thinking.[28]

The same is true of Cézanne. His elegant paintings are in a way more elegant than those of Van Gogh. Yet here, too, that elegance conceals great profundity and an extremely radical point of view. The same can be said of Debussy, and his unquestionable elegance.

Behind this elegance—which is seldom truly attained—one can discern an exceptionally radical perspective. But for me, the interest of these great works lies beyond their elegant style. I've nothing against that style, but I can't say I consider it an end in itself. There are descendants of Debussy, Ravel, and company who've simply been content to write in a vaguely elegant manner, and because of that they've produced nothing but boutique music, ready-to-wear music.

There's a curious change of partners going on at present. In France we swear by international design[29] at the very moment when Germany, heir to the subtle Bauhaus style, is fascinated by its French contemporary, Art Deco—by the Ravels of Deco—which, despite appearances, is horribly ponderous and suspect—

Yes, well, you know how fashions come and go. I think at present people are tired of radical research, of looking radically at society. This is giving rise to a canned-product, crumb-picking kind of art, an art of public letting-go. People gather up all manner of bits and pieces and say, "O.K., I'll put a Corinthian column on a metal base and it will look postmodern." Obviously this is all quite superficial. There have been certain exaggerations of structuralism and of functionality in architecture, as in design generally. But one can't fight this excessive and certainly sterile functionality by adding entirely superficial elements that were functional in another era, but no longer are. All right, maybe it will last only for the blink of an eye, but you know, if you spend your whole life blinking it can ruin your eyesight.

That holds true for composers too.

Exactly.

And for those young conductors who've begun using crazy semaphore signals, as at the turn of the century.

I don't think that will last long. We're experiencing a moment of fatigue, that's all.

Our conversation is moving toward the composer. Wouldn't you say that the ability to learn and master the text thoroughly, to decide on an interpretation after reading it, are attributes of a composer, rather than a conductor? Isn't your own interpretive ability that of a composer?

I don't draw much distinction between the composer and the conductor.

What about your mastery of the written score?

That's true. But most conductors have studied composition. George Szell composed, Furtwängler composed, Klemperer too. They may not be good at it, but they are at least aware of the mechanics of composition, and from that perspective their approach can be quite intelligent. Like any other interpreters, however, they'll have more difficulty with scores by composers such as Berg and Schoenberg than with a score by Stravinsky.

In Stravinsky, the hierarchies are very quickly established. They're very well thought out and the music is not all that complex because it rests essentially on two dimensions, melody and accompaniment. Of course, it's more complicated than that, but Stravinsky doesn't really pose enormous problems. That's why conductors don't generally experience difficulty with his works, except for the mechanics of beats. This was evident when Scherchen had to conduct Stravinsky's beats, and Munch too, and the results were rather shaky, the balance was unstable. You see, they didn't have within themselves that irregular pulsation you need to conduct Stravinsky. It's something one acquires—probably a question of the generation one belongs to, I would say.

But at least Stravinsky doesn't present any textural difficulties. Berg's Opus 6 Pieces, for example, present serious problems in analyzing the text. You really have to know what's important and what's less important. You have to be able to balance the different parameters of the music so that the texture is always clear. You mustn't be afraid to sacrifice a voice so that the most important one can be heard and understood. Naturally, there aren't many people who can analyze these problems clearly, especially while they're actually conducting.

It's almost like the prerogatives of a fraternity: Berg is your equal, and you're the equal of Berg.

Yes, but having said that I really don't advance myself as anybody's equal. Based on personal experience, I simply tell myself that I know the composer spends a lot of time, at any rate, some time, in writing the full score, in setting down a certain hierarchy of values, if I may speak in the abstract. And that's the hierarchy I want to hear.[30]

If you know that, it's because you're a colleague.

It's perhaps because I'm a fellow composer that I'm more aware of it, yes. At least I know how much effort the composer's put into it, and that I must respect that effort. But yes, in that sense, composing does promote exacting behavior as a conductor. Especially in the twentieth-century repertoire, especially in the Viennese repertoire. As I was saying, neither Bartók nor Stravinsky present such difficulties. Webern is fairly clear, but Berg and Schoenberg certainly pose enormous problems. The first time I conducted them, a long time ago, sometime in the sixties, Berg's Opus 6 Pieces caused me a lot of problems because I didn't really know how to go about them. There are times when respect for the musical text alone doesn't serve much purpose. You might have a secondary part written for a relatively weighty instrument, and a principal part written for a much lighter instrument. You have to actually change the dynamics. I have no qualms about doing that. As a fellow composer, I say to myself, "That's what he wanted to hear, but he didn't have enough experience to write down the exact dynamics." So I change them, that's all.

This "keenest ear"[31] you have for arranging the different structures of orchestral sound, this ability to bring out the full range of orchestral color—is that still part of your collegial respect for the text?

For me, it's really a matter of finding what I want to read in a score. I think the composer—and this probably isn't one of my obsessions, but I do nonetheless pay great attention to it—has included certain elements in composing his score. He's written a certain number of instrumental lines and on the whole, he hasn't done so just to make a general amount of noise. He's composed those lines so that we can hear certain things, so that we distinguish a certain hierarchy that's dependent on his writing. What I try to do is bring out that hierarchy in a very precise way, even when it's difficult.

In some scores this task is relatively easy. For instance, if you're conducting Stravinsky's *Chant du rossignol*, the right balance is obtained almost automatically; there isn't much you have to do. In a work like Berg's Three Pieces for Orchestra, Opus 6—especially in the third piece—the task is very hard. First of all, the orchestration is very dense, and the relationships between the instruments are rather risky. By that I mean that the secondary lines contain a lot of orchestral weight, whereas the principal ones contain relatively little. Therefore you have to re-establish a proper balance, and since the orchestration is constantly being modified, you also have to modulate that balance so that it corresponds to the relevant bars. But whether the work is crystal clear or very involved, I personally feel a duty to clarify its contents as far as possible, so as to obtain an intelligible reading of the score that is then transmitted aurally. I don't want to be the only person who can read it—I want everybody to be able to, even without a score.

The objective-versus-subjective theme again. Does the priority you give to orchestral sound structures stem from an ideal reading with the eye, or does the subjectivity of the ear enter into it?—because many conductors favor certain structures, for the sake of an "interpretation," even when other structures should predominate according to the actual score.

Interpretation does exist, of course. You never have a totally objective reading of a work, given that you perceive it yourself and thus put something into it. I don't think this subjectivity is necessarily detrimental to the text. It can emphasize certain connections and make them more apparent—preferably not too apparent, because when they're too apparent they're no longer interesting—make them more apparent, but without sounding false. So at times one does ponder the problem.

There's a particular passage toward the end of the first movement of Debussy's *La mer*, involving cello and English horn. The phrase is repeated twice. So one could think to oneself, "I'll do the same thing twice, I'll try to make the timbres blend completely and produce two phrases that are uniform." Or one can say, "I could vary the balance slightly between the cello and the English horn." So what should one do? There are two other possible solutions, apart from that of total balance that I explained first. Either favor the English horn in the first phrase and the cello in the second, or else favor the cello in the first phrase and the English horn in the second. I base those decisions on timbre. In that register, I think the timbre of the English horn sounds more full-bodied than the cello's. Therefore I let the English horn dominate in the first phrase, and then in the second, I emphasize the melodious though less full-bodied timbre of the cello, at the expense of the English horn.

Actually I think it would be more logical to decide to emphasize the thinner timbre first because it has more vibrato and so is more immediately expressive. Then make the English horn sound not colder but less immediate (in any case, its expressiveness has nothing to do with vibrato—and that's the difference between the two instruments), so it will sound a little more direct. But then, I find the difference between the "direct" concept of timbre and the "vibrato" concept of timbre less important than the full-bodied/less-full-bodied character of timbre. And so, if I think and listen as I go along, I eventually decide on a personal interpretation. It's not Debussy's at all. In these two phrases I give precedence to the English horn first and then to the cello. It's a purely personal choice, purely subjective—and yet it's based on the actual text, or at least doesn't contradict the text.

To make a text speak like that, using as much intuition as erudition, is not interpretation—it's clairvoyance.

I'm sensitive to the phenomenon of sound, that's all. In music, two things are ineluctably linked, at least for me: the actual writing of it, which communicates by means of signs and thus implies a certain logical relationship between them, in addition to coherence and affective power; and the sound quality. And it's through sound that you discover the text. For example, supposing you have a text that's extremely strong and brutal in meaning, and the brass section is not as incisive as you want, or else there's a drum whose skin isn't tight enough, or a *ponticello* missing from the strings. If that happens, the aggressiveness that the composer truly intends will be badly conveyed. Or suppose you have, on the contrary, some passages of an extremely refined sonority, but that sonority is out of balance and not as consistent with the text as it should be—then the text is equally badly represented.

For me, an orchestra's lack of discipline is always reflected in a feeble dynamic range. An undisciplined orchestra will not have very quiet *pianissimo*s, or very strong *fortissimo*s. What you'll hear is music that always stays within a relatively limited range, and this greatly reduces its expressive power. Something I do very often in that case—and I'm not exaggerating—is to push the dynamic register to the absolute maximum, until it reaches what I think are appropriate levels for a given work. Some pieces are not based on an enormous contrast, and so one doesn't need to go that far. But in *The Song of the Earth*, for example, the instruments have both *ppp* and *fff*. That's how it has to sound and there's no other way to go about it.

Some conductors spill their guts out, thereby detracting from the credibility of the sound levels. But with you, one is aware more of a preoccupation with the structuring of sound.

I think of music not so much in its different structures or as details, but more as a totality. That's as true when I'm writing as when I'm conducting. In my view, the only way to conduct is to conduct with a purpose. If I hear something that has remarkable moments but no general design, it leaves me unsatisfied. I hear those moments and appreciate them, but if I can't really link them with something continuous that joins one moment to the next, then I'm unsatisfied. In rather disconnected music, such as that of Webern, those moments have to be joined in an extremely evident manner. Even in music where the sound is not continuous, I still try to obtain a certain continuity through discontinuity. By that I mean that there may be interruptions, or ruptures, but there is still an underground rumbling one does not hear, and it links up with something one then hears anew.

As far as all that goes, then yes, I am extremely sensitive to the way music is constructed. I think of it as being a form of architecture, and it's true that music is architecture in motion, for architecture is like music that's been turned to stone.[32] Yet you have to retain in your own memory or mind the entire sum of moments—you may, at a certain point, favor one of them, but you must not forget the others. You have to have a sense of perspective.

Among the panoply of virtues proper to a conductor, we almost forgot to mention phrasing. But is that really an omission? It seems to me to be contained in everything we said. Or could it be, as some people maintain, that phrasing isn't part of your technique?[33]

No, we didn't include it, and that was a gross error on our part. Phrasing is an element of continuity, of distinction between structures, as its name indicates. There isn't just melodic phrasing, though usually when people speak of a phrase, that's what they mean. It's one of the definitions of a phrase: a melodic phrase needs to be articulated. If we're talking about phrasing in general, let's talk about articulation, because articulation does indeed relate to a particular phrase, but also to a rhythm, to a form or segment of form. It also relates to the delineation of timbre and to the delineation of polyphony. In other words, phrasing, or articulation, really applies to all those categories.

In general, then, when people speak of phrasing, they ascribe it far too narrow a meaning. What is phrasing? Phrasing consists of showing, without pedantry or unpleasant emphasis, that the structure of a phrase— for example, the structure of a melodic phrase—hinges on several important points, that it has a certain drive, that it follows a momentum and trails off again, that, in effect, it really follows a curve. And a curve hinges on points of retrogression; that is, it has all the characteristic features of a curve. *That's* a melodic phrase.

A rhythmic phrase occurs when you emphasize, for example, the relationship of diverse rhythmic cells. If you're conducting *The Rite of Spring*, there comes a point where there's nothing but rhythmic phrasing, period. Because all the other dimensions are subordinated to the rhythmic one.

To speak of Webern is to speak of the articulation of form, in other words, the phrasing of form, and this is the most important aspect. If one doesn't indicate this articulation of form, then the form becomes incomprehensible.

Phrasing also applies to polyphonic articulation. In Schoenberg the score indicates principal voice and secondary voice. But there are all the other voices too. Schoenberg gives two, but there are all the rest to consider, and "the rest" isn't just some vague accompaniment you can forget about. If there's polyphony, each of its elements has to be studied and indicated so as to be heard properly. Phrasing then develops through the quality of the legato, the quality of minor articulations and of cuts, and through the dynamics. It develops from the intensity of intervals—from many things. There are a great many components in phrasing: it isn't just a line you happen to see, it's a line that must render its maximum expressive potential by having all those elements respected.

The confusion between phrasing and melodic line is such that even recently I've heard it said of you—and by professionals, too—that your work is solid and well structured, but it remains rather upright. In short, they missed the flowing feeling of a torrid stream.

It's simply that their perceptions of music are extremely rudimentary.

And outdated, I would say.

Rudimentary, above all, because even Beethoven is not like that. Beethoven is more than a melodic line. The *Coriolanus* Overture, how would you describe that? It's made up of chords, without a melodic line in sight at the beginning. And what about the end of the Fifth Symphony? Or the Third Symphony? It's all chords. What do you make of the two chords that begin the Third Symphony? That's also an articulation. There's a phrasing to those chords that prepares the melodic phrase. Beethoven's music is, precisely, one of the least rigid and one-dimensional types of music that exists. There's an extraordinary degree of direction, and change of direction, between the different phases of the development. In the last quartets, particularly, there are moments when the rhythmic phrasing is far more important than the melodic phrasing. The melody develops in small units, so there's not much phrasing to do; there is the possibility of phrasing, although the rhythmic impression is far more refined.

It's the fight between clarity and verve.

That depends on what you mean by verve. Verve accompanied by confusion does not appeal to me at all. What's needed is energy. If I do *The Rite of Spring*, I don't think it lacks energy or verve or anything like that. That's true of the Berg pieces too—wonderful, they are, really. As to energy, that depends, too. Not all pieces of music have the same kind of energy, that's obvious. And if that energy—it's not something out of control, I don't really like the word because energy should always be an untamed force that's nonetheless controllable—if that energy is not dispensed at the right moment, if it's wasted, then it no longer has the power to seduce. Energy should be well used. That's obvious, really. In my

> "Verve accompanied by confusion
> does not appeal to me at all.
> What's needed is energy."

Pierre Boulez in rehearsal with the Cleveland Symphony. Photos by Peter Hastings.

view, the great conductors are those who know how to use it sparingly when some is needed, and not to inject it when it's not needed.

Is misusing it mere bluff?

It isn't even that. I grow weary of its misuse very fast, because I wonder why all that flailing about is necessary. It's like actors gesturing wildly in a situation that docsn't call for it.[34] Whereas, in fact, when you have to summon up intensity, it's not a matter of huge gestures or frenzied movements. Intensity can even be entirely motionless. For example, in traditional Japanese music, you can see a fabulous intensity being obtained with hardly any movement and the results are far more intense than any amount of the babbling and upheaval, which is often taken for intensity.

I used the word "clarity," you say, "energy and intensity." Are these the source of phrasing?

Absolutely. They're essential. A phrase lives essentially through the distribution of energy. If the energy is badly distributed, the phrase is badly executed. As I said, phrasing isn't just a matter of legato; it's literally a distribution of intensity, of dynamics. There are phrases with minimal dynamics, and others that require a vast dynamic range.

When you conduct works from the Museum, some listeners experience the heavenly surprise—or hellish disappointment—of seeing the Sistine Chapel after it was cleaned. The whole thing suddenly becomes too clear; they miss the successive layers of ancient varnish, the rushes of enthusiasm.

I think those listeners don't know the scores. They probably know the music from other people's recordings.

Or else they don't read the scores properly. After all, the Catholics did eventually discover the Bible, but they still don't respect it.

They don't really go back to the text. What does a musical text mean, and what does it really mean to us? Those are two questions I ask myself, though not systematically, in that form—I don't say to myself each time I pick up a score, "What does it mean to me?"—but I do make it mean something to me. I'm always mistrustful of judgments that aren't based on thorough study of the text. Those judgments are based purely on recollections and on what I call *postcards*, picture-book impressions. And that doesn't interest me at all, not even remotely, because there's absolutely nothing behind them.

Pleasure and Authority

In essence, conducting is pleasure: pleasure in music, pleasure in power.

I don't think there is any pleasure in power. In any case, I don't feel it. First of all, I'm not interested in power. What really interests me is how accurately and well one can perform a given work. I remember performances I've conducted with some excellent orchestras, the Cleveland orchestra especially, when I used to tell myself, "Yes, what I hear now is an almost ideal performance of this work." We were perfectly coordinated, the orchestra and I, in those performances—the best I think I've managed to obtain. Next to that, power leaves me cold. It's of secondary importance, compared to the excellence of the music and the ideal interpretation one aspires to.

Isn't there simply pleasure, in the normal meaning of the term?

That's what that is.

The sensual pleasure afforded by the work?

An accurate performance of the work includes that. It also involves translating it into sound, and when that's done properly, it satisfies you intellectually and physically. In the end, that's all that counts. That's what you strive for, and it requires both discipline and inner tension. When one gets as close as possible to an ideal performance, I think one has achieved a goal that exceeds all other satisfactions, without doubt.

And that's pleasure?

Oh, it's far more than pleasure. If that's the vocabulary you want to use, it would be better to say "joy" rather than "pleasure."

A psychiatrist expressed astonishment that you don't use a baton, that symbol of power and pleasure, although you embody both as a conductor.

Ah well, the baton is rather a slender symbol of virility, as such things go. (*Boulez laughs.*) A century ago, around the time of Berlioz, you could have called it that. They used batons that were quite weighty and substantial. But now, you know, as a sign of virility, it's dwindled away to almost nothing—more like a useless little appendix.

No, I don't think conducting has much to do with virility. I think it's much more a question of somebody's personality being absorbed into a work, and corresponding exactly to that work. That seems to me essential. Until you've reached that level of perfection, well—I don't need to reiterate Diderot's paradox of the actor, but it may well be that when we can distance ourselves from a work, we understand and perform it better. Perhaps one enjoys doing it less, precisely because one watches it taking shape, rather than seeing oneself take shape with it. But the first few times you conduct a work and are only starting to understand and master it, when you're still involved and not yet detached—that's maybe the best time of all.

That's why I don't envy conductors who've performed the same piece three hundred times; one can sense them gradually distancing themselves from it.

So it's the pleasure felt in conquest.

Oh, I think it's less than that. It's simply the pleasure one derives from professional skill and from producing a well-finished piece of work. I don't think it's like a conquest at all. It's a professional skill, like a baker producing a nice symmetrical loaf. That's why I criticize people who stick to a particular repertoire. Frankly, they have no curiosity. They're like specialized workers who have no large-scale vision. That sort of professionalism doesn't attract me in the slightest.

Leaving aside pleasure and power, there's still authority.

Power no, authority yes. By authority, I don't mean authoritarianism, even though you have to display a little of that from time to time. Authority essentially resides in one's knowledge of the scores. If you don't correct mistakes right away, at the entry level you might say, the musicians will notice immediately, and they won't have much respect for what you're doing. Once you're past that literal stage of studying the score, the other important way of manifesting authority, in my opinion, is to say what you want—what you want to hear, how you want to hear it, and sometimes why you want to hear it sound like that. In other words, you have to explain your expectations fully to the orchestra. That's what creates such an intense relationship with the musicians.

If they don't know the work, there's even more to explain. Even if they've looked at their individual part, they can't possibly imagine what the whole score is like. Musicians often apologize (sometimes it's also an excuse) for not having practiced their parts by saying they didn't know how I was going to conduct the work, how they would fit into the whole ensemble. And that's usually true. Until they know the full score, the musicians don't have a precise idea of their function. And so you have to explain their individual part in relation to the full ensemble, and how you want it performed. I find that very important. It's there that one's opinion as a *composer* asserts itself, and that always creates an authoritative air.

In the major orchestras, you deal with major soloists. You have to perform *with* them, not rap out orders as if they were babies. They're accomplished musicians and they have their own ideas. If they've achieved that stature, it's usually because they have great ability. So you must never try to dictate to them in any way at all. You simply listen to what they do, and if you like it you don't need to say anything. If you find that a passage doesn't correspond at all to what you believe suits the ensemble, then you say, "I prefer this," and you work it out between you. There's a relationship of mutual consent, of give-and-take, between the person conducting and whoever is playing, especially a soloist. What's fatal is to show up without having an opinion and let yourself be swayed by what you hear. The musicians notice that at once. Not only will they lose confidence in you, but they'll mistrust what you do—or what you don't do, for that matter.

Rehearsing

So the musicians arrive and you can start the rehearsal. What then?

The actual work depends on the pieces you're going to perform. For example, if you're doing a repertoire piece that you've often played with the orchestra before, then naturally you don't need to spend much time on it. Take the BBC Symphony Orchestra: whenever we were to perform *The Rite of Spring*, the players knew beforehand which passages I would rehearse, because they were the passages that always deteriorate first. They're a little more difficult and the orchestral playing tends to have deteriorated, whereas there are other passages the orchestra can pick up again very quickly, and which need to be rehearsed only once.

So first of all one has a certain personal familiarity with the musical text, and one knows more or less where to expect problems. Something I always insist on doing, even with a work the musicians know well—unless, of course, it's one we've recently performed—is to provide an overall view. I think that's very important. It's something I picked up as I went along. At first I shared the fault common to all beginners: I used to stop at the first mistake. There's nothing that annoys a musician more, especially at the beginning, because it prevents him from getting a sense of the work's continuity. So, the first time I conduct a work, regardless of how well the orchestra knows it, I have them play it from start to finish, at least, playing each movement right through. Even if it's a very long work, I do that.

While that's going on I can talk to them and say things like, "You were late," or, "Careful! You come in here." In other words, I do point out mistakes but I don't stop, unless there's total confusion. I stop if they're completely puzzled by an error in the score, by a repeat that isn't marked or cuts that are badly indicated. When that happens you really have to stop, and that's fine. But in general I try to battle through and I try to create at least an initial impression, even if it's rather blurred, and even if it's an impression of impending disaster! At least people will subconsciously retain a feeling of the ground that's been covered.

Like a seamstress, tacking the outline of a dress.

Yes, absolutely. You have to go on to the end, without stopping. Afterward, you can repeat passages. If it's a work the orchestra's already played, even if it was some time ago, you know exactly where the difficult points are. You pick out certain details, but since you don't want to hold up the entire orchestra for hours on end you don't pick them all out in isolation from the entire work. You take a certain passage, correct it, and then have them play it, because what the orchestra likes is to play, not to sit and wait. What you have to do—and here again, experience teaches one—is, above all, to play, while concentrating on just a few details. Even if the details aren't perfect, you go on to the next bit, and then on to a larger bit, and so on. So that later on, when you've gone through the whole work that way, you can repeat it all.

In very lengthy works, when stamina and breathing become important factors, I go through the whole work as often as is necessary. In Schoenberg's *Pelleas und Melisande*, for example, you have to keep going for forty-five minutes. Even with the wonderful Chicago Symphony Orchestra, I went through the whole thing once before the dress rehearsal, and again during the dress rehearsal. The first public performance was the third time we'd played it right through with full understanding, after sightreading and all the intermediary work. When you show up at the concert with that kind of secure mastery of continuity, the performance is inevitably stronger and more sustained than if you'd prepared it in bits and pieces, without attempting any continuity until the dress rehearsal.

Even in disconnected works, such as Berg's Three Pieces for Orchestra, Opus 6, where the segments are separated, I look for continuity. The orchestra still has to grasp the sense of one piece following another. It's become less necessary now, but even so I play the work at least twice before a concert, to give the players that sense of continuity. Especially with short pieces like Berg's Three Pieces, I systematically rehearse them twice at the dress rehearsal. The first time, you see, the players expect it; they're not surprised but they still have this impression of disconnectedness. When they play it through the second time, they have a far better sense of continuity. And whether the pieces are separate or continuous, I believe the sense of continuity is the most important element of performance.

Attention to detail matters too.

Yes indeed. For new or difficult works, I hold rehearsals where we pay a lot of attention to detail. We might, for example, concentrate only on the strings. Quite recently, at the BBC, the orchestra was sightreading my *Visage nuptial*.[1] I had two rehearsals just for the string sections, because I knew they had a lot to do; a single rehearsal for woodwinds and brass, because their parts were easier; and two rehearsals for percussion, harp, and keyboard instruments because their parts were also more difficult. After those rehearsals I began with the orchestra as an ensemble, and then we added the vocal parts.

You see, there is a systematically developed method for approaching works the orchestra has never played before. As Berlioz said, attention to detail is crucial.

Would you rather be overprepared, or slightly underprepared, so that luck can play a part?

Underprepared, no. I don't like being underprepared. It always entails the risk of catastrophe. You have to be ready. But you mustn't be overprepared, either, because that risks a certain lassitude and lack of interest. Too many rehearsals aren't good. And you have to be able to work quickly, in my view, to keep the players interested. The worst thing of all is when you have too many rehearsals and there comes a point when you don't know what to do next. The musicians notice, and you can start all over again or mess about with some detail, but that won't really help the interpretation. So I'm not at all in favor of overrehearsing. But under-rehearsing certainly won't do either.

You're saying good quality obtained through solid work is better than dazzling brilliance obtained in a day?

As for dazzling brilliance, I don't believe in it at all! I can't point to any specific conductor, but how can you be dazzling with disorderly phrasing, with out-of-sync chords and tempos, with muddled entrances? I wouldn't call that dazzling—I'd call it a coverup.

When you're conducting an ensemble, social and professional relationships must necessarily be separate.

Yes, especially since I was the one who, together with Michel Guy and Jean Maheu, founded the Ensemble InterContemporain.[2] It wasn't a personal objective, but something directly related to my own activity.

In a way, it's a continuation of the Domaine Musical.

That's right. It's not an institution I took over in full swing; it's one I created. People who join this group know very well that I'm in charge and that I have been from the start. That's the first thing that distinguishes it from institutions where I was just a transient phenomenon. Maybe I won't be connected with the group forever and ever, but we've been together now for many years, and, equally significantly, we've been together from the start. Secondly, it's a contemporary music group. People who join it have made a deliberate choice and are thus highly motivated. At some point in their lives they've decided to commit to this group. The third distinguishing feature is that the group is rather small. You get to know far more people than in a large orchestra, where, out of a hundred and ten players, you get to know only a certain number well. When there are only twenty, you inevitably get to know them better, especially since you seldom work with the full complement in these smaller ensembles. I don't know the exact figures, but usually the group has between eight and fifteen people. It's highly unusual to need more, or to use the full resources of the ensemble.

Do relationships become more fraternal, or does the conductor's authority remain the same?

I think authority is something one shouldn't make a show of. One doesn't need to overdo it—it's just there. Anyone who has been to our rehearsals can see how coherent the Ensemble is. There's no need to call people to order or rely on discipline. Everyone is in agreement and we hardly ever have problems—at least, I hardly ever do. Sometimes with younger players, or even not-so-young players, who haven't much experience or who haven't shown sufficient talent, there can be trouble, naturally. That's entirely normal.

The age difference enters into it, inevitably.

Yes, of course. The Ensemble is very young, compared to me. I'm practically old enough to be everybody's father. And certainly the age difference plays what you might call a tutorial role. Except for two or three older musicians who'd already acquired a lot of experience, I hired very young players. A few of them were only nineteen, twenty, or twenty-one when they joined us, and therefore totally inexperienced. They gradually acquired experience, mainly with me. That's why they developed a relationship of apprenticeship, rather than being on an equal footing.

In such a gathering of experts, doesn't the conductor's role change?
Doesn't he become a soloist among other soloists?

No, not at all. If he does his job properly, he really has to give very precise guidance when confronted with seven or eight different personalities, even with the strong personalities found among chamber music players. Rehearsing takes less time, of course, because there's less to say when you have interpreters of the highest caliber, particularly with music they know well. Even so, the principle of unification still has to be respected. It's not a question of authority, then, but of unifying a certain number of personalities by means of a central personality. If that person doesn't do his job, the musicians will resent it. I'm not saying they always need to be led by the nose, like horses; indeed, they often play chamber music, where there isn't a conductor at all, and they themselves take the initiative. From that point of view they don't get hassled, any more than they do for their career or their musical choices. But in ensemble playing, you have to make sure the bowing coincides, and that the dynamics, balance, and intonation all agree. In short, there has to be someone who hears all that, and who gives clear directives to the ensemble.

I'll dwell on just one entirely objective problem, that of intonation. There are no subjective indications to give there, as there are in phrasing. Intonation is either accurate or not; you can almost measure it. If the conductor doesn't assume that responsibility, if he doesn't tell people they're playing sharp or flat, that they need to make this or that adjustment, if he doesn't do that, then first of all the musicians feel uncomfortable, and second, they'll be forced to take action themselves. And musicians always take it badly when one of them suddenly says to a neighbor, "You're out of tune." It doesn't go down well at all, and someone is needed as both guide and arbiter. I think musicians trust someone who displays professional qualities, and that person is seen not as a nuisance, but as a necessity.

You're an ensemble conductor who blossomed into an orchestral conductor. Is your experience with a full orchestra helpful or harmful when you turn back to a small ensemble?

Neither one nor the other. You change gear, that's all. I imagine it's a bit like being a bus driver who switches to a passenger car. The smaller vehicle will handle differently, but that doesn't alter the basic principles of changing gear and braking.[3] One difference is that with an orchestra, you have less time to concentrate on detail than with a chamber ensemble. The orchestral repertoire does not assume a high level of preparation—the players don't spend hours practicing their parts before they arrive, except for the soloists, of course. Very often you have to accomplish a great deal of what you might call textual work during the rehearsal. Furthermore, no matter how good the orchestra may be, you have to take into account the different levels of proficiency, because all the players aren't equally skilled. You have to make the best of them and come up with a formula that makes the best performers lead and the others follow. This leads to a homogeneous blend of the different qualities and skills.

"You have to explain your expectations fully to the orchestra. That's what creates such an intense relationship with the musicians."

Boulez talking to players during a Cleveland Symphony rehearsal. Photo by Peter Hastings.

Then again, rehearsals last only a given time. Never, or very rarely, does one have time to study the difficult works as thoroughly as one would wish. That is far different from chamber music. When a quartet prepares a piece, it can take all the time it needs, and that might mean two years. That means the quartet plays the piece as well as it can be played, because they've taken the time to study it, and their own economic status and internal management permit this. With an orchestra it's as if someone is always saying, "Hurry up with that letter! Federal Express is here!" or, "Come on! The train's about to leave!" One always feels a bit thwarted by managerial imperatives, by factors that aren't really musical.

With a group like the Ensemble InterContemporain, however, we don't generally suffer from any of those ills. There are ample rehearsals. I even tend to avoid having too many of them, especially for our standard pieces, which are beginning to be known. As I was saying, I prefer to maintain the freshness necessary for performance. Otherwise, fatigue and lassitude set in, and the works are *overrehearsed*.

For harder works, ensemble players get ready in advance. Obviously, they don't sightread the parts for Schoenberg's Serenade with the ensemble. They practice, either before the first rehearsal, or at least in between rehearsals when they realize what problems lie ahead. If they don't, I point it out, very simply, at the following session, because I'm not there to teach them to read music. In a small ensemble, accuracy of notes and problems of that level and literalness have to have been resolved previously. There are problems of a different nature you have to save time for in chamber music. The others can be taken care of by the individual.

What about the orchestras you've spent some time in molding? Haven't you been tempted to consider them as large ensembles?

Yes and no, naturally, depending on the works.

There are contemporary works in which almost everyone is a soloist.

There are indeed contemporary works that require more attention to detail. One provides that through rehearsals with the individual sections, and here the similarity is obvious. All the same, orchestral style rarely resembles that of pure chamber playing. There are a few chamberlike moments in Schoenberg's Variations, for example. There are indeed variations that are real orchestral variations, and others that are chamber music. In those cases I rehearse all the orchestral variations, I send home part of the orchestra, and I select ever-smaller groups for the chamber variations, so as to rehearse in ever-greater calm. When you have a work like that to rehearse you can't leave anything to chance, and it's best to prepare a rehearsal schedule, so that people don't waste their time. If you keep the main body of the orchestra waiting—even if it's only for fifteen minutes—while you perform a chamber variation, that obviously isn't going to be very popular. Therefore you have to organize rehearsals in such a way that the players don't waste time, or at least don't think they're wasting time. You don't need the whole orchestra listening to you while you rehearse what's really a chamber variation. The orchestra will hear you quite enough during subsequent rehearsals and the actual performance.

What about opera? It's not easy to rehearse. Munch flopped badly in Pelléas.[4]

You know, there are some conductors who can't get used to opera, just as there are some excellent conductors who make poor accompanists, in the solo concerto repertoire. Conversely, there are some quite unremarkable conductors who make gifted accompanists—pilot fish, as it were. The gift of accompanying is multifaceted, and conducting opera presupposes not only a mastery of the orchestra, but, above all, an interest in theater and a certain knowledge of staging.

I haven't had a bad experience like Munch; that hasn't happened to me. In my opinion, one needs to take one's time. When one has the requisite experience it may be possible, though not particularly useful, just to attend the final week of rehearsals, when the production is almost ready. I was always involved right from the start in my own operatic ventures. I attended the individual rehearsals, those with just the singers and director, to get to know the staging and to see if it contradicted the music, to see if I could make any suggestions, and to become visually accustomed to what was happening on the stage. Then I would watch for the singers' gestures and expressions, because what they do on stage corresponds to the music. If you miss this whole preparatory phase and don't become "routiniert," as the Germans say, then you certainly won't be able to keep up.[5] Orchestral rehearsals on a stage don't prepare one for opera at all. You feel a bit frantic because all of a sudden not only is there something directly under your control that you expected, but something quite different that's also under your control. I can well understand why some people are thrown by that.

When we did *Wozzeck* I went to all Barrault's rehearsals. So when I had to make the connection between stage and orchestra pit, I wasn't terribly surprised. It's true I had some experience behind me, with the Barrault company, but it wasn't anything like having to conduct an opera. If one doesn't attend rehearsals, one may be caught unawares. If an old hand at conducting opera turns up at the last minute for a production he doesn't know, he'll still be able to adjust very quickly and indicate the entrances. Mechanically speaking, it will work very well. But if he doesn't participate in the staging, it's reflected in the music, which becomes quite unrelated. I've seen productions like that, when the staging was interesting but the orchestra was utterly schizophrenic in its lack of connection with the stage. You can tell at once, and the production loses all interest.

You use the word "participate." Do you mean, get involved with the visual representation?

I don't get involved, no, I watch and pay attention. I am happy merely to watch, because it's not my job to do more—it's the director's job. Presumably he has pertinent reasons for his ideas. Once they've been physically translated onto the stage, then I can say, "Yes, I see it that way," or, "No, I don't see it like that." In other words, there may come a moment when I don't think certain movements are concordant with the content of the music, and I say so. But to tell you the truth, I've never had enormous problems with directors, or even little ones.

Hasn't there ever been a moment of barbarism when you said, "I can't possibly agree to that"?

No, never.

Then you've always had good directors.

I've always chosen them myself. For me it would be unthinkable to agree to conduct an opera without knowing who the director was. The music director and the stage director absolutely must choose each other and complement each other, in a reciprocal exchange.[6]

Doesn't it throw the singers off, that you conduct with just your hands?

No. Not having a baton doesn't make the slightest difference. Disagreements with singers can stem only from differences in concept. I'm not at all authoritarian about that, but I do believe that if singers perform in a way that doesn't suit the musical context—if they stretch something out quite incongruously or, conversely, rush through it—then you have to be firm. It's imperative. It's like riding a horse. Good riders let the horse lead and at the same time keep it in check, because otherwise it will dash off wherever it wants. I've gotten along very well with most singers.

There are a few I haven't gotten along with at all, but, after all, that's to be expected.

You've always got the better of histrionic performers.

When necessary, yes, because the musical director is nonetheless in charge. I must admit, I've never worked with the big Italian stars, because I've never tackled that repertoire. I'd love to know what would happen.

What happens when you conduct your own works—are you more critical? Do you feel embarrassed? Do you feel the work's slipped away from you, or do you rethink it?

No—well, it depends. If it's an old work, I feel more distanced, but with a more recent work I am still involved. The more a work recedes into time, the less I consider it, not with a critical eye, but with a view to remodeling. The work is completed. I am, however, critical of several recent works that I now find in some way unsatisfactory. So I take mental notes as I rehearse and conduct, and I know that if I rework a new version, it will owe a lot to my experience of conducting it.

Do you ever want to reshape a work when you see it from the podium?

Not exactly. Once I start conducting it, I know if there's a problem. If I do conduct it, it's precisely because I want to see that problem clearly. Once I've seen the problem, it's up to me to solve it.

Even so, a scene took place some years ago that made a big impression on the players of the Orchestre National. It happened during a rehearsal of Visage nuptial.[7] *They told me you arrived, opened the score, looked horrified, and immediately closed it again.*

No, no, the story's been completely changed. I had indeed put *Visage nuptial* in the program, precisely to see what was wrong with it. I began to play through the first movement, just using the strings, and I saw it was going to require an effort quite out of proportion to the work's quality. I held two individual part rehearsals, one for strings and the other for winds, brass, and woodwinds.[8] I thought to myself, "This is going to waste my time and everybody else's time as well. I'm going to examine this extremely closely." I hadn't really expected that. When I had looked at the score, I'd told myself I'd play it one last time and rework it afterward. But when I saw how much work would be involved in playing it, and what a nuisance it would be for me and the musicians, I decided, "O.K., I'm going to close it up again."

Was it because of the players?

No, it was because of the score, not particularly because of the musicians. It would have been the same with another orchestra.

It made a big impression on them.

Did it? I think when you feel something has to be done, you have to do it. That's why I wrote the new version of *Visage nuptial.*[9]

A concern for the musicians crops up often in your conversation. You're very demanding, but you'll do anything to keep up the morale of the troops, to the point of planning violations of the rules.

I think that, in large orchestras especially, less so in smaller groups, there's a tendency to grind everyone into a kind of anonymity. I'm not referring to the winds, who always get a chance to perform either as soloists or in small groups, nor to the percussionists, who are always rather independent, especially nowadays;[10] rather I'm thinking of the strings.

String players have little opportunity to show their individual personalities. They're always enclosed in an ensemble, always anonymous. String players either have difficulty accepting this, or they accept it with resignation, which isn't a good formula for living either. In the orchestras I've conducted, I've always managed to divide them into two, so as to perform works for a small orchestra or for a chamber orchestra. As far as was possible, I've always favored chamber music groups because I feel it's essential to good health.

I would actually call this a self-serving way of seeing things, because if you have groups of musicians working in chamber music formats—as in the Ensemble InterContemporain, where there's a wind quintet and a brass ensemble[11]—the ensemble as a whole benefits enormously. People work harder, their technique improves, and their interest in programming is stimulated too.

According to you, specialization becomes a motivating factor.

Yes, in the sense that people study a repertoire they choose themselves, or that someone helps them to choose. They may ask your advice, but it's still their own initiative, their own personal work. No one guides them, although sometimes they may ask, "Could you be here for this?

We'd really like to work with you." That's fine, but I don't force myself on them. As far as possible I encourage these groups to bloom and I ask my colleagues to do the same. When the players have a difficult work to play I have them rehearse it and perform it again, naturally, because the investment has been so huge. It would be a pity to restrict so much effort to a single performance, and so we try to place them in various circuits, so that they can play these works a certain number of times and get some return for their work.[12]

In thus instigating or accepting specialization in orchestras, be it baroque or contemporary, you're really directing people to break rules.

Of course. I'm inclined to think that, rather than having musicians act on their own authority, against the central institution, it would be far better to have the central institution collaborate with them, giving them help and breathing space and aid in doing what they want. There's always a hostility toward a big institution. It is seen as devouring the individual and that individual's interests. I think big institutions should actually cater to these supplemental activities, even the more important ones, and this requires a looser kind of organization than has existed previously. In short, it requires less of this total supervision of the musician, who's supposed to be constantly available. That implies a far more subtle organization than you find in our present large institutions.

If subversion is too readily involved, it loses its attraction.

I don't think it loses its attraction. Musicians break rules because they have to, most of the time, faced with structures that tell them they owe so many hours. When you face an enemy like that, taking an hour over a bite to eat can seem like a subversive act, or even a great victory. I think this worker-boss attitude, an attitude that, if not overtly hostile, at least separates people into camps, is very harmful economically. And so I don't just think it's the appeal of forbidden fruit that motivates musicians, but also the means of earning a bit more money. Their salaries are not exactly wonderful, and they obviously enjoy playing music of a particular period in small groups, so why not allow them to?

You've institutionalized such infringements at the Ensemble Inter-Contemporain. The musicians have a workload of two-thirds the norm.

We half institutionalize them, because if they create chamber music groups, we will employ them ourselves. As for their individual activities, if they decide to go and play elsewhere, I give them the green light if it's an interesting project. If, on the other hand, it's some very minor engagement, such as playing in a tiny place just to make a few cents, then I tell them to beware.

You're the musicians' accomplice.

It's not complicity, it's that I understand them. If I were in their shoes, I'd do the same thing. I understand their situation and their desires. I want to avoid frustration.

You come across as someone really professional, really understanding.

I've been so close to these problems I must understand them. I tell you, I really dislike the kind of power that says, "I want these players two-thirds of the time, and that means two-thirds of the time." There are moments when you do have to remind people, because when there's too much elbowroom, the dinghies tend to row away from the main boat, and suddenly you find you're a few hands short. So there comes a point when you have to remind them rather firmly, and say, "Yes, it's a pity, I know you'd like to do that, but the institution does have first call on you and you're accountable to it first and foremost, just as I am." Once these occasional reminders have been issued, there aren't usually any problems in dealing with people.

Frankly, when you are viewed with such respect and awe, is it always as easy as that? Don't some orchestras have to be won over?

Yes. But naturally, in my present situation, it isn't like it was before. Even if I were to go and conduct an orchestra I didn't know at all, I would not be unknown to the orchestra. There's the matter of one's reputation, which indeed sometimes stems from a false image. People say, "Good heavens, look at the things he's done, it seems he has an excellent ear and he's going to make our lives miserable because of it." There are always clichés attached to one's reputation, that's certain, but on the whole, I never arrive as a complete unknown. If I don't know the orchestra—and that rarely happens now—I usually have them play a work right through. I see how the musicians play for me, to start with, how they react to my gestures, what sort of individual attitudes they have, and how I should adapt to them. You can't achieve all that in a second, you need fifteen or twenty minutes. But, as you know, that is hardly ever necessary now, because I almost always play with orchestras I know.

The musicians told me, "He's difficult, but we gain by that."

Yes, I do try, at a certain level, to make things more dispassionate because there's a job to be done. First you deal with the mechanical aspect, then you deepen the musical appreciation. If you get angry or tense while doing so, it's quite useless. You either waste your time or you don't obtain very good results. I sometimes get annoyed, but it's very rare. I'm very patient at that stage, even if things sometimes progress more slowly than I would like. But once we are past the stage of discovering the text together, then yes, one has to put some passion and vigor into it.

On the other hand you can't rehearse at breakneck speed for three hours—it isn't possible. You have to watch out for your muscles. I often compare people in my profession to athletes, and in particular, to acrobats. Acrobats don't do their turns in a state of passion; they practice very precise movements so as to perform perfectly. Then when they perform in public, they do so with the panache that's peculiar to acrobats.

This being said, there are of course hours of preparation, and they can become tedious. You have to avoid that by working as rapidly as possible. Speed is the most important thing, for me. A highly professional person knows how to work as efficiently as possible.

Recording

There's another activity that requires you to work fast, and that's record-ing. Here, however, you may no longer be the only person in charge. The sound engineer is like an extra conductor.

Yes, you have to work with an excellent sound engineer, or "pro-ducer," as they say in the States. The best producer I ever had is probably Andrew Kazdin.[1] He did practically all the records I made in New York. I took him to Bayreuth to do the *Ring* cycle with me. There's an initial process of adjustment which can sometimes take a long time. First of all the producer and I determine which extracts are the most important for judging the balance on the recording, and then the musicians and I play them. Afterward, the recording goes relatively fast, especially in the United States where the industry is very well organized. In England too. We stop and listen to the tapes—I always listen to each take—and then start again. It all goes very quickly and it's highly professional.

Are you really safe from mistakes?

I haven't been disappointed often. The *Gurrelieder* was a complex work to record, with all the soloists and massed choirs it involves, and I'm not really happy with the results. It was to have been recorded at the Royal Albert Hall, where such enormous numbers of musicians sound perfectly all right. But the hall wasn't free, so we recorded it in a church that, in my opinion, was too small.[2] You can tell because the sound re-verberates in the recording, and at the same time it's a bit too compressed; everyone is jammed together like sardines in a tin. That's one of the few times I've been disappointed.

The other time I wasn't very pleased was when we recorded *Pierrot lunaire* in the church of Notre-Dame-du-Liban.[3] There again, the church made the sound echo quite inappropriately for such a work. Sometimes one is a captive to circumstances. To abandon the recording would have meant having to start all over again, but no one was free, myself least of all, and so we'd have had to wait another two or three years.

A recording is an interpretation. Do you try to have complete control of it yourself or do you hand it over to somebody you trust?

You trust someone to do it but you still act as a witness. Naturally the ones you trust are the truly competent producers. There's an excellent producer in Paris too, Kadar, and I've made some very good recordings with him.[4]

And you follow the actual recording process as far as possible?

Yes, because I listen. First they give me the test recordings after they've been edited. I don't do the editing, of course, but I usually discuss it with the producer. One knows as one goes along which takes should be used, and after that there aren't too many questions. For instance, if I hear something I don't like in the final cut, it's usually that there was nothing better. But sometimes we've still been able to find a slightly different way of editing the problem. Then there's the test cut, and after that it has nothing to do with me.

In a studio, the sound structures you're so keen on become a matter of balance. Do you take into account what the microphone picks up, or do you arrange the orchestral palette as usual?

I arrange it as usual. What the microphone picks up has to be real, because if you start manipulating the microphones in an exaggerated way, the reality you convey is not a very good one. It's absolutely indispensable that you begin with a well-performed, real object. In variety shows, the sound-takes are entirely different because there is no real object. They separate the performers and record everything on separate tracks; the acoustic blending is done afterward, not at the beginning—whereas I think instrumental music has to be presented as it is written. Naturally, you sometimes have instruments that sound weaker than others, such as the celesta. Since you can't put it on a platform, you have to put a microphone beside it. You need some extra assistance like that, but it mustn't sound artificial: it must be as close to reality as possible. You can assist reality just as you can emphasize some feature in a photograph without disfiguring it. It would be different in the case of music that required, for example, a different kind of typesetting or some exceptional kind of typography, corresponding to separated sound tracks. But as far as instrumental music is concerned, one is responsible for the musical object, and the recording engineer is responsible for transmitting that object as faithfully as possible within limits that are naturally scaled down. Even in stereo, you don't get the same impression as when you hear fifteen instruments that are separated only by air.

Does it bother you to play without an audience?

It's not very exciting, but in general, most of the recordings I've done were made after concerts. There are two reasons for that: first, record companies can no longer afford to have an orchestra or an ensemble sightread a work and then record it in a studio. Second, it would be crazy from an artistic standpoint, too, because you have to take advantage of the combination of elements that proved successful in the heat of the concert. And so what you reconstitute in the studio is a combination you've already obtained.

Of course, the great problem of studio recording is how to maintain the impetus, the vital impulse of performance, without making any mistakes. People often sing the praises of live recordings, and they obviously have a vigor and unique quality you never find in studios, but at the same time there are always a few small errors, not to say large ones. To hear the same mistake in phrasing, the same wrong note or an untidy entrance or even a fault in intonation—to hear it once is bad enough, but to hear it on a CD that you listen to again and again is utterly intolerable.[5]

It has a documentary use.

It's a document, yes. But one doesn't listen to a record the same way one listens to a concert, especially not the third or fourth time. In a concert you know it's over and done with, whereas everyone knows you don't buy a recording just to listen to it once. Especially if it's a work that's an outstanding document, but rarely performed. During the recording, therefore, you have to try to blend fire and water—you have to maintain the momentum of public performance, with all the excitement that implies, and at the same time control all the mistakes. You can't let the musicians be so careful that it becomes deadly dull, nor so careless that you have to keep doing everything again.

I generally record fairly long passages. I'd rather play a longish passage two or three times, and if something's really wrong—something that was particularly difficult—we make an insert later. That's a technique I find extremely useful.

But if one of the players starts to stumble over a note, then everyone gets nervous and irritated and they start to stumble. When that happens, it's better to stop for twenty or thirty minutes, until people's nerves settle down, and then begin again. No one feels like playing it again at that point, and you risk losing the tempo and the energy level and the phrasing and even the meaning of the work.

So the documentary principle applies to the studio.

"The great problem of studio recording
is how to maintain the impetus, the
vital impulse of performance,
without making any mistakes."

Boulez recording with the BBC Symphony Orchestra, London, 1984. Photo by Alex von Koettlitz, courtesy BBC Symphony Orchestra.

You try to reconstruct in the studio what you did during the concert, rather as if you were galloping after an image. You really have to concentrate on the work and what it means, at that point. There isn't the feeling of working without a safety net that you get when you play in front of an audience, but the feeling is present in another way because of the excitement of a potentially flawless product.

Settings

An element of concert performance you often emphasize is placement.

Yes. Most of the orchestral compositions written in the last thirty years or more are limited by placement, because a certain orchestral topography is necessary to highlight the actual musical text. We highlight it by an arrangement, by a musical mechanism that enables the written text to assume its full meaning. For example, certain instruments are placed close together, or conversely, others are placed far apart. There's a sort of geography or topography that makes the music clearer. And, of course, our rigidly designed Italianate concert halls don't lend themselves to that. I must admit that operatic directors of the generation that appeared during the sixties have made a great effort to vary locations. But there again, as is always the case, varying the settings has led to some very extravagant, mannered choices of locale. It's almost as if the locale justifies the production.

A warehouse, for example, or an old grotto.

Yes, exactly. They drag you into a patch of forest somewhere and play you *A Midsummer Night's Dream*. And everyone exclaims, "Oh! It's wonderful!" But it isn't. Theater is a marvel of illusion: it should create an illusion out of nothing, like a magician, and that's far preferable to having people go and sit in some old factory.

In terms of a concert, it's strange to add visual elements to music when the music doesn't need them.

Yes, compared to the effort one has to make, it is all something of a smoke screen. What bothers me about these excessively exterior forms of expression is that when there's no functional justification for them—when they remain outside the music—it's almost like an activity planned by Club Med.

Sometimes locale is used as sugar coating to make people swallow the pill of contemporary music.

But that doesn't make them swallow it either, because the only people who go to things like that are already devotees. Twenty-five years ago, Grotowski[1] used to do performances for fifteen or twenty people—he wouldn't accept any more. By all means, let someone be so intent on his or her work that they let only twenty people see it—it's not as though I'm aiming for an audience of twenty thousand, though twenty does seem a little restrictive to me.

The Strasbourg Musica Festival and the Avignon Festival often resort to the formula of location.

Well, you can do that from time to time to demonstrate something. I'm simply saying that when it becomes the only formula, something's very wrong. (*Boulez has sensed the trap.*) It's true, I did play in the stone quarry at Avignon one summer. That's certainly not an auditorium, but the site lent itself to musical performance. And above all, there was no auditorium in Avignon that was suitable—it was as simple as that.[2]

There was an effect of superfluity, as if the eye had too much to take in.

Not at all, because everything was in darkness, so there was nothing to see. One could merely see the rock walls, just as one would normally see walls—I mean, you don't listen to music while gazing at the stars. No, no, there were just enough visual elements for the surroundings to be like any other surroundings, like the courtyard of the Palazzo Farnese was in Rome. There comes a point, yes, when you see what it is, but when what's going on inside is more interesting, one pays attention to that and not to the surroundings.

When new concert halls are built, unfortunately, they still tend to be built with forward-facing stages.

Yes. In the case of La Villette, however, and also the variable hall at the Bastille, plans were drawn up for what you might call transformable venues.[3] These halls can accommodate different seating arrangements and topographies and are far more flexible than our existing auditoriums, which can't be adapted at all.

You've referred to the case of Piscator in Germany, where the movable facility has never been used. Force of habit proved stronger than the new facility there.

That's what happens when the apparatus is very hard to move, or very uneconomical. If you have to close the theater for five days and hire a team of twenty workmen to change all the seating arrangements, it's obvious you'll use it once or twice and that will be all. I haven't seen the technical arrangements of the Mannheim theater; I've only read a description of them. But in all the theaters I've visited, the equipment is far too heavy to maneuver. Heavy to maneuver means it's a burden economically. And if it's a burden economically, it won't be used.

Will the nonstandard venues of the future be used as intended?

Certainly. I've spent a lot of time making sure that the equipment is very light and that the room can be transformed very quickly. The old Théâtre National Populaire, the Théâtre de Chaillot, offers an example of how equipment that was intelligently conceived yet too heavy has almost never been used.

What about these rather modern and companionable concert halls, such as that of the Berlin Philharmonic, where the spectators sit all around the orchestra?

It works and it doesn't work. For an orchestral piece, it's O.K. For a piece that has a soloist, it works only moderately well.[4] Try listening to something like the Brahms Violin Concerto there—since it's part of their repertoire—and sit right behind at the back. You will get a completely distorted impression of the balance between violin and orchestra. For one thing, the violin sound will be projected in the opposite direction, toward the public sitting in front of the orchestra, and it won't project backward at all. For another, the orchestral wall, particularly the winds and brass, will make your acoustical perspective extremely unsatisfactory.

Of course, you'll tell me there are other compensations, because one can see the conductor and because one feels caught up in what the orchestra is doing. That reminds me of the Concertgebouw auditorium, where there are far fewer seats behind than in front, but where people are very drawn to the ones behind, because they want to feel part of the orchestra's activity.

It's a form of voyeurism, then?

It's a form of participation rather than voyeurism. People are there, they watch, they know the works, they see how the works are being conducted, they can follow the conductor's facial expressions as he looks at the musicians—they certainly participate more fully and I imagine that this kind of visual participation makes up for the acoustical distortions.

And what about you? Does it make a difference to have the audience in front of you?

No, you soon forget about them entirely. They're sitting quite far away, and besides, you're so taken up with what you're doing, other people scarcely matter at that point.

Audiences

The audience is ultimately the orchestra's partner. Are there many types of audience, or are they all the same?

I wouldn't even say there were audiences. There are people. Really. You know, an audience is made up of about fifteen hundred people, something like that. I don't know if you recall the fine passage from Claudel's book *L'échange*. In about ten or twenty lines an actress describes theater and the theatrical audience. You should read it, because it's exactly what I believe.[1] There is indeed an audience, united by its presence in the house, by the mass it forms, and by the kind of emotional movement you get inside a group. But listen to what people say as they come out of a concert, and you'll hear opinions that are diametrically opposed—even the opinions of professionals are sometimes extremely divergent. That's why I don't think there are types of audience. I think there are individuals who suddenly see themselves in the same mirror, but apart from that—

I've been present at auditions for stringed instruments in New York. There's a sort of internal jury, comprised mainly of other string players. And then when you hear the jury reading their notes, you really wonder if they've been listening to the same person. One of them will say, "Bowing very rigid, not much virtuosity in the right hand, not much sound," and another says, "Ample sound production, very flexible bowing, virtuosity." Really, it's as divergent as that.

Does that apply to critics, too?

It applies to anyone who listens, I would say. There are so many elements involved, as in Pirandello: in the end, no two people tell the same story. I think that's a good thing—if everyone uttered the same opinion emerging from a concert, it would be deadly. Instead everyone tells you, "It was wonderful," but it's like after a play, when one person will say, "That scene was superb, but this one wasn't as good," and someone else will say exactly the opposite. Naturally, there's unanimous agreement about excellence, but it is expressed through innumerable points of view.

Do people's comments have national or social overtones?

Social overtones, certainly. For example, there are people who go simply to hear a great name. So, whatever that artist does, they'll be thrilled, but in fact they barely listen.

They can say they were there.

They were there, and the concert fulfilled the social function of having people meet each other, as they do at the theater. They go to hear Monsieur X or Madame Y and they're thrilled. That's all right—it corresponds to the behavior of a certain social class, to certain notions spread by glossy magazines, or even to a certain form of culture. You have to remember that some social strata are extremely superficial, and the people in them flock like geese toward some spectacle, and all they're really asking is to be expensively amused in some way. All right, fine—I don't actually see how one could eliminate that tendency, given that the power of money plays a part in it. It's simply not what I consider really important in the musical life of a country.[2]

What about the other classes of society? Haven't you yielded to working-class experiments?

No. First, it hasn't been done. Secondly, it would be like trying to spear water. What do you expect to achieve when people have absolutely no culture? Your spear will maybe bring a drop or two of water to the surface. But does one have time to do that—time for events where five hundred people will show up, and not even one of them will really be interested? There just isn't the cultural substratum. Personally, I think this is an educational problem. It really needs to be grappled with and taken very seriously. If working people are going to come, they need to be involved in a certain number of leisure activities. And then they mustn't have the feeling they're being helped; they must feel they have chosen freely because they have already acceded to a certain area of knowledge. When that happens, they'll enjoy going to concerts.

It's quite obvious that rock groups address a very elementary cultural level, and that the working class is more or less obliged to be content with that. I'm not at all demagogic in that respect. I say it's fine to give them this outlet—because that's really what it is—this new opium of the people. But in my opinion, the people who make the decisions shouldn't be content to say, "We're interested in your problems so we've built you a venue for rock concerts." The decisionmakers should be told to go ahead and build the venue, but at the same time to try to give these people the same culture they have themselves. What bothers me is the demagoguery implicit in their attitude and the lack of respect they have for working people, who are supposed to be content with this primitive form of culture.

"Naturally, there is unanimous agreement
about excellence, but it is expressed
through innumerable points of view."

Boulez conducting the Chicago Symphony Orchestra, 1995. Photo by Cheri Eisenberg, courtesy Chicago Symphony Orchestra.

So playing at the Renault factory reveals just a preoccupation with the baseness of the working class?

It's meaningless, that's all. It's meaningless because it defies logic, or even absurdity. It's simply to have a clear conscience. Let's hit the Renault factory. What's the point? There isn't one. It's what used to be called slumming, when rich ladies would distribute candies to the poor. Personally I think we've got other things to do.

But rock audiences are mainly young. You've invested a lot in young people and have been generous with your explications. Is that enough?

Yes, I still try to assume educational responsibilities, though at a rather restricted level. I've done so in New York, in London, in Paris, you know. But I no longer have the time. If I absolutely had to spend it that way, then I'd do that and nothing else. I think, however, that these activities can be performed by persons other than myself.

Have you been aware of national characteristics in your audiences?

No, they're more or less the same wherever I go. I don't see huge differences between audiences. Yes, some audiences may feel closer to certain pieces, the way a German audience may feel a greater affinity with certain German compositions. But these are not reactions I find particularly striking.

Some performing artists mention the enthusiasm of German audiences or, conversely, the slightly chilly intellectualism of French listeners. Are those mere myths?

Yes, they are myths. That's the way the performers tell themselves those audiences react, how they imagine they react. There's no more intellectualism in France than there is more this or that in Germany or England. Obviously, you can distinguish between an audience in London and one in Rome. In Rome the public tends to be noisy but very enthusiastic, whereas in London it's also very enthusiastic but much quieter and more disciplined. So, you have to adjust to that—it's like going into an English restaurant or an Italian one.

You've had a taste of opera audiences, especially at Bayreuth.[3]

They're rather special audiences, I have to admit. You know, some musical audiences are very compartmentalized, even now. There are people who go only to the opera and almost never to a concert. Then there are people who are interested—or at least, passionately interested—only in chamber music, and who seldom attend orchestral concerts. Obviously there are others with a rather broader horizon, but I'm sometimes astonished at how compartmentalized audiences can be.

Opera audiences are evidently drawn by certain vocal qualities. Anything can happen—the staging can be dreadful, the orchestra inadequate—but as long as there are voices, that's all that interests them. They also tend never to venture beyond a certain repertoire, so if they're used mainly to hearing Italian operas, the German repertoire annoys them. I have to say that this indicates a very narrow vision, and not much musical intelligence at all. The opera-going public is very sensitive to what I would term the sensual qualities of the music. I don't mean qualities that appeal to sensibility, but immediate, physical qualities. From that point of view, I find them very narrowminded. It's very unusual, among opera-goers, to find people who appreciate the staging as well as the singing and the musical direction, who have a general sense of the production. There's a real lack of curiosity and concern in that kind of audience, I find.

Hence the shock at Bayreuth.

Hence the shock at Bayreuth, certainly. Because when we did *Lulu* at the Paris Opéra, there were no protests at all.[4] But that audience had come specially to hear *Lulu*. And since it came for *Lulu*, it knew perfectly well it wasn't going to hear *La bohème*.

France and Its Orchestras

What if we took stock of the orchestras in France?

It's difficult for me to do that. I suppose I would say French orchestras have good points and bad points. Bad points rather than good points, on the whole, because it's been difficult to attract big names to France, big names who'll take charge of an orchestra for a long time. The Orchestre de Paris is probably the only example of that at the moment. Several big names have paraded through the Orchestre National, but either they didn't stay long or they didn't take up the musical director's duties sufficiently firmly.[1]

I think the life of an orchestra depends essentially on both its musical director and on its manager, and thus by extension on the manager's efforts to expand its audience. There's still a dearth of managers in France, a dearth of people with the requisite profile as you would find in England and the United States. The managers I know well in places like Los Angeles or New York or Boston or Chicago just don't exist in Europe—at least not in France. I think it's execrable to entrust the administration or management of music to people who have absolutely no knowledge of administrative problems, who haven't given proof of their ability in that domain.

Except for the Orchestre de Paris, the French radio orchestras have had a lot of problems to overcome. One of them, the New Philharmonic Orchestra, has pulled itself together since it acquired a musical director,[2] and I hope the Orchestre National will do the same with Maazel. Even so, French orchestral administration really needs to reach the same level as in America. The conductor should be present for between sixteen and eighteen weeks per year, which is at least four or five months per year, or almost half the season.[3] Until that happens, you really can't expect marvelous results.

What about the regional horizon?

Frankly, I don't know too much about that. I know the French papers keep mentioning several names, particularly Lille, then Strasbourg and Toulouse. Those are the three poles they speak of, together with the Lyons opera. So I think there must be degrees of excellence in all those cities, but I can't really tell you because I haven't followed either their programs or their performances.

Is there any reason why you can't or won't take a hand in those orchestras?

It's not my place to, really. If I have to do something, I'd rather be selfish and accept an invitation to Chicago for two or three weeks for some special project.[4] At my stage of the game that's really far more interesting. I'd gladly go to Lille, but only with a visiting orchestra—as when I went with the Ensemble, for example.

The Future

Let's talk about the future. You've said some very interesting things about the future role of the orchestral conductor. According to you, his task will be less to disseminate information than to absorb it, to take it in.

The contemporary repertoire already requires this. Normally, one directs people toward synchronism and centralization. But there are works, particularly works of our generation, in which musicians must, on the contrary, assume a certain freedom, a certain individuality. This is the sort of decentralization one must strive for, while simultaneously seeing to it that people don't get lost, that they're still under the surveillance of the lifeguard, so to speak. They can go a certain distance from the beach but they're still under supervision. And so when they return to the group, they can do so with security. I actually think that for certain works, it's as important to know how to wander off as it is to come home, in my opinion.

Could this be applied to music of the standard repertoire?

Certainly not. You can leave the reins, well, extremely loose—as I was saying earlier about soloists and the solo players in great orchestras who have extensive musical culture and strong personalities. When they have a big solo passage, yes, you leave them alone: if you have a horn solo in Mahler, for example, you're not going to beat away like a madman—you let the soloist go ahead and then simply connect the solo passage to the music. In a way, there's already a feeling of freedom in relation to the group in the great orchestral literature, but it's a freedom which is nonetheless still very much connected to the center.

Do you still maintain that the conductor is an expert, a real virtuoso?

Yes, absolutely. There *are* virtuoso conductors. Moreover, the term can be applied to several areas. I mean, a conductor can have virtuosity in execution, in the sense that he interprets well, that he has the ability to raise the orchestra to a superior level, that he carries things through and sees to it that things are carried through. In short, he's so demanding that, with him, even things that are very hard for the orchestra are well performed. Then there's a kind of virtuosity in the gestures a conductor makes: I'm speaking in regard to myself, because I have a lot of experience there. When there are a lot of free expressive gestures to make, in fact, and these free gestures really have to determine each individual response, it takes a high degree of virtuosity to trigger an entirely personal relationship with the players. For example, when the music isn't metrical, there are no longer collective gestures, there are simply individual gestures that you have to make with absolute dependability and brilliant technique. That is virtuoso conducting, certainly.

Then "conducting" can be taken in the spatial as well as musical sense?

Yes, absolutely. Even in a normal orchestra, with normal conducting, you have to keep track of everyone, of the people sitting in front of you, hence, of their topography. But if you happen to be conducting unconventional things, then topography becomes essential. In the course I taught in Avignon, what bothered the students most was not remembering where the musicians were. They would suddenly make a gesture without knowing where to direct it, because they hadn't made a mental note of where that person was.

You've even called conducting a "science."

Yes, it is a science, like a virtuoso's science, for the most part—well, it's not a particular science, it's a virtuoso's science, a technique the virtuoso has.

And in 1966—the same year you used that term—you went so far as to devise an orchestral part that was all gestures.[1]

Yes.

Wouldn't it be constricting, to have a kind of extra line in the text?

When I add gestures, I do it just for certain scores, not for all, but for some of them. In *Répons* for example: when Peter Eötvös first conducted it, I went to the rehearsal and I told him which were the best gestures, the most effective gestures. I wrote it down, of course; it's written down that here, for instance, you conduct left hand right hand, the left hand does this, the right hand does that, and so on, so that in effect there's an orchestral score consisting of gestures.

So there's a coding, a kind of language involved?

It isn't a grammar really, but it consists of beats one has to give, purely and simply, left hand right hand, and it tells you how to beat them, if the music is not specifically metrical. If it is metrical, there's no problem, but if it isn't metrical then one has to indicate what one wants.

Is that by way of advice, or is it really an order?

Let's just say that if you don't follow it (*Boulez laughs*), you'll get into a lot of trouble.

A true Boulez answer. The question is an important one, because at this point, the composer merges with the conductor and the conductor's action becomes an element of the composition.

Indeed it does. But it's not the first thing to consider. It's something that crops up along the way, when one says to oneself, "If I write that, how am I going to conduct it?" If I conduct it, I will try that, and if it works, then I'll leave it in the score, that's all.

Just as Wagner indicated the "Takte," you indicate the gestures.

Yes, but they're very simple indications—it's not a special grammar. Read the score of *Éclat* or the score of *Répons*: they're things one does oneself. For example in *Répons*, there's quite a long section with a metrical direction for the main orchestra and an absolutely nonmetrical direction for the soloists, who surround the conductor, and the two are superimposed. And if you don't do it the way I say, you'll simply get into difficulties.

With the possible risk that in a hundred years some iconoclast will exclaim, "What do I care about old Boulez and his gestures?"

If he discovers better ones—

But you yourself say that Wagner's metronomic markings don't interest you at all.

He didn't provide any. After *Tannhäuser* I don't think he gave any.[2] He didn't give any more metronomic markings and he explained why. He believed metronomic markings basically give rise to the wrong interpretive impulses; therefore one shouldn't indicate them. Debussy's the same. Although he doesn't explain it, he didn't give any metronomic markings toward the end.[3] Curious, isn't it?

These written parts for gestures, aren't they really a way of imposing your interpretation?

It's as if you indicated fingering, nothing more. In critical editions of Liszt and Chopin, they give the fingering used by Liszt and Chopin. Here, the beat is indicated, that's all. There's no more to it than that.

Isn't the aim actually to make conductors' gestures more aesthetic?

No, not at all. No, it's truly the equivalent of fingering.

Then there's no risk of theatricality?

No, no, no. That's impossible. It goes by too fast. (*Boulez laughs.*)

Our virtuoso conductor of the future will need a concept of the ideal orchestra. For a while you conceived of it as a consortium or a cooperation, though not simply a cooperative. Do you still see it that way?

It's rather a utopian entity, because to tell you the truth it's harder to bring about than it is to think up. I once gave a rather lengthy talk on the subject, in a conference on the orchestra of the future at the European Broadcasting Union in Frankfurt. My remarks were published in their account of the proceedings. I'd already stated the problems that would occur.[4]

I start with a number. Then I imagine an ensemble, a sort of pool—it wouldn't really be an orchestra at that point—yes, a pool of about 150 or 160 musicians. There would be a large proportion of strings, of course—I can't say exactly how many, I haven't gone as far as to investigate the statistical breakdown of the repertoire—and there would have to be more wind instruments than usual, at least six or seven wind instruments in every section, an equal quantity of brass, several keyboard instruments, and so on.

And there would be problems—first of all, the problem of historical specialization. As I was saying, taking into account people's affinities and likes and preferences, there would have to be a certain number to whom one could entrust, say, baroque music, or even music older than baroque, music dating as far back as the sixteenth or fifteenth century—medieval music. Then among those people there would need to be a core group who could make a thorough study of the musical texts and style of execution. So that really presupposes a certain number of specialists.

And then there would be people who would work with the standard repertoire, and others more attracted to the twentieth-century repertoire and especially to research—people who would work, that is, with an institute like IRCAM. The whole affair would have to be linked to an institute of that kind, so that with such a large body of musicians one could cover practically the entire repertoire. Of course, that would create a staffing problem. You wouldn't have an orchestra of 160 musicians all the time; it's just not possible. But in the great works of the past, or even of the present, you can have as many as 110 or 120. So there would be a kind of breakdown, or rather a timetable, for splitting up the more specific activities of the reduced group and the activities of the whole. I think this way of organizing things would be very useful, first and foremost because it would involve the principal musicians in the whole range of history. Even if they have a preference for one period or another, they would still experience the entire repertoire. In my opinion—and what I'm saying is really very *omnivorous*—one would have to arrange performances of opera as well, so that the musicians would also cover a part of that repertoire. It isn't proper for a musician in a symphony orchestra never to have played through an entire work by Wagner; it's really very harmful to his development. Then again, as far as possible one would have to promote the formation of various chamber groups. So there you have it, that would be the project. Of course it's rather a utopian view of things.

One encounters many problems. To start with, you can't change instruments just like that. If you've been playing a baroque instrument for a while, then you have to get used to the present-day instrument again, because the distances between the fingers aren't the same, the sound isn't the same, ditto for bowing and breathing. In other words, you'd need some time between the preparation needed for such works and for the normal or contemporary repertoire—I should say, the historical or contemporary repertoire. For example, the people who might do a series of seventeenth-century concerts would need time to readapt to modern instruments, to the sound they make and the sound of the group. I think that in this regard, one would have to arrange for periods of intense personal preparation. It's obvious that when people play a different instrument, even if it's only the fiddle in Mahler, when it's tuned up a tone to

D in the Fourth Symphony, the violin soloist needs several days to adapt to the instrument's new tone and a different fingering, and it's obvious what different practice habits that implies.[5] Thus, there's a problem in apportioning the time needed for preparation and time needed for execution, and the time needed to make the transition from one repertoire to the next. That's the first thing.

Second, homogeneity occurs in an orchestra because people are used to playing in the same seat. It's almost like home, and, although seating isn't literally prescribed in a certain way, it's nonetheless an extremely strong component of the orchestra. And people sharing the same music stand can get along very well or very badly together, sometimes that happens. There have been clashes. You can't keep changing stand partners, because once you do, the homogeneity and the quality of the orchestral playing suffer enormously. So you have to find a system that allows you to modify the orchestral body while keeping some elements constant. And there again, it isn't easy to have variable and constant elements at the same time.

I have never looked into the problem further because in the case of those institutions where I had responsibility I could go only so far—separate the orchestra into two, as I said, and try to create smaller groups. But we didn't for instance go as far as to specialize in early music. So from that point of view, we really need to look into a way of distributing the resources—it would be inconvenient but I do think it's possible.

It remains to be seen whether such a consortium would be very onerous to administer. Obviously it's easier to manage a small ensemble, a normal-sized orchestra, and another small ensemble, because you have three distinct bodies. But I think with present-day methods of business management, it is possible. I think that managing the personnel and the artistic side would be much harder than the administrative management—or even than a joint administrative-artistic management. But with practice one can do it. Naturally, you couldn't arrange for constant exchanges, because, as I said, there wouldn't be enough preparation time, but I think you could schedule a season with enough separate compartments and enough time for assimilation. I think that in a large city, a major organization could really benefit from this type of concentration of activity.

So will it come about or not? I don't know. It isn't the right moment now for concentrated activity, because everyone likes to get funding for themselves, and, of course, the more individual groups there are, the more sources of money there are to tap into. It corresponds to a particular type of patronage. A large organization like that, however, would require massive patronage—collective patronage, I would say. So is it viable or not? In any case I think that even if one didn't have the consortium, with its musicians apportioned into different groups or activities, it would be very useful to put a small administrative board in charge of a city's various musical bodies. The board could make sure that their activities didn't overlap, keeping them separate while at the same time ensuring the existence of a common audience, when the opportunity arose.

From the standpoint of conducting, such an organization presupposes a kind of collegiality, since no single conductor is capable of encompassing four centuries of repertoire.

No, certainly not—not well, in any case. It can be done, of course—a measure is always a measure and a group of musicians is always a group of musicians—but it's done badly and without period expertise. I think one can risk it occasionally, precisely when one's trying to establish a kind of osmosis between various organisms. Having said that, obviously people do specialize. There are conductors who are quite remarkable with chamber orchestras and utterly lost when they conduct full orchestras. That has occurred and will continue to occur, just as there are conductors who perform superbly with a nineteenth-century repertoire and a large orchestra, and who have absolutely no sense of fifteenth-century style.

Would there be a sort of collegial self-management, or would there still be a conductor in charge to determine the quality?

No. If there was a level of understanding between people of high quality, the arbitration—and some would indeed be necessary—could be settled fairly easily by the same people. It's not about competition or rivalry; it's about not stepping on each other's feet. It's a matter of apportioning the time and of seeing how many thousands of spectators correspond to a particular repertoire. Because however much you try to improve communication with the public, it's quite certain that music from the fifteenth or early sixteenth century will attract a smaller audience than Mahler.

As far as revenues are concerned, you would definitely have to monitor the ratio between audience interest and the repertoire performed, because there's a ratio that has to be considered extremely realistically. We know that an opera can be performed ten times, whereas a concert can be repeated only two or three times. You can try to improve a few numbers, knowing all the while that there are circles that are certainly not concentric, as in Dante's *Inferno*, but which get larger or smaller in proportion to the repertoire you play.

Looking at the map of Europe, how many such focal points do you envisage?

I think there are several groups that could develop. Unquestionably, you could only give reality to these consortiums in relatively large cities. Such cities would be the true centers for these groups because that's where you find adequate resources in terms of instruments, musicians, and also the stringed-instrument trade—the things you couldn't find in a small town of fifty thousand, for example. But even in the smallest towns it would be possible to organize—I sound like a supermarket manager—a system of concerts. The most specialized orchestras could give regular series there.[6]

Naturally, this implies a fair amount of traveling, but if each region possessed a strong lead city, the distances are never so vast that they are not easily manageable. You would simply have to define the head of each region very clearly. Since each town wants its own hegemony, that's rather difficult. The towns would have to see that they couldn't realize more than a certain amount of their potential—and that this would depend on the size of the urban area involved.

And how many centers could there be in France?

As many as there are regions, more or less—that is, about seven or eight, of varying degrees of importance. It's difficult to equate Rennes with Paris, that certainly can't be done, but I think if each region were to be organized in relation to its size and wealth, the plan would be quite feasible.

Above all, it involves reforming the way people think. Education would have to accompany this reorganization and be disseminated throughout the regions. For even in Germany—and, God knows, Germany's a federal country—where the Berlin Philharmonic is, some schools are far superior to others. There will always be different levels of quality, that's inevitable, but I think considerable improvement can occur, if there's a plan. What I find regrettable is that behind these big institutions, there's rarely any plan. Or else the project is very limited, or sporadic, or it depends on a particular person, lasts a certain time, and then vanishes—whereas if there was a more permanent plan, I think the institutions would be far better off.

TWELVE

Education of Conductors and the Changing of the Guard

Let's turn to education.

I'm not at all a specialist in education; I've never been much involved myself. Only rarely have I taught conducting: twice in Basel and once in Avignon.[1] I've always taught it with an orchestra, with players who have to respond very precisely. That's because I think trying to teach conducting by means of a piano, or two pianos at the most, is absolutely useless. First, you don't obtain the real sound, and second, you're not working with a large group, which is very important. Third, it doesn't correspond to the psychology of conducting an orchestra. Two people playing a reduced version of the work on two pianos may provide a tiny bit of training, but afterward you have to go straight to nature, as it were. You have to give future conductors the opportunity to conduct. A champion swimmer practices in a swimming pool; an orchestral conductor practices with an orchestra. Until there are proportionately more opportunities for would-be conductors to conduct, we won't make much progress.

This being said, some things are very hard to understand. Genetics can be mysterious, you know. I don't think Italy has better conservatories than France—they may be better distributed, since the country is less centralized—yet there are far more international conductors from Italy than there are from France, or even from Germany. Why were they all born there? What's more, they've sometimes been educated outside the country. Abbado studied in Vienna and so did Sinopoli, in part.[2] So it's clear that, from one country to the next, the same conditions produce different results.

I have lots of faith in education, but I'm very skeptical about it too! If I told you good teachers are all you need in order to have good students, it would be far too simple. And even teachers who bear the stamp of genius—that is, very great interpreters or composers—don't necessarily make great professors. They haven't time; they have other interests in life. Because it's specialized, pedagogy runs the risk of remaining a peripheral activity, especially in the interpretive arts, yet obviously we can't do without it. So, it's problematical. You don't see famous conductors spending two days per week teaching students, and it would surprise me if they ever did. They have too many commitments, too much traveling to do. So we certainly need to put together some sort of basic pedagogical program. It might not be very exciting, but at least it would be there. We could inject it with hormones periodically—although that's banned (*Boulez laughs*)—so that the students would suddenly make progress, or at any rate receive a shock! I don't know what kind of shot in the arm we could give them—some kind of stimulus to relieve the monotony of regular education.[3]

What about a privileged relationship between master and student, or else an assistantship?

Assistantships are not ideal either. When you know the risks that orchestras and organizers of concerts take in order to attract large audiences, you can't entrust much to an assistant. That's the problem. You give them something to do only when you're ill.

Which is what happened to you.

Yes—it's illness that finally drives the rats out of the ship. When you fall ill, you're forced to hand the conducting over to the assistant. If I fall ill two days before a concert and they can't find anyone, the assistant is there. He usually knows the scores, he's followed the rehearsals, and he can still jump on board the train, as it were. In general, however, the assistants don't get many favors. They always get the odds and ends—you'll say, well at least that's something—they get the concerts and parts of concerts that the conductors don't want to do. If a conductor doesn't like contemporary music, he'll give the contemporary pieces to his assistant, which is not exactly a gift vis-à-vis the orchestra. The assistant will also conduct things like children's concerts, where the kids are often rowdy and it's hard to hear, and the program consists of insignificant extracts from this or that. In short, they won't be very interesting concerts.

Perhaps you'll tell me that the assistant will still get an occasional chance to become familiar with a certain literature, but the opportunities really aren't too glorious. That's why an assistant of average ability will stay with you a long time, because it's a way of earning a living, and such a person isn't going to do much better. But if you have a very good assistant, the first thing he or she will do is try to make it alone, try to find something more advantageous. It's very difficult to give assistants interesting tasks that aren't too risky. You can't expose them to criticism too suddenly, because the reactions of audiences and critics can be extraordinarily harsh and can prove detrimental to the assistant for a long time. So you have to try to give them tasks gradually. Unfortunately orchestral institutions don't lend themselves to that, one has to admit.[4]

Are you pleased or disappointed with the new generation of conductors?

That depends on each individual. I think some of them do perform a more interesting repertoire than others, while at the same time there are some very conventional ones, who are apparently devoid of curiosity and who are prematurely old at thirty. I wouldn't want to mention any names, although there are several on the tip of my tongue, but I've recently seen people I met ten years ago, when they were about twenty, and they've become hyper-conventional.

Doesn't the current state of the market rather encourage that?

The market leads to conservatism, yes. But you know, if you have a strong personality, you're the one who'll change the market, instead of the market changing you. If these conductors are prepared to conform to the market, it's because they were always prepared to be molded in that way. I think it comes from their own attitudes.

Colleagues

How do you view your colleagues generally? Are you optimistic or pessimistic about their conducting?

Both, I would say. First of all I consider them from a professional standpoint, and from that point of view there are undoubtedly some really excellent conductors. There aren't hundreds of them, but there are certainly some who are excellent, particularly in their regular repertoire. I can judge them with adequate detachment—without envy or jealousy—because I'm not personally involved. From a professional viewpoint, then, there are quite a lot of highly competent conductors, but what I find regrettable in most of them is their total lack of curiosity and absence of culture. They tend to view conducting as mere work: artistic work, obviously, but work that's devoid of adventure. Even in relation to the historical repertoire so dear to them they're entirely lacking in culture. They're not familiar with the lesser-known works, or minor works, and very often they don't have the imagination to make up a good program. They have a certain amount of imagination in regard to what they play, but none at all for programming, or incorporating musical life into cultural life generally. If people of their talent possessed more curiosity, they could do musical life a lot of good. They perform the works well, agreed, but what's left afterward? It's like a pastry cook who makes good cakes, period.

So they should risk their reputations by playing a few more recent works?

Yes indeed, but they won't. Most of the time it's not even through fear of risking their reputations—it's simply because it's too much bother, because they're devoid of curiosity, because they don't like that sort of music, because they won't make an effort.

Do you think perhaps they're incapable of it?

They would be capable if they worked. I'm absolutely convinced of that. Contemporary music has nothing savage about it. You just need to work, and be possessed of a more curious turn of mind than they have. It's due to laziness, to lack of curiosity, to lack of culture.

Have they perhaps been caught up in the machine, as well?

Exactly, they've been caught up in the machine because they don't have sufficiently powerful individual personalities, that's all. (*Boulez laughs.*) I don't think it's possible to have a more severe attitude than mine. In no way do I take issue with their undeniable professional qualities; it's their lack of curiosity and lack of culture that I reproach them for. I find it terrible to see.

In the end, that may not be such a bad thing. They're actually killing off a part of the standard repertoire.

They're not really even killing it off, because they doubtless correspond to a segment of the public that's as uncultivated and incurious as they are. If lack of curiosity and culture were self-vitiating vices, they would no longer exist. But not only are they not self-vitiating vices, they are, on the contrary, embellishments of society.

By playing the older repertoire too often, they may cause it to shrink and disappear.

Alas, I'm not as optimistic as you are. On the contrary, I think it corresponds exactly to what the Germans call "Unterhaltung" and the English call "entertainment." What's tragic at times is that even the noblest music—the very same music that was the most daring music written in past centuries—is treated like a kind of dessert. I find that really appalling. It reduces music to the most trivial gastronomic level.

Can your special relationship with Barenboim really convert him to contemporary music? [1]

Yes, certainly. Barenboim possesses curiosity and he realizes you can't always live on the standard repertoire. Besides, he's interested in what's going on—just as, in opera, he's interested in directors who are really adventurous, whose work really means something. That's because he has a sense of curiosity.

Can any of the others be saved?

A few, maybe five or six at the present time. That's not many, you'll tell me, but at least it's something.

What about von Karajan, the Commander of Berlin?[2]

Oh, yes! He was the perfect example of the superior professional. I'm sorry that a person of his caliber did not marshal his forces in favor of a richer and more interesting activity.

His recordings of Schoenberg and Webern have been reissued.

Yes, he recorded them once. Just once.

His interpretation leans heavily toward romanticism.

I've never listened to them, so I can't comment. Even so—the problem is not that he interprets them this way or that. I think the fact that he recorded them at all indicates he made quite an effort. It's a pity he didn't keep going in that direction. Contemporary music could have benefited not only from his prestige, but from his experience and personal magnetism too.

You haven't said anything about the Berlin Philharmonic.

I've been invited to conduct the Berlin Philharmonic several times.[3] But you know, visiting an organization like that to do a contemporary music series, solely because the orchestra feels duty bound to make that concession, is not very interesting to me. It's much more interesting to visit an organization that considers contemporary music a significant part of its activity, even if it can't be considered the central part of it. I've always preferred to visit orchestras that have the latter attitude.

Was the Berlin Philharmonic shaped too much by one person?

I don't think so, no. Great orchestras aren't fashioned by a single person. Orchestras of such distinction react very well to a change of conductor.

When one of your colleagues deigns to conduct your works, when they're conducted by somebody besides you, do you feel the works are slipping away from you? Do they disappoint you? Or do you discover them anew?

It depends. I can be pleased and even interested by a good performance, but sometimes I'm in the position of being the backseat driver, the passenger who's used to being the driver and can't help reacting. Even if the performance goes well, there's always a passage where one thinks: I'd have slowed down sooner, I'd have done this. I mean, one has a kind of physiological reflex. It would be better if one couldn't drive at all. It's all right with good performances, but sometimes I'm put through bad ones, too.

Don't you mind if the interpretation contradicts your own idea of the work?

In general it doesn't contradict it. If I suffer, it's because it's nowhere near the idea. (*Boulez laughs.*) It's because people don't pay attention to what I wrote, or else they're incapable of performing it with any depth. If a tempo is taken too slowly, for example, or if the players hold back at a moment when they should go forward—things like that. It's very annoying. I have to admit I'm rarely satisfied. But sometimes I am.

Does that mean you would permit your works to be interpreted only one way?

No, I don't think so. Besides, what I hear most of the time is not another way of interpreting them, it's simply an inadequate way. I expect performances from conductor and musicians that are as vivid as my concept was; I expect the balance between the instruments to be truly as I imagined it. You could say I expect the work's continuity to be as I conceived it; that is, there has to *be* continuity. All that is indispensable to me. And if those elements aren't there, I find it very annoying.

I feel the same annoyance when I listen to works I didn't write, but which I've often conducted. It bothers me enormously sometimes when I hear things that I don't think really fit the music. At times I'm a bad listener. Then again, sometimes the work gains the upper hand and I become more interested in the work than in the person conducting it.

Even if it's one of your own recordings?

Oh—I'm not terribly good at recognizing my own recordings. I must tell you, someone tried that on me once, and I couldn't recognize myself. It's especially hard if people play me little bits and pieces, or if it's a record I made twenty years ago. Then I don't remember what I did at all.[4] And as I've changed in the interim and would certainly do things slightly differently, I think of what I would do now and not at all of what I did then. Besides, there's an element of narcissism in listening to one's recordings. Personally, I never do.

You're lucky in that you have an equal mastery of conducting and composing. Most of your colleagues who compose haven't really been successful with the baton.

That's simply because it's not their profession, because they haven't worked at it, because they've never done enough of it. It's not a trade those conductors are going to learn through conducting their own works once or twice a year.[5]

It's become proverbial to say that composers are bad conductors. Is it a matter of subjectivity?

No, it's a matter of experience and of having the right gift. There are people who aren't very gifted. I won't mention their names, but I've seen some composers conduct who really aren't gifted at all.

You see, they tend to be very emotional. They don't possess that kind of tool acquired through professional experience, and so they conduct solely by means of passion. And passion isn't really the best way to conduct. You need to have passion, but you also need the professional tool. (*Boulez laughs.*) It's as if you were cutting a windowpane: either you do it properly, with a diamond, or you don't know how to go about it and you use your fist. You'll hurt yourself, and the pane will be cut badly, that's all.

Body Language

by Paul Griffiths

It's hard to say who learned more: the four young conductors who became Pierre Boulez's apprentices for a couple of days with the Cleveland Orchestra at Carnegie Hall in March, 1993, or the audience at this Professional Training Workshop, since the need to explain himself obliged Mr. Boulez, one of the most undemonstrative of conductors, to show his hand—or, rather, his two hands, his two hands capable of maintaining different rhythms independently, of thinking apart. That was one problem for his would-be disciples. Mr. Boulez's advice was directed solely to matters of technique, and to musical issues technique can address. Without his technique, the four young men stood little chance of rising to his expectations of them, however straightforwardly and encouragingly those expectations were expressed, and however much support and good will was coming for the brave volunteers from both orchestra and audience. (The only bulls at this corrida were the mutely demanding scores, by Debussy and Messiaen.) No closer approach to the Boulez ideal could have been expected from conductors early in their careers: few seasoned professionals can chop or mold time with his virtuosity.

But the concentration on the purely musical—on the printed notes, on what can be determined from the printed notes, and on how the fruits of observation can be realized with an orchestra—was at least an education in Mr. Boulez's approach. In the introductory session, of classroom study, he rapidly passed over the scenario of Debussy's ballet *Jeux* and said hardly a word about the bird songs of Messiaen's *Chronochromie*, about that work's concern with the projection of color through harmony and

Originally in *The New Yorker*, 12 April 1993. Paul Griffiths has written extensively on Pierre Boulez, including *Boulez* (Oxford University Press, 1978).

instrumentation, or about its use of sound to, as the title suggests, give a color to time. What Mr. Boulez asked his trainees to notice was, rather, Debussy's way of transforming motifs, and his own way of transforming Messiaen's metronome marks in order to make the music playable.

In elucidating the Debussy score, he was following what he had learned fifty years before, when he was a student in Messiaen's class. Messiaen, he told us, had pointed out how threads of connection pass through the fugitive melodic ideas of *Jeux*: how an important theme may become secondary or vice versa, how the same theme may recur differently harmonized, how rhythms can be expanded or contracted. "Maybe you can have an intuition of this, but I doubt it. The relationships are to be"—and here he brought a heavy downbeat emphasis on the participle—"discovered." There, in a word, was the passion of Mr. Boulez's engagement, and also the objectivity, the view of the score as something to be inspected, learned, and understood. Once discovered, the motivic relationships are, for him, to be conveyed to the orchestra wordlessly, simply by rehearsing thematically connected passages side by side. Analysis is for the conductor to do in his workroom; rehearsal is about making things happen, about the activeness on which Mr. Boulez was constantly insisting, both in what he said and in his examples of productive gestures.

When, later in the exercise, the question of the baton came up, he looked physically pained at the idea of becoming, as he put it, a sort of Captain Hook of the podium, losing the fluidity and immediacy with which he can work with his hands on the orchestra. Time and again, he stressed how the conductor must play the orchestra, must use his hands with a keyboard player's feeling for qualities of attack and volume ("You do yourself what you want to hear"), but always with a sense not of controlling the players but of enabling them, of giving ("You give and you receive. You receive what they play: you listen. And you give them what they need"). To offer a cue, the right hand slices swiftly forward on the horizontal, palm down, and then, at the last moment, the digits spread, giving the signal to the musicians, not grasping it close to the body, tight-fisted, as Mr. Boulez criticized one of his junior colleagues for doing. "That's not only in order to be precise. That's much more important than to be precise: that's to be"—again an intense final emphasis—"acting."

Another fault would be—and here, too, an example was provided by one of the students—to do more with the hands than is required, to "put too much lace around the gesture." Mr. Boulez's gestures, famously economical and exact, are at once controlled and loose: controlled in that the arms move in a shallow vertical space, from waist height to head height, and from a stationary torso; loose in that the hands are held well away from the body, and in that the whole arm, from shoulder to fingertips, works in a single, smooth flow. By comparison with his pupils, whose hands flailed high and elbows chugged, he often appeared to be conducting more slowly, even when his tempos were faster. But though he evidently prizes elegance as a virtue in itself, and said so, there are other reasons for it. A distinct vocabulary of movement clarifies communication with the orchestra. And the extension of the arms is the outer manifestation of an inner attitude: one of giving, of generosity to and care for the players, but also of distance from the score, of holding the music explicitly at arm's length. Don't come too close: "You have to be looking at the painting and making the painting at the same time."

Beyond that, the fluidity of the Boulez style is needed—following his idea of the conductor as super-player of the orchestra—to achieve fluidity in the music, and especially in Debussy's music, and most especially in *Jeux*. He urged his students to find a "flexibility which does not destroy rhythm," and on another occasion remarked how "the arabesque in Debussy should be always precise but not rigid," those contrasted adjectives again opening a verbal window into his whole way of thinking. Everything must be thoroughly considered and rigorously executed, and yet the feel must be supple. In his talk about the Debussy piece, and in his answers to questions, another phrase kept recurring: "But not too much, but not too much."

Apropos of Messiaen, we heard those words much less. The hurdles for the young conductors in *Chronochromie* were, rather, those of acquiring coordination and keeping it all the way through irregular rhythms that would pass at high speed and be suddenly supplanted. Mr. Boulez's cavalier reinterpretation of the metronome speeds was a help, relaxing the extreme prestissimos and adjusting neighboring tempos to simpler proportions—though one was left wanting more justification than the glib assertions that, first, Messiaen never objected, and, second, composers' metronome marks are always wrong (except in the case of Stravinsky's *Les noces*).

But, even with the path thus smoothed, pitfalls abounded when we came to the practical session on this piece. At an awkward point in the first movement, where an imitation of the narcissus flycatcher requires a quick rebound—from high woodwinds and xylophones to low brass, bassoons, and percussion, then back again—Mr. Boulez asked his student to find the substance of the motif not in imagining the bird but in himself: "You must live the rhythm in your body." This incorporation of the music—he shook as he spoke—is probably necessary to the active conducting he demands. Then, there was a passage in the Coda where one of the young conductors kept experiencing difficulties with the simultaneous combination of values: thirty-second notes in the woodwinds, triplet thirty-second notes in xylophones, longer durations in bells, gongs, and cymbal, and an entry for the brass. "You forgot your trombones!" The apprentice nodded; it was getting to be too much. Quietly, ruefully, Mr. Boulez brought the trial to an end: "You must try to think of everything."

The trouble is that these matters—living in avian rhythms, thinking of everything, and then acting everything for the orchestra—depend on qualities of mind and physique that are particular to Mr. Boulez and not easily communicated. *Chronochromie* dates from a period in Messiaen's life, that of the late fifties and early sixties, when he was listening not only to birds in the woods and fields but also to Mr. Boulez's performances in Paris. Since the sea change in the senior composer's orchestral style occurred between *Réveil des oiseaux* (1953) and *Oiseaux exotiques* (1955–56)—across the time of his pupil's debut as a concert conductor—it's tempting to conclude that there was some link, that now he knew it would be possible to compose differently, since he had seen and heard the necessary performing technique in action.

Anyone else who faces an orchestra with *Chronochromie* on the music stand therefore has to become Mr. Boulez a little, and it was no surprise that each of the workshop conductors in turn should have found the accommodation tricky when the model was standing behind his left shoulder. If, nevertheless, the four remained good-humored, that was due not only to Mr. Boulez's determination on their behalf but also to the interest, care, and honesty of the Cleveland players. The orchestra's musical readiness in the two workshop scores must have been helped by the experience of performing both pieces in Cleveland the previous week under Mr. Boulez's direction, in concert and for Deutsche Grammophon. But its responsiveness was just as remarkable: each conductor could see his different exaggerations and faults, and occasionally his different successes, in a perfect mirror.

The permanent mementos of Mr. Boulez's time in Cleveland should be interesting. Meanwhile, the Debussy recordings he made there in 1991—of the *Prélude à l'après-midi d'un faune*, *Images*, and *Printemps* —have been released (on DG 435 766-2), and show the grand sweep and the luxury texture of his current preferences. The contrast with his Debussy of more than a quarter of a century ago, when he recorded the *Images* with the same orchestra, is startling: speeds are much the same, which is to say generally brisk, but the sound is fuller and the continuity more traditional; there's not the quasi-Japanese feeling for fierce tension in a formal gesture, for fire in ice, or the willingness to sound out the weirdness in Debussy. Where Mr. Boulez's sixties view was that of a fellow-composer, his new recordings are those of a master conductor, and they provide a more sumptuous sort of pleasure. One also gets a vivid impression, in sound alone, of those separately mobile hands as they trigger an entry or wave in the air an arabesque that's precise but not rigid.

Notes to the Interviews

ONE **A Journey** (pages 19–31)

1. This was in *Hamlet*—incidental music for wind instruments, percussion, and Ondes Martenot by Arthur Honegger (first performed 17 October 1946 at the Théâtre Marigny). Boulez took lessons in counterpoint from Andrée Vaurabourg-Honegger, the composer's wife, between the winter of 1943 and the autumn of 1945.

2. The tour began after the first performance of 24 October 1946. Joseph Kosma (1905–1969) was known for his film scores (*La grande illusion*, *Les enfants du paradis*) and for the songs he wrote with Jacques Prévert.

3. Inaugural concert, 13 January 1954. With the help of Jean-Louis Barrault, Madeleine Renaud, and several patrons of the arts (among whom Suzanne Tézenas, wife of the industrialist, figured prominently), the group began a concert series, the Concerts du Petit-Marigny. In 1967 Boulez entrusted the Domaine Musical to Gilbert Amy; it was dissolved in 1973.

4. Roger Desormière (1898–1963) founded the French Association of Progressive Musicians in 1949 with Serge Nigg, Charles Koechlin, and Louis Durey. Hans Rosbaud (1895–1962) conducted the Southwest German Radio Orchestra in Baden-Baden from 1948 until his death. Ernest Bour (b. 1913) conducted the Strasbourg Municipal Orchestra between 1950 and 1964, and the Strasbourg Opera beginning in 1955. In 1964 he succeeded Rosbaud at the Southwest German Radio Orchestra in Baden-Baden, where he still lived in 1989. Hermann Scherchen (1891–1966) cofounded the International Society for Contemporary Music in 1923 and, in 1954, the Electronic Studio in Gravesano.

5. First public performance on 21 March 1956 of *Le marteau sans maître*, for voice and small instrumental ensemble. This debut was carefully prepared with a view to posterity. As a program note states, "This concert is being recorded by

141

Vega records and will appear in the collection entitled 'Contemporary Musical Presence.'"

6. In addition to Rosbaud, Bour, and Scherchen, early conductors of the Domaine Musical included Rudolf Albert, Serge Baudo, Marcel Couraud, Robert Craft, André Souris, and Igor Stravinsky.

7. Contract of 1 January 1959 with the Southwest German Radio Orchestra. Boulez granted them the right to a first hearing of his new works and agreed to take up residence in Baden-Baden (where he henceforth owned a house).

8. 4 December 1957 in Cologne. The West German Radio Orchestra and Chorus in *Visage nuptial*.

In fact, Boulez had already conducted the Venezuelan Symphony Orchestra, Saturday, 16 June 1956, at the Caracas Municipal Theater, during the Renaud-Barrault Company's second South American tour. The program, which the company continued to perform henceforth, included Debussy's *Jeux* and *Ibéria*, Stravinsky's Symphonies of Wind Instruments, and Prokofiev's Classical Symphony (a last-minute replacement for Bartók's Music for Strings, Percussion, and Celesta). The Cuban writer Alejo Carpentier, a friend of Barrault's and an enthusiastic admirer of the Domaine Musical, was the force behind this event. He had already tried, in vain, to invite Boulez to the first Grand Festival of Latin American Music in Caracas in 1954. He was music critic for the Caracas daily paper, *El Nacional*, and on 26 February 1955, in an article entitled "A Foreigner in Caracas," he announced:

> A premiere in Caracas. In a letter which arrived yesterday, Jean-Louis Barrault announced the extremely pleasant news of his next season in Caracas, consisting of six performances. In addition, there will be a supplementary program in collaboration with the composer Pierre Boulez, who is coming to Venezuela as the company's musical adviser. This program will offer nothing less than the entire stage version of Stravinsky's *L'histoire du soldat*, with Barrault in the principal role.

Meanwhile, on 21 March 1956, Boulez had conducted his first nontheatrical performance, *Le marteau sans maître*, at the Domaine Musical. Had Carpentier convinced him, or was Boulez feeling ready for a decisive course of action? *L'histoire du soldat* was no longer an issue, with its small force of musicians and ties to the theater. In December 1955, the administrative director of the Renaud-Barrault Company wrote to the French foreign minister concerning the company's tour plans for 1956: "Note about Caracas. . . . It is possible that we may organize a concert of French music [*sic*] in the open-air theater of Concha Acustica, conducted by Pierre Boulez."

A few days before the arrival of the troupe, Carpentier was finally able to declare in an undated article entitled "Pierre Boulez in Caracas":

> In a few days Pierre Boulez will be back in Caracas, accompanying Jean-Louis Barrault and Madeleine Renaud on their tenth Latin American tour. As maestro Pedro Antonio Rios Reyna has opportunely announced, the young maestro is to lead our symphony orchestra in a program of contem-

porary music consisting of four major scores to be heard for the first time in Venezuela, each of which constitutes in its own field an essential expression of the current trends.

The concert took place on 16 June, five days after the Renaud-Barrault Company left for the Antilles. The one extant commentary on the tour's incidental music is this undated account in *El Nacional*:

Under the expert leadership of Pierre Boulez, the music was generally restrained, as is fitting in the theater. In the midst of the general perfection, I must nonetheless point out that in the "Gardener's Lament," the music frequently drowned the actors' voices, and in important passages at that. This flaw could easily have been remedied.

Boulez told Joan Peyser that he thought to himself, "To conduct so far from home is not dangerous." Joan Peyser, *Boulez*. New York: Schirmer Books, 1976, p. 133.

9. 4 December 1957 with the West German Radio Orchestra and Chorus.

10. Heinrich Strobel (1898–1970).

11. Memorial concerts on 17 and 18 October in honor of the Prince of Fürstenberg, the festival's patron, who had recently died. First performance (in part) of Boulez's *Tombeau*; first performances of Stravinsky's *Epitaphium* and Wolfgang Fortner's *Prelude and Elegy After Hölderlin*.

12. July 1959 at the Parc Rambot, with the main orchestra of the Belgian National Radio Institute. The program consisted of orchestral music by Webern, three excerpts for voice and orchestra from Alban Berg's *Wozzeck*, the first performance of Henri Pousseur's *Rimes pour diverses ressources sonores* (Rhymes for Diverse Sound Effects), and Hindemith's Concerto for Orchestra.

13. Individual concerts on 24, 25, and 27 February 1960 and 6 July 1961; full seasons 1962–63 to 1964–65; single concert on 29 June 1966; full season, 1966–67; concert on 8 March 1968—all this as guest conductor. This complemented but did not replace Boulez's activity at the Residencie Orchestra of The Hague.

14. Hans de Roo, artistic director of the Residencie Orchestra. Boulez conducted there from 1961–62 to 1967–68, leading three to six concerts a season, with an exceptional twenty in 1968, including a European tour. He also conducted at the Holland Festival the summers of 1965 and 1968. It seems that the end of Boulez's time in Amsterdam was not entirely harmonious.

15. 27 November 1963. J.-L. Barrault directed.

16. For performances of *Parsifal* (2, 12, 18, and 21 August 1966) and to replace Hans Knappertsbusch, who died suddenly on 25 October 1965. Wieland Wagner (1917–1966), the German opera producer, was a son of Siegfried Wagner.

17. From May 1964, Boulez periodically conducted the BBC Symphony Orchestra. In accordance with a contract signed 1 January 1969, he succeeded Colin Davis as principal conductor for three years, beginning in September 1971, with the possibility of two renewable contracts of one year each (renewed once, in

1974, from which time Boulez was principal guest conductor until 1977). Boulez insisted that the BBC's controller of music, Sir William Glock, be allowed to remain at his post despite the age limit; Glock stayed on through 1972. In 1952 Glock had published Boulez's famous article, "Schoenberg is Dead," in the English magazine, *The Score*.

18. From 11 March 1965. Appointed principal guest conductor 20 February 1969, effective from March through the end of the 1971–72 season. Boulez committed himself to five weeks in residence plus one on tour for the first season; six to eight weeks, divided into two segments, for the two following seasons; and a minimum of three weeks at the Blossom Music Festival each season. His participation ended 3 December 1971.

19. George Szell died 29 July 1970 at the age of seventy-three, three weeks before Heinrich Strobel died at the age of seventy-two.

20. In September 1971, for three years, with two possible renewals of one year each. The contract was proposed on 1 April and announced 1 June 1971—something of an April Fool's hoax, in view of Boulez's remark of 9 March, reported in the *New York Times*: "I couldn't possibly accept it. New York has bad musical habits, and to change bad habits you have to know them all." At that time Boulez was a guest conductor in the middle of his probationary period; from 1970 he was musical advisor and principal guest conductor.

21. Boulez also appeared with the French National Radio Orchestra, the Lamoureux Orchestra, the Conservatory Concert Society Orchestra, the Berlin Philharmonic, the Vienna Philharmonic, the London Symphony Orchestra, the Orchestre National, the National Youth Orchestra of Great Britain, the Chicago Symphony Orchestra, "Musica Viva" of Radio Munich, the "New Works" program of North German Radio, Hamburg, and the Ulm Concerts.

22. Gaëtan Picon was general director of arts and letters at the French Ministry of Culture; Émile Biasini was responsible for the administration of theater, music, and letters. A national commission to study problems relating to music was set up by André Malraux—the first official French minister of culture—on 27 December 1962. The commission delivered its report (undated, printed 26 March 1965) two years late. Forty-five experts gave testimony, forty-one others took part in group discussions, and a further eight submitted the report, making ninety-four specialists in all, not counting Boulez. The commission made thirty recommendations (number fourteen proposed a substantial increase in subsidies for the four major symphony orchestras and recommended transforming the Conservatory Concert Society Orchestra into a state orchestra and increasing the subsidy for the other three main bodies). These recommendations had no effect on the budget of 1966.

In the spring of 1966, in an atmosphere rife with crisis and intrigue, Biasini—supported by Picon—suddenly asked Boulez for another "Plan to Reorganize French Musical Life," apparently without notifying Malraux. Boulez proposed concentrating Parisian musical activities into three main centers: radio; a double orchestra at the Opéra, which would be available for concerts; and a double orchestra sponsored by the city of Paris and available for opera. The minister did not reply. According to a memorandum of 28 March 1966, confirmed by a decree of 28 October 1966, "The office of music is being withdrawn from the management of theater, music, and cultural activity, with the exception of lyrical arts and dance." In May, the composer Marcel Landowski became head of the musical service (which soon became an administrative department). The rest fell to Biasini, who transferred to the Ministry of Finance on 19 November 1966. "Biasini was made to resign, Picon resigned," observed Boulez to Michèle Cotta and Sylvie de Nussac (*L'Express*, 13 April 1970).

At this point Boulez unleashed his famous "Why I Say No to André Malraux," which appeared in the *Nouvel Observateur* of 25 May 1966:

> Waving a weary hand, André Malraux has just made a decision which affects music in France, . . . the worst possible decision, and one fraught with compromise. Not wishing to repudiate Biasini, but wanting to appease the "official" musicians, he has split the apple in two: one half, the theater, stays in Biasini's hands, and the other half ends up in Landowski's claws. . . . I consider the present solution to be the worst, the laziest, and the stupidest possible. I am therefore going on strike with regard to any aspect of official music in France.

23. A collaboration with Vilar, who founded the Théâtre National Populaire (TNP), and Maurice Béjart. Three volumes of typescript were prepared. The sole existing copy, which is in the Maison Jean Vilar (Bibliothèque Nationale, Avignon), is labeled "Proposal to Reform the Paris Opéra," by Jean Vilar, 30 May 1968.

According to Sir William Glock, Boulez devoted all his weekends between October 1967 and May 1968 to this project. In an interview with Michèle Cotta and Sylvie de Nussac (*L'Express*, 13 April 1970), Boulez said, "Vilar withdrew from the project in June 1968 for political reasons. I had no interest in going on without him. Especially since, a week later, the BBC's representative came and asked me to be artistic director of the BBC Symphony Orchestra." During this awkward time, Boulez also stepped up his visits to the Residencie Orchestra of The Hague. In the interview, Boulez justified his attempt to return to France in late 1967, after his tumultuous 1966 departure. "I agreed because Vilar was who he was, and because the Opéra was then under the ministerial direction of theater, not music." The theater section was run by a top bureaucrat, Francis Raison. Boulez's sudden passion for the Opéra resembles the story of the Trojan horse. Could it be that the Opéra was later officially transferred to the department of music, voice, and dance by a decree of 23 December 1970 precisely to avoid this kind of maneuver?

In his book *Vilar* (Paris, 1987), Jean Roy writes:

> Vilar's apparent cessation in 1963 was a pause, not a retreat. . . . The new departure conceived by Vilar would have been a large national lyric theater intended for the people—an opera house, in short. The Fifth Plan released in 1964–65, and Malraux himself in 1967, charged Vilar with studying the situation of lyric theater in France and presenting a proposal for reforming

the Paris Opéra. In 1968, Vilar recommended a triple form of administration for this reformed Opéra: Pierre Boulez as musical director, Maurice Béjart as director of ballets, and himself as theatrical director.

In the report he submitted in 1965 to the Commission on Cultural Facilities and Artistic Patrimony of the Fifth Plan (1966–70), Jean Vilar explains: "The proposal recommends having 3000 equally good seats; in other words, an amphitheater in which every spectator, even the last ones to arrive and be shown in, would find seats where they can see and hear."

The commission's general report quotes Vilar:

Too often, lyrical art has been limited to the art of singing, or even of simple vocal performance, and has become the victim of its own "literary drowsiness." Lyrical art must rediscover its true identity as authentic musical theater. . . . By simultaneously subjecting lyrical art to an aesthetic transformation and broadening its popular appeal—the two processes being indissolubly linked—this art form would be brought up-to-date, and would, in addition, benefit from the renewal and enrichment of its apparently stale repertoire.

The 1968 project completed the picture:

The highest quality must be attained throughout; at the very least, an international level. . . .

This reform proposes what might be called a major rotation between the two main disciplines that fall within the province of this type of theater: dance and lyric theater. The monthly or annual playbill will announce an equal number of performances of both. Regular concerts will also be announced. . . .

Finally, we must clarify and define the connection between music and theater, beginning with the connection between conductor and stage director—a subject frankly broached in only a few rare operatic situations. This duality, which is inherent in stage productions, is often a source of conflict that harms both the public performance and the smooth daily workings of the company. It will be noticed that the schedule calls for an almost equal number of orchestral and production rehearsals. . . . This current reform of artistic life cannot be tolerated. It is necessary to take things in hand, and it is inconceivable that groups of artists should continue to be treated as minors—these are artists who have mastered their art and whose skill and imagination are invaluable to the prime movers in the theater.

Proposed conductors for a preliminary season (1969–70) were Boulez, Bernstein, Barenboim, Abbado, Previn, Mackerras, Lombard, Semkov, Oistrakh, Maazel, Ormandy, Giulini, Schmidt-Isserstedt, Zender, and Rozhdestvensky. Vilar's plan included the following (the question marks appear in the original document):

Monday 22 and Tuesday 23 September 1969: J. S. Bach, Cantata no. 50; Gustav Mahler, Symphony no. 2, with Christiane Eda-Pierre, Janet Baker. (New Opera Orchestra), conducted by Pierre Boulez.

Monday 29 September 1969: Haydn, Symphony no. ?; Bartók, Piano Concerto no. 1, with Daniel Barenboim, piano; Stockhausen, *Gruppen*. (New Opera Orchestra), conducted by Pierre Boulez and two others.

Monday 6 October 1969: Haydn, Symphony no. ?; Béla Bartók, Piano Concerto no. 2; Hector Berlioz, *La mort de Cléopâtre*; Claude Debussy, *La mer*, with Nelson Freire and Josephine Veasey. (New Opera Orchestra), conducted by Pierre Boulez.

Monday 13 October 1969: Monteverdi, *Vespers*, soloists? (New Opera Orchestra), conducted by Pierre Boulez.

Monday 12 January 1970: Béla Bartók, *Cantata profana*; Joseph Haydn, *Nelson Mass*, soloists Edith Mathis? Yvonne Minton? Robert Ilosfalvy? Donald McIntyre? (New Opera Orchestra), conducted by Pierre Boulez.

Monday 19 January 1970: Joseph Haydn, Symphony no. ? Béla Bartók, Piano Concerto no. 3, soloist Malcolm Frager; Igor Stravinsky, *The Rite of Spring*. (New Opera Orchestra), conducted by Pierre Boulez.

For the 1970–71 season, the proposed operatic conductors were to be Boulez, Colin Davis, and George Szell. Included in the program would be Berlioz, *The Fall of Troy* and *The Trojans at Carthage*; Debussy, *Pelléas et Mélisande*; Gluck, *Orfeo ed Eurydice* ("If we are prepared to admit that this opera, although composed by a foreigner, conforms definitively to the rules of the eighteenth-century French school"); Schoenberg, *Moses und Aron* (first performance in France); an unpublished work by Berio; and Mozart's *Don Giovanni*.

Vilar's second career and his hopes of founding a popular national opera house with Béjart and Boulez (who wanted to call it the Center for Music and Theater) were cut short after a radio broadcast of 30 May 1968 when General de Gaulle, whom Vilar nonetheless admired, heaped invective on those who were "preventing students from studying and workmen from working." Vilar immediately wrote to André Malraux, declaring that "the broadcast speech just delivered by the president of the Republic forces me in all conscience to reconsider the provisional acceptance I had given you." (Letter of 31 May 1968. The "Proposal to Reform the Paris Opéra" is dated 30 May 1968.)

On 25 February 1970, Vilar took part in another debate on power and culture, this one with Georges Conchon and Roger Louis, held during a series of meetings on socialism and society at the Maison de la Mutualité. The moderator was François Mitterand.

Mitterand's first cultural undertaking as president, in 1981, was the Opera of the Bastille. With its quantitative purpose (including the small experimental theater dear to Pierre Boulez), it is an echo of the popular national opera house imagined by Vilar. In charge of completing this project was the state secretary for major works—none other than Émile Biasini.

24. Its principal sponsor, Volkswagen, abandoned it in 1966, in the midst of the recession. This Klangstudio project, which was associated with the name of Paul Sacher, was still alive in 1970. Its failure is a remarkable example of how a project can get bogged down in administration. The Max Planck Gesellschaft's re-

cords on the subject are still under a thirty-year injunction, but the following is currently known.

Discussions about founding a music institute under the auspices of the Max Planck Gesellschaft were begun in 1964 by members of the MPG and a number of musicians, including Boulez. A memorandum was drawn up in 1966. On 9 March 1967, Paul Sacher presented the MPG board with a memorandum about the institute, which was to have four departments: a) musicology; b) fundamental research into sound, electronics, and the development of instruments; c) composition; and d) performance or interpretation. To test the validity of this project and to perfect the plan, a commission composed of company presidents and musical experts met on 7 June 1967. The project was presented in late 1969 to the administrative board of the MPG; they passed it on to their humanities branch for an opinion. The problems it posed seemed so formidable that in 1970 a commission was set up to ponder the proposal. This commission included members of the biological-medical and chemical-physical-technical sections. In 1974 the commission advised the governing body of the MPG not to carry out the project, but to consider contributing to the Paris institute instead!

According to Joan Peyser (*Boulez*, p. 229), Boulez said that he shared his thoughts with the newspaper *Le Monde* in late 1969. Reading this article in 1970 supposedly inspired Georges Pompidou to invite Boulez to found the future IRCAM, which—for the time being—would be identical in substance to what the German plan proposed.

Boulez made a similar remark during an interview with Michèle Cotta and Sylvie de Nussac in *L'Express* on 13 April 1970. Boulez said, "There ought to be a research institute established, following the necessary study." The remark was not allowed to pass.

> If you were made director of such a research institute tomorrow, would you accept?
> "Immediately, and I'd give up conducting without any regrets."
> And in the meantime?
> "I carry on."
> Are you, on the whole, fairly optimistic about it?
> "If you offer me ten million dollars, yes."
> Do you think these ten million dollars are likely to appear?
> "Very likely."
> It's perhaps not accidental that you're speaking in terms of dollars.
> "I could just as well have spoken in terms of deutsche marks. I think this research center will appear either in Germany or the United States."

25. Though both men were composers, Boulez devoted the years 1964 to 1974 mainly to conducting, whereas Marcel Landowski spent them in administration at the Ministry of Cultural Affairs.

26. Inaugural concert 14 November 1967. This subsidized orchestra replaced the bankrupt Conservatory Concert Society Orchestra, founded in 1828.

27. Boulez has commented:

When people talk about prestige, the last rites aren't far away! I'm not interested in patching things up the way Malraux does. What's taken place at the Opéra or with the Orchestre de Paris is as depressing as the Maginot Line and about as effective. At best, it's a caricature of what Biasini, Vilar, and I had proposed. (Interview with J. L. Martinoty, *L'Humanité*, 22 February 1972.)

A month after being founded, it claimed—inspired by Coué [the pioneer of autosuggestion]—to be the best symphony orchestra in the world. . . . France's tragedy is that she lost her colonies. Before that, the more lamentable bureaucrats could all be shipped off and absorbed into colonial ministries. (Interview with Claude Baignières, *Le Figaro Littéraire*, 29 April 1972.)

28. Daniel Barenboim was musical director of the Orchestre de Paris from 1975 to 1989. Boulez conducted it as early as 5 January 1976. Jean-Philippe Lecat, then minister of culture, intended to make him the orchestra's president, but that triggered a general outcry.

29. Amy took over from Boulez at the Domaine Musical in 1967 and remained its leader until the group was dissolved in 1973. He conducted Radio France's New Philharmonic Orchestra from its inception in 1976 until 1981.

30. The Mozart Festival's first opera was *Don Giovanni*, 23 June 1982.

31. Boulez held the position between April 1965 and May 1968. *Journal de l'Artiste Musicien*, "official organ of the Musical Artists' Union in Paris, founded by Gustave Charpentier; honorary president, Pierre Boulez," declares in its April 1966 issue:

There is a serious need to consider a reform project, fairly close in principle to the statutes of the Vienna Philharmonic and Vienna State Opera Orchestra: a double orchestra, or else one consisting of about 180 musicians. One establishes a rotation between the orchestra's theatrical activity and its concert activities, and this greatly improves the orchestra's intrinsic quality. A concert orchestra is more brilliant, more virtuosic; it plays like a soloist, for its personal prestige. An operatic orchestra is more flexible, because it has to adapt to its dramatic function, as well as to its musical one.

32. Michel Guy was secretary of state for culture from June 1974 to June 1976. First concert of the Ensemble InterContemporain was 15 December 1976 at Villeurbanne. IRCAM (Institute for Research and Coordination in Acoustics and Music at the Centre Georges Pompidou, Paris) was incorporated 30 April 1976; its first event took place Thursday 13 January 1977, with the Ensemble InterContemporain.

33. "I'm very attached to an idea I hope to develop—probably in Paris—in the coming years (1975?): a center for acoustical and musical research adjoining Beaubourg. Contemporary music seems to me to be stagnating through a failure to pose a number of technical and theoretical problems and to resolve them, scientifically if need be." (Interview with J. L. Martinoty, *L'Humanité*, 22 February 1972.)

34. Speech broadcast on the day of the concert, 5 January 1976. Palais des Congrès, Paris. Program: Beethoven's Piano Concerto no. 5 ("Emperor") (Daniel Barenboim, soloist); Stravinsky's *The Firebird* (complete ballet, original version).

35. Carlos Du Pré Moseley (b. 1923). In 1971, he was forty-eight and: "his working relationship with Boulez has been a model of how artistic and administrative activities can unite to achieve a result that is both artistically fruitful and appropriate to the needs of the time." (Patrick J. Smith in *The New Grove Dictionary of Music and Musicians*. London: Macmillan, 1980.)

36. "The Boulez era . . . can certainly be seen as a key period in the musical life of Britain in this century. It opened up several paths leading to renewal; yet it had little effect on the conservative way musical life is organized. It was a strange phenomenon, a revolution which altered nothing." (Nicholas Kenyon, "A French Revolution? 1971–75" in *The BBC Symphony Orchestra*.)

37. From June 1974 to 1977, Rug Concerts—informal concerts with discussions—so called because "we'll take out the seats from the Philharmonic Hall and create a more relaxed atmosphere," (John Rockwell, *Music and Musicians*, quoted in *Le Monde*, 27 March 1973).

In the same vein, Boulez had already created his Prospective Encounters, transposed from the Round House in north London to a room in the theater complex at the New York Shakespeare Festival.

In favor:

> An innovation that gets talked about, provoking both sarcasm and praise. I'm speaking of the Prospective Encounters which take place between 7 o'-clock and midnight, not at Lincoln Center but in Greenwich Village. During these long sessions—which Boulez refuses to call *concerts*—everyone is free to come and go as he or she pleases, to sit where and how they want; free, too, to question the musicians and composer. The idea is to emphasize discovery. "We have to get rid of the idea that in listening to new music we're discovering masterpieces for the twenty-first century," says Pierre Boulez. "The aim is to explore what's happening today." (Nicole Zand, *Le Monde*, 3 February 1972.)

Against:

> His Prospective Encounters were criticized on account of the inconvenient places where they take place, and because of the reportedly misplaced interest they evince in certain schools and composers. His "informal evenings" attract only modest audiences (unless a well-known artist is announced in the posters); Boulez's explanations of a given work hesitate, sometimes uncomfortably, between a rather rigorous technicality, and general observations indicating his good will toward the masses—who aren't there! (John Rockwell, quoted in *Le Monde*, 27 March 1973.)

There were also his conversations with students at the famous Juilliard School of Music. Again, John Rockwell, 1973:

His so-called "destruction" of the scarcely developed arguments put forward by the Juilliard students did not perhaps give them much immediate encouragement, nor did it reveal much sympathy on his part for ideas different from his own, but the experience nonetheless gave them a new look at the way a great musician works.

38. Four months in residence with the BBC Symphony Orchestra (instead of the five originally planned, that is, thirty-two concerts instead of forty) and four months in New York (seven weeks in 1971–72 to start the English season), with a promise not to accept other engagements—such was the gentleman's agreement between Moseley, Glock, and Boulez.

39. Arranged by S. Hurok, January 1969. Boulez had already been on tour with the BBC Symphony Orchestra, between 24 April and 16 May 1965, giving concerts in Boston, Stamford, New London, Hartford, New York, Durham, Philadelphia, Washington, Syracuse, and Corning. The conducting was divided between Boulez and Antal Dorati. "Yet, until that tour with the BBC Symphony Orchestra, Boulez had never conducted in New York, despite his extraordinary reputation as a conductor of twentieth-century 'classical' music." (Benjamin Boretz, *The Sunday Times*, London, 16 May 1965.)

40. Boulez also conducted the London Symphony Orchestra from time to time.

41. Twenty-six years, from 1912 to 1938.

42. Forty-four years, from 1936 to 1980.

43. Leonard Bernstein stayed eleven years, from 1958 to 1969. Zubin Mehta was their conductor from 1977 until the arrival of Kurt Masur in 1990.

44. *Souvenir à la mémoire*, BBC Symphony Orchestra, 16 December 1976 (date of French broadcast). *Tombeau d'amour* no. 2, Orchestre de Paris, Palais des Congrès, Paris, 3 November 1977.

45. "I refused to conduct in Chartres Cathedral before de Gaulle and Malraux, and I hate idiotic patriotism. A patriotism that's on the rise, furthermore—an imbecilic nationalism." (Interview with Martine Cadieu, *Les lettres françaises*, 10 July 1968.)

TWO   Conducting to Compose (pages 32–35)

1. Incidental music for *Oresteia* (Aeschylus), adapted by André Obey for the Renaud-Barrault Company, Bordeaux, 1955.

2. From 1946 to 1955.

3. Other effects conducting has on composing: The composer-conductor can revise unsatisfactory works in the light of performance problems, and he can curtail the instrumentalists' freedom to improvise. As Dominique Jameux wrote in 1986, "Boulez's extraordinary realism with regard to 'the musician's craft' has been largely influenced by his conducting. This has given him the ability to

test a composition (so much so that his penchant for revision leads him to spend even more time on scores he deems inept: *Visage nuptial,* which [was] being rewritten [as of 1986], and *Improvisations III,* revised in 1984–85). It has also fostered his growing conviction that a group of instrumentalists is ill-equipped for the games and pleasures of improvisation: they don't know what to do, or when, or how to do it together. The scores of *Rituel* and *Improvisations III* will henceforth be devoid of any hint of 'variability.'" (Dominique Jameux, Musica Viva program, 1986.) Revised version of *Visage nuptial* was first performed in its entirety by the BBC Symphony Orchestra in London, November 1989, conducted by the composer, according to Dominique Jameux in *Pierre Boulez* (Fayard, 1984, translated by Susan Bradshaw. Cambridge, MA: Harvard Univ. Press, 1991).

On instrumentalists and improvisation, Boulez declared:

> Instrumentalists are executors who carry out intentions but do not invent them—if they did, they would be composers themselves. When one hears them improvising in sequences where almost nothing has been written down—gratuitous sequences, let's say—one finds that they repeat what they've played previously—commonplace clichés from contemporary music. For when push comes to shove they cannot invent; they can only present an unexpected aspect of a work—a "freshly painted" aspect as it were, of a work they've played. And so one can recognize, in this passage from *Rites*, the staccato style the instrumentalist has borrowed from the work. Indeed, what one hears is not in fact an instrumentalist improvising: one does not hear an actual work; one sees the patchwork colors of a Harlequin, so much so that the personality of the composer almost disappears. The improviser provides a musical outline which may be entertaining but is nonetheless far less satisfying if one tries to view it as a completed work. (Unpublished lecture, Studio 111, Strasbourg, 1966.)

4. *Le marteau sans maître,* for voice and small instrumental ensemble, 21 March 1956, at the Domaine Musical. First performed by Hans Rosbaud 18 June 1955 in Baden-Baden.

5. Conducting also has a cathartic effect on a composer: "I conduct because I'm a composer; I learned the art of conducting through conducting. Now that I'm familiar with the technique and have assimilated the works of the past through personal experience, I can completely purge them from my memory, and move forward." (Interview with J. L. Martinoty, *L'Humanité,* 22 February 1972.)

Yet Boulez possibly entertained the opposite opinion as well. In a 1969 *New York Times* interview with Joan Peyser, he said: "When I compose, I have Debussy, Stravinsky and Berg in my background. For an audience to listen to my compositions, it must have the same background as that. So I conduct early 20th-century music to prepare people to listen to more advanced pieces." (Peyser, *Boulez,* p. 183.)

6. Boulez's returns to France have been dramatic and even more numerous than his departures. "So! The young maestro has left Elba, and nothing leads us to suppose this is the start of his Hundred Days. The concert he conducted yester-

day at the Odéon earned him a warm reception. Pierre Boulez has created several scandals in his lifetime. The second to last one caused a particular stir: mortified by a setback, the hot-headed conductor announced his irrevocable decision never to collaborate again with official musical channels in France. The Domaine Musical stopped accepting its state subsidy and Boulez condemned himself to a cozy exile, with foreign orchestras rightly jockeying for the honor of being led by his prestigious baton." (Clarendon, *Le Figaro*, 17 November 1966.)

"In fact, Boulez has too often sworn 'never to return to France' to be able to go back on his decision without making nonsense of his words." (Clarendon, *Le Figaro*, 15 March 1968.)

7. "Ten years ago, when you weren't very active in France and I expressed surprise over that, you replied with your customary humor: 'I'm not as Francophile as you are.' But since then you've given fresh impetus to musical life in France and today I think we're all 'Boulezophiles'." (Daniel Barenboim, program tribute for concert in honor of Boulez's sixtieth birthday, 3 October 1985, Salle Pleyel, Paris.)

8. "No, I don't really want to go back to France. . . . I prefer to be completely marginal, that is, completely outside it, rather than being marginal inside it, which would serve no purpose at all." (Interview with Louis Dandrel, *Le Monde*, 12 September 1970.)

9. "The French system brings everything down to the lowest level, for want of decisiveness and responsibility. Whether you're any good or not, the mechanism of promotion keeps on turning. . . . Fortunately, IRCAM will be completely cut off from French musical life and will not be subject to the same controls." (*Newsweek*, European edition, 3 March 1975.)

IRCAM nonetheless experienced several crises and budgetary threats.

In 1980, IRCAM was the target of criticism and questions whose importance stemmed from IRCAM's position in the French musical landscape (its budget amounted to about twenty times the amount granted in subsidies to other research centers in France). Although his concerts were recognized as excellent, Boulez was criticized for concealing the "total absence of a plan (Jean-Claude Éloy) behind his policy of disseminating the contemporary "classical" heritage of Stravinsky, the Vienna school, and so forth. He was criticized, too, for his ignorance regarding contemporaneous or previous research projects; and for the absence of real discovery, leading to a "ponderous impasse for the entire musical world." (Iannis Xenakis, in *Dictionnaire de la musique*. Paris: Larousse, 1982.)

THREE   **Choosing the Works** (pages 36–63)

1. "In preparing his individual programs, Boulez seemed to resort to a process of suggestion and counter-suggestion; it was rather like a game of tennis one can't play by oneself. I have always considered the choice of a good program to be a small work of art, even if there aren't many which deserve that term. I think

Boulez had an attitude that was similar in many ways." (Sir William Glock, *Pierre Boulez Symposium*. London: Eulenburg Books, 1986.)

2. In New York, Liszt and Berg were paired for the first season: little-known works: Berg's *Der Wein* and Liszt's *Totentanz*; Haydn and Stravinsky were paired for the second.

3. Pre- and postromantic pairings for the third New York season (1973–74), playing on affinities and contrasts between Schubert, Weber, and Berlioz, on the one hand, and Mahler and Schoenberg, on the other. *Doktor Faust*, opera by Busoni (1916–24, completed in 1925 by P. Jarnach).

4. Monday 25 January 1988, concert of the European Broadcasting Union at the Royal Festival Hall in London. (See Selection of Programs Conducted by Boulez.)
    George Benjamin (1960–) was a former student of Messiaen. He was invited by Boulez to work at IRCAM in 1984 and 1986 on *Antara*, which had been commissioned for IRCAM's tenth anniversary in 1987. Benjamin is considered the heir apparent to Boulez. The Southwest German Radio Orchestra of Baden-Baden has commissioned a work from him.

5. This concert took place on 14 September 1988, shortly after these interviews.

6. "This mania for period playing has now reached such proportions that one can't perform a work without lighting a candle, as it were." (Boulez, Conference on the Future of Radio Symphony Orchestras, European Broadcasting Union, Frankfurt, 2–4 April 1984.)

7. "The intelligentsias who think they are pure gold often do a lot of harm. Witness the intellectual milieu Stravinsky frequented in Paris in 1930, which pushed this unintellectual realist down the slippery slope of preciosity." (Interview with J. L. Martinoty, *L'Humanité*, 22 February 1972.)

8. A statistical check of all the programs Boulez conducted in Cleveland, London, The Hague, Amsterdam, New York, Paris, Ulm, and Baden-Baden, up to the time of these interviews in 1988.

9. *Daphnis and Chloé* (1912); *Rapsodie espagnole* (1907–08); *Tombeau de Couperin* (1919); *Bolero* (1928); *La valse* (1919–20). The *Mother Goose Suite* (1908–12) and the Concerto for Left Hand (1929–30) were performed in Cleveland and New York; Boulez also recorded *Mother Goose* in New York and the Concerto for Left Hand in Cleveland.

10. "Batavians" could refer to an ancient people of the Netherlands or to inhabitants of the Javanese islands, perhaps, loosely, natives, remote islanders, or even primitives.—Ed.

11. The Concertgebouw Orchestra, 25 January 1965, in Tilburg; 27 and 28 January, Amsterdam; 30 January, Scheweningen.

12. *Heterophony for Orchestra* (1959–61); *Variations Without Fugue* (1971–72).

13. Remark made in a radio broadcast, 20 October 1974.

14. Lecture in Saint-Etienne, 13 May 1968. In a third version of 13 April 1987, the Museum becomes the future sanctum of modernity (through commissions): "Let's not confine ourselves simply to maintaining the Museum, however carefully; let's try to enrich it with new acquisitions. For that is what will be remembered later, when our everyday occurrences have been replaced by future ones." (*Von Heute auf Morgen.*)

15. The "notorious" interview, quoted below, appeared in *Der Spiegel*, 25 September 1967. In a French broadcast of 4 March 1971, Boulez reiterated the substance of his declarations to *Der Spiegel*. According to the radio broadcast:

> Since I've conducted works from the past, my views on history have altered completely. I like to stroll through the Museum from time to time, but I personally see no point in anything more than that. For example, if tomorrow you were to tell me, "I won't listen to any more music written between yesterday and the preceding century," I wouldn't care at all. There comes a time when I think one can be very well rid of culture; indeed I am, increasingly. That's why I once expressed admiration for the Chinese Red Guard, because they'd actually had the courage to destroy the temples and break statues. There's a point where civilization collapses or becomes apoplectic and there's far too much thick blood.

Der Spiegel (25 September 1967):

> In the provincial town which Paris really is, the Museum is very badly maintained. The Paris Opéra is covered with dust and *merde*, if you'll pardon my French. . . . So let them calmly bring on a whole gang of Red Guards— don't forget that the French Revolution also smashed a lot of things, and that was very healthy. When too much tension builds up, there's only one thing to do, and that's to let blood.

16. Despite an obvious attempt to find the rare work. Does originality equal modernity? "My main concern was to transform the current concept of concerts; to promote atypical works, both classical and modern, and also new ways of programming them." (Interview with Alan Field, *Newsweek*, 3 March 1975.)

17. No.

20 September 1964, with the Concerto in C major (unpublished) by Pachelbel and the Overture in B-flat major BWV 1067 by J. S. Bach. The concert was sold out, as was the concert of contemporary works on 18 September (Stravinsky, Webern, Debussy, Boulez). The Concerts of Ulm are organized by a music lovers' society, Gesellschaft 1950, led by the industrialist Hans Zumsteg and the architect Martin Stroheker. Boulez felt so comfortable there he returned faithfully in 1966, 1968, 1970, 1982, and 1988.

The concertos of Vivaldi comprise at least 422 opus numbers; his masses and oratorios come to sixty-one, according to the Ryom catalog.

18. "Verdi is stupid, stupid, stupid!" Boulez in English to a reporter for the *Indianapolis Star*, 8 September 1972.

19. Goffredo Petrassi (b. 1904).

20. Interlude intended for the unfinished opera *Sorochinsky Fair* (1874).

21. First performed 8 March 1984. Jean-Albert Cartier was director of the Châtelet musical theater in Paris between 1980 and 1988.

22. *Islamey*, oriental fantasy for piano (1860), transcribed for orchestra.

23. Boulez on Rameau: "I love composers who construct their works." (*Candide*, 15 October, 1964.)

24. When asked in 1983, "Has Webern gone back into Purgatory?" Boulez replied, "Did you think he'd ever been out of it? In reality, he's never been played all that much. But it's true that he's become less attractive to young composers lately. It's probably that people have already gleaned all they could from his style and approach, and now we'll have to wait some time before rediscovering what he has to offer." (Interview with Brigitte Massin, *Le Matin*, 21 July 1983.)

25. Six Pieces for Orchestra, Op. 6 (1909, revised in 1928); Passacaglia for Large Orchestra, Op. 1 (1908).

26. Five Movements for a String Quartet, Op. 5, (1909, arranged for string orchestra in 1928; revised in 1929).

27. Of 1940. On numerous occasions, particularly in Los Angeles, Boulez performed the *Fuga ricercata* from the *Musical Offering* by J. S. Bach, transcribed for orchestra by Webern (1934–35), as well as Webern's transcriptions of Schubert's Six German Dances. Both works were recorded, but the Schubert-Webern was omitted because of an extant version conducted by Webern himself. He also performed Webern's works for voice and orchestra: *Das Augenlicht*, Op. 26, for mixed chorus and orchestra (1935); the Cantata no. 1 for soprano, mixed chorus, and orchestra (1939); and the Cantata no. 2 for soprano, bass, mixed chorus, and orchestra (1941–43). Boulez conducted the works for voice and orchestra several times at the BBC as well as with the London Symphony Orchestra, with whom he recorded them.

28. Symphony, Op. 21, for an instrumental ensemble (1928); Five Pieces, Op. 10, for chamber orchestra (1913).

29. *Pelleas und Melisande*, Op. 5, Symphonic Poem, was performed in London and Chicago; *Transfigured Night*, Op. 4, for string sextet (1887, arranged for orchestra in 1917 and revised in 1943) was performed in London and New York, recorded in New York, and recorded again by the Ensemble InterContemporain (EIC) in the version for solo strings. Boulez has also performed and recorded Five Pieces for Orchestra, Op. 16 (1909); Variations for Orchestra, Op. 31 (1926–28); Incidental Music to a Motion Picture Scene, Op. 34 (1929–30); the orchestral transcription of the Piano Quintet in G Minor, Op. 25 (1937); the orchestral transcription of Bach's Prelude and Fugue for Organ in E-flat Major (1928); two Organ Preludes by J. S. Bach, also transcribed for orchestra (1922); and the Second Chamber Symphony (1912–14), which was performed by the Southwest German Radio Orchestra and recorded by the EIC.

30. *Erwartung*, Op. 17, for Soprano and Orchestra (1909); *Die glückliche Hand*, Op. 18, drama with musical accompaniment (1913).

Boulez performed and recorded *Gurrelieder* (1900–11) in London; *Jacob's Ladder*, an unfinished oratorio (1917–22), was performed in London and Paris, recorded in London. The Four Songs with Orchestra, Op. 22 (1913–15), were played and recorded in London with Yvonne Minton and the BBC Symphony Orchestra; they were also performed in Paris with the National Orchestra in 1964. *Kol Nidre* for Narrator, Chorus, and Orchestra, Op. 39 (1938); Prelude for Orchestra and Mixed Chorus, Op. 44 (1945); *A Survivor from Warsaw* for Narrator, Chorus, and Orchestra, Op. 46 (1947); *Israel Exists Again* for Chorus and Orchestra (1949, unfinished); and *Modern Psalm* for Narrator, Mixed Chorus, and Orchestra, Op. 50C (1950, unfinished) have all been performed and recorded in Paris, London, or New York.

With regard to Boulez's presumed dislike of Schoenberg's later works, Robert Siohan writes: "Arnold Schoenberg's String Trio, Op. 45, bears a distinguishing mark. According to Pierre Boulez, this work of 1946 and the Op. 42 Piano Concerto of 1942 appear to be rare islands emerging from a period of weakness in the master's thought." (*Le Monde*, 14 April 1965.)

31. Concerto for Violin and Orchestra, Op. 36 (1934–36); Concerto for Piano and Orchestra, Op. 42 (1942), recorded for Erato with Pierre Amoyal and Peter Serkin. One might also include the Cello Concerto, after a harpsichord concerto by G.-M. Monn (1932); and the Concerto for String Quartet and Orchestra, after the Concerto Grosso Op. 6, no. 7, by Handel (1933).

32. The Round House, Chalk Farm, north of London. Former depot (built 1847) for the locomotives of pioneer G. L. Stephenson. Scene of informal concerts with discussions; previously the site for Peter Brook's experimental theater and for the total nudity of *Oh Calcutta!*

33. In the countries in which he conducted regularly—Great Britain, the United States, the Netherlands—Boulez was always careful to program works by first-class composers, whether ancient or modern. Some American composers deemed themselves insufficiently represented and protested vigorously.

34. Inventory of programs from 1976 through 1987. This tendency was already becoming apparent while Boulez headed the Domaine Musical.

35. Hungarian composer and conductor (b. 1944). Appointed musical director of the Ensemble InterContemporain in 1979.

36. Hugues Dufourt (b. 1943), Tristan Murail (b. 1947), both founders of the group L'Itinéraire. Marc-André Dalbavie (b. 1961).

Boulez conducted *Diadèmes*, a work originated at IRCAM, on 7 and 8 February 1990 at the Salle Pleyel. Boulez placed much emphasis on young composers during the 1989–90 season of IRCAM and the EIC.

37. Also Gérard Grisey (b. 1946), three times; Jacques Lenot (b. 1945), once; and Kimi Sato (b. 1949), also once.

38. Philippe Manoury (b. 1952), Philippe Durville (b. 1957), Philippe Hurel (b. 1955), and Frédéric Durrieux (b. 1959) have contributed to IRCAM's efforts.

39. The Rug Concerts and Prospective Encounters, mentioned above.

40. "What is needed in America is a musical John Kennedy. As long as you have no Kennedy in music, you have no future of music in America." (*New York Times* interview with Joan Peyser, 1969, quoted in Peyser, *Boulez*, p. 183.)

41. Boulez spent much time in the orchestra library trying to unearth rare works. In his second season in New York (1972–73) he scheduled these works by Haydn: Symphonies 28, 31, 49, 60, 75, and 86; scenes from the *Incontro Improviso*; the *Theresienmesse*; and the *Harmoniemesse*.

The following season, he programmed Schumann's First and Second Symphonies as well as Beethoven's Third and Fifth Symphonies and Mendelssohn's "Reformation" Symphony, but offered Mahler's First Symphony and Bruckner's First Symphony only in Paris.

42. Boulez has said:

> The Museum shows us the entire cultural life and visual heritage of a given era. I see a work by Rembrandt, and with it, paintings of the guilds; this helps me to understand why the Rembrandt is not an isolated phenomenon in time, but a general phenomenon magnified by genius. Now in the musical world, we usually choose to show some extreme tendency and we neglect almost everything else. Just as history is sometimes taught by showing nothing but the battles won by a few great men, with no concern at all for social continuity, music is taught by showing only a few of the loftiest pinnacles. Which really leaves some gaps in the landscape! (Boulez, Conference on the Future of Radio Symphony Orchestras, European Broadcasting Union, Frankfurt, 2–4 April 1984.)

43. According to "La musique et ses problèmes contemporains," in *Cahiers Renaud-Barrault*, no. 41, 1963, first performances of the following works took place before 1963 at the Domaine Musical. Several exceptions are noted in brackets.

Alban Berg
　　String Quartet, Op. 3 (1909–10): 1955
　　Three Pieces for Orchestra, Op. 6 (1914, revised 1929): 1957
　　Three Pieces from *Lyric Suite* (1927): 1958
Arnold Schoenberg
　　Suite for Piano, Op. 25 (1924): 1954, first public performance
　　Three Satires, Op. 28 (1925): 1954
　　String Quartet no. 4, Op. 37 (1937): 1957
Igor Stravinsky
　　Canticum sacrum (1955): 1956, French premiere
　　Agon, ballet (1957): 1957, European premiere
　　Threni (1958): 1958, first performance in France
Edgar Varèse
　　Hyperprism (1924): 1960
　　Equatorial (1933–34): 1963

Anton Webern

> Passacaglia for Orchestra, Op. 1 (1908): 1958 [first performed in 1923 by Concerts Straram]
>
> *Entflieht auf leichten Kähnen*, Op. 2 (1908), a cappella: 1954
>
> Five Movements for String Quartet, Op. 5 (1909): 1955 [first performed in 1922 by the Pro Arte Quartet]; version for String Orchestra: 1955
>
> Six Pieces for Orchestra, Op. 6 (1910): 1957
>
> Two Songs for Voice and Eight Instruments, Op. 8 (1910–11): 1956
>
> Four Songs for Voice and Instruments, Op. 13 (1914–18): 1956
>
> Six Songs for Voice and Instruments, Op. 14 (1917–21): 1960
>
> Five Sacred Songs for Soprano and Instruments, Op. 15 (1917–22): 1960
>
> Five Canons on Latin Texts for Voice, Clarinet, and Bass Clarinet, Op. 16 (1924): 1960
>
> Three Traditional Rhymes for Voice and Instruments, Op. 17 (1924): 1960
>
> Two Songs, Op. 19 (1926): 1954
>
> String Trio, Op. 20 (1927): 1957
>
> Symphony for Chamber Ensemble (1928), Op. 21: 1955
>
> Quartet, Op. 22 (1930): 1956
>
> *Das Augenlicht*, Op. 26 (1935): 1955
>
> Variations for Piano, Op. 27 (1936): 1954, first public performance
>
> Variations for Orchestra, Op. 30 (1940): 1955
>
> Second Cantata, Op. 31 (1941–43): 1956
>
> Posthumous Movement for String Trio (1927): 1961
>
> *Fuga Ricercata for Six Voices*, no. 2, of the *Musical Offering* by J. S. Bach, transcribed for orchestra (1935): 1954

The early Webern performances noted in brackets above are testimony to the lively discovery of scores that took place between the two world wars, resembling the activities of the Domaine Musical years later. Most of the records of the Concerts Straram (1925–33) disappeared after the basement of the Théâtre des Champs-Elysées was transformed into a ticket office in 1987.

44. Exactly thirty-five years. Early April 1922 with the Orchestra of the Pasdeloup Concerts, conducted by André Caplet at the Théâtre des Champs-Elysées. Schoenberg himself conducted the Paris premiere of Two Bach Chorales and *Pelleas und Melisande*, Op. 5, at the head of the Orchestre Colonne on 8 December 1927. On 5 March 1933, Dimitri Mitropoulos led the Paris Symphony Orchestra in the premiere of *Transfigured Night*. In 1935 Alban Berg died. The first performance of his Lyric Suite was organized by the group called Triton on 13 June 1936 in the Salle Perret (possibly played several days earlier at the Spirale). Berg's violin concerto, "To the Memory of an Angel," was performed at the Salle Pleyel on 2 November 1936 by the Philharmonic Society Orchestra under the direction of Charles Munch, with Louis Krasner as the soloist. The score had just been published.

45. Boulez was educated as a Catholic at the little seminary of Montbrison, Institut Victor-de-la-Prade. Even so, Joan Peyser heard this exchange during the intermission of Boulez's first concert in New York, September 1971: "Is Boulez Jewish?" "Heavens no! I think he must be the son of a Swiss watchmaker!"

46. Director of the Los Angeles Philharmonic Orchestra. Born in Frankfurt in 1924; conductor in Johannesburg from 1942; opera conductor for the South Africa National Opera, then for the Cape Town University Opera and the Libya Grand Opera Company from 1948 to 1955. Became manager of the Los Angeles Philharmonic in 1969.

   Boulez is thus putting the organizational function before the conducting function here.

47. Paul Sacher (b. 1906), conductor who founded the Musikakademie and the Paul Sacher Foundation. Playing on an exaggerated historical awareness of contemporary composers, this foundation intends to supplant public collections and store these composers' documents. Its methods and its passion for secrecy are to musicology what Swiss banks are to the global economy. Boulez has deposited several documents there.

48. 23 November 1963; Jean-Louis Barrault was stage director.

   Wozzeck had been staged in Paris at the Théâtre des Champs-Elysées in a Vienna State Opera production, in which Karl Böhm conducted the Vienna Philharmonic Orchestra. On 5 December 1959, the Strasbourg Municipal Orchestra performed *Wozzeck* in a production of the Munich Opera, conducted by Ernest Bour.

49. For a composition course at the Musikakademie in 1961.

50. *Parsifal* in Bayreuth in 1966, 1967, 1968, 1970, giving a total of seventeen performances. In 1967 Boulez conducted *Tristan* in Osaka with the Bayreuth Festival Orchestra, for the first International Music Festival there. *Wozzeck* was performed in Frankfurt on 20 April 1966.

51. Other plans: a *Don Giovanni*, a *Boris*, and a *Ring* cycle, all interrupted by the death of Wieland Wagner in 1966. Boulez conducted Debussy's *Pelléas et Mélisande* at Covent Garden on 4 December 1969, in a production staged by Vaclav Kaslik with sets by Svoboda.

52. The *Ring* cycle in Bayreuth, from 1976 to 1980, in a production staged by Patrice Chéreau with sets by Richard Peduzzi. *Lulu*, 24 February 1979 at the Paris Opera, staged by Patrice Chéreau with sets by Richard Peduzzi. Also a concert version of Schoenberg's *Moses und Aron*, 4 December 1974 at the Royal Festival Hall with the BBC Symphony Orchestra.

53. On 13 October 1964 at the Théâtre des Champs-Elysées, National Radio Orchestra and Chorus. "Two do not a couple make," announced a review.

   > One can only glean a feeble idea of progress made in bringing to light music of the past because the most immediately noticeable innovation of the performance was its record speed. Boulez, who conducted, adopted tempos

which were sometimes twice as fast as those which performers, conductors, or virtuoso soloists and ancient theoreticians all agree upon. . . . But there's no need to bring in historical considerations in assessing the harm this performance did to the singers, who frequently did not have time to judge their breathing properly or let their voices resonate fully, much less control their articulation and shading. And there was another peril: thanks to a worthy concern with authenticity, the score was performed at the pitch prescribed by Rameau at a time when the diapason in Paris was one of the lowest in Europe, almost a full tone lower than it is today. This resulted in a heightened tension in the upper register for our modern interpreters. . . . His technique as a conductor remains beyond reproach. Wherever clarity, precision, and rhythmic steadiness were called for, Boulez met his own high standards. (Marc Pincherle, *Les Nouvelles Littéraires*, 22 October 1964.)

In announcing the concert, Boulez told Claude Samuel:

No, the great composers of the past are not modern; they belong to their own time. Rameau represents the state of French music at a certain moment in the eighteenth century. Unfortunately, the nationalism preceding the 1914 war created a misunderstanding: the musicians of the Schola Cantorum, and even Debussy, wanted to find a French equivalent to Bach. Rameau was the blue blood of the Vosges. In reality, however, this style of opera is now terribly dated. For me the most interesting aspect of it is the tragic side (not the mythology), together with the choruses and great flexibility of the construction. I love composers who construct their music.

Messiaen, who was present at the interview, concluded: "Basically, you have very French tastes." (*Candide*, 15 October 1964.)

54. Performance 24 February 1979 at the Paris Opera. Staged by Patrice Chéreau, sets by Richard Peduzzi.

55. Friedrich Cerha (b. 1926), Austrian conductor and composer. Asked to perform this task, Boulez refused.

56. Act III, scene 1.

57. Act III, scene 2.

58. Boxed set of LP records: Debussy's orchestral works, recorded December 1968 in London; 18 April 1969 in Cleveland; and 29 September in New York, with the respective orchestras of those cities.

59. *G-sharp*, by Kimi Sato (b. 1949). Work broadcast 11 December 1980.

60. Sonnet no. 217 by Petrarch in the Serenade for Seven Instruments and Bass Voice, Op. 24. In bar 3, a B-flat played by the guitar has a question mark beside it.

61. I was lying.

62. Boulez's main publisher is the same as Schoenberg's, the Austrian Universal Edition. The Serenade is published by Hansen of Copenhagen.

63. The Bibliothèque Nationale in Paris. Boulez contributed to the correction of *Jeux* (Durand-Costellet, publishers, 1989) in the monumental Debussy edition overseen by François Lesure, honorary director of the Bibliothèque's music department.

64. *Suite*, Op. 29, penultimate bar. Ledger line added in pencil above the two highest notes of the violin part. The B-flats become D-flats, and the F-sharp that follows becomes a G-sharp. In the following bar of this painstaking edition, an asterisk refers to a variant in the manuscript, scrupulously indicated.

65. Schoenberg, *Suite*, Op. 29. Bars 224 (5/8) and 225 (6/8) redefined as a bar in 4/4 time and one in 3/8.

When the composer is still living, Boulez's corrective parricide verges upon farce. In a scene in the documentary film *A Stravinsky Portrait* by Rolf Lieberman and Richard Leacock (North German Radio, 1963), Boulez and Stravinsky are seated at a table, discussing *Les noces* in English. Boulez says that he "discovered some things which are not really right, in my score at least." He shows Stravinsky a place at the end where "there is one bar too much." Stravinsky replies, "I hadn't noticed it." Soon Lieberman appears:

> Lieberman: What did you find out?
> Boulez (thrilled): A mistake.
> Lieberman: A mistake?
> Boulez: Yes.
> Lieberman: And you found it, the first one who found it!

66. Cover of Columbia LP record 7206.

67. John Eliot Gardiner (b. 1943) also established new editions of Monteverdi's *Vespers* and of Rameau's *Dardanus*, *The Feasts of Hébé*, and the *Les Boréades* suite.

68. André Cluytens was then its musical director.

69. 29 May 1913 at the Théâtre des Champs Elysées.

70. On 23 October 1934 Hermann Scherchen, conductor of the Strasbourg Municipal Orchestra, confided to his wife: "Today I spent the entire day . . . until 7:30, studying with the bassoon (the difficult solo passage from the beginning of the *Rite*), and at 8 o'clock I began the rehearsal, which went on until 11."

FOUR **On Gestures** (pages 64–86)

1. Charles Munch, speaking to his assistant, Serge Baudo: "Do you think it's a good idea, when people conduct without a baton? I think it's stupid." (October 1968, quoted in *L'orchestre nu*, by François Dupin.) Serge Baudo, who uses a baton, was among the first to conduct at the Domaine Musical, before Boulez had decided to do so.

2. "Instrumental music . . . has temporarily abandoned the full orchestra and

flung itself madly into chamber music, an area in which research could still be undertaken. For that very reason, moreover, my entire activity in Paris has been limited to chamber music." (Interview with Louis Dandrel, *Le Monde*, 12 September 1970.)

3. André Cluytens (1905–1967) was music director at the Opéra-Comique from 1947 to 1953. He conducted the first performance of *The Rake's Progress* by Stravinsky in 1953.

4. The English composer Cipriani Potter (1792–1871) was the first to conduct standing up and without a baton.

The New York Philharmonic Orchestra seems accustomed to conductors who did not always use a baton. Before Boulez, the Russian conductor Vassily Sofonoff (1852–1915) made news by not using one, between 1906 and 1909. Leopold Stokowski (1882–1977), a guest conductor of the Philharmonic who had given some two thousand first performances in the United States, abandoned his baton for a while around 1925, perhaps under the influence of jazz. The case of his successor, Dimitri Mitropoulos (1896–1960), oversteps the bounds of anecdotal erudition. Predecessor, between 1949 and 1957, of Leonard Bernstein—who preceded Boulez at the New York Philharmonic—Mitropoulos conducted without a baton, though mainly before and after his tenure in New York. He resembled Boulez not only in character, but also in his insistence on presenting contemporary music and in the criticisms he received. His conducting of avant-garde music in France between the two wars makes him an essential link in the French modernist tradition, of which Boulez is now the trustee.

A critic observed of a Straram concert conducted by Mitropoulos on 24 April 1934:

> Truly this conductor is unlike any other. His fingers hold no baton; and rather than transmit some imperious indication his two hands seem freely and equally to seize diverse configurations of a moving mass of waves, shaping and ordering them through this double and all-enveloping gesture which alternately scoops and soars. A sovereign and invisible instrument, of which every visible instrument is like a departure, a component, or a symbol. (Claude Altomont, *Le ménestrel*, 4 May 1934.)

Mitropoulos returned to Paris, where he conducted the New York Philharmonic Orchestra on 19 September 1955. (In December 1955, Pierre Boulez's first orchestral concert was announced; it took place 16 June 1956 in Caracas.) The Mitropoulos program consisted of the Overture to *Der Freischütz* by Weber; Beethoven's Piano Concerto in E-flat with Robert Casadesus, soloist; the French premiere of Shostakovich's Tenth Symphony; and, as an encore, Kabalevsky's *Colas Breugnon* Overture.

> The concert given at the Théâtre des Champs-Elysées by the New York Philharmonic Orchestra brought us great satisfaction. We were particularly delighted to see its conductor, Dimitri Mitropoulos, finding the form he displayed at the podium of the Orchestre Symphonique de Paris. I still recall [Florent Schmitt's] *Tragedy of Salomé*, performed in February 1932 as I

remember, which showed us one of the best conductors one could ever hope to know. We rediscover a Mitropoulos unchanged by the past twenty years: he still possesses the same fire, the same power to control the instrumental body, the same lucidity which never becomes dry, the same restrained and precise gestures. As for the hundred or so performers grouped before him on the stage, Dimitri Mitropoulos seems positively to hold them in the palm of his hand. (René Dumesnil, *Le Monde*, 20 September 1955.)

And again:

Using a minimum of gestures, Dimitri Mitropoulos excels in giving a maximum amount of expression to the works he conducts. From the first bars of the *Freischütz* Overture, ample proof was given of his own mastery and the perfection of his hundred players. (Jean Mistler, *L'Aurore*, 19 September 1955.)

Years later, by leaving New York to return to Paris and found IRCAM, Boulez barely escaped the same rejection that Mitropoulos suffered in New York because of his programming. In the contemporary music review, *Melos*, Robert Breuer sketched a portrait of Dimitri Mitropoulos that calls to mind many aspects of Boulez, another southern European who migrated to the north:

He possessed an essentially Greek mind, conditioned by German discipline, a mind that had adapted to the "practical" realities of life in America (but without their commercial flavor). He was not a dictator, wanting to enslave the world with his ideas, but an educator, guiding it toward new shores on the perpetually renewed if apparently erratic current of musical creation. . . . A world of mystery seemed to surround this very private being, who kept apart from women and was said to lead an austere and monastic life. . . . The abiding purpose of his life was to encourage talent. A staunch friend and counselor, he was perhaps even more a benefactor, a patron of the arts who never flaunted his almost boundless generosity.

This encomium, accompanied by photographs of Mitropoulos conducting without a baton, appeared in *Melos* in April 1961; Pierre Boulez contributed to the journal several times during the same year.

5. "In ten to fifteen years, orchestras will no longer have recourse to the baton!" (Vassily Sofonoff, 1909, in Georges Liebert, ed., *L'art du chef d'orchestre*.)

6. Diego Masson (b. 1935): "His restrained and precise hand technique, without a baton or excesses of expression, reveals the school he was formed in." (C. S., *Candide*, 7 March 1966.)

Boulez's most obvious descendants—whether he likes it or not—are the "baroque" conductors, the American William Christie and the British Roger Norrington. In 1988, for example, Norrington recorded the *Symphonie fantastique* by Berlioz for EMI with the London Classical Players, on period instruments and without a baton.

7. See chapter 12, "Education of Conductors and the Changing of the Guard."

8. Course at Villeneuve-lès-Avignon, from 4 to 20 July 1988.

9. Monday 3 August 1987, Promenade Concert at the Royal Albert Hall, and previously on Friday 10 August 1973 and Sunday 21 July 1974. (See Selection of Programs Conducted by Boulez.) Recorded on 6 December 1974 in West Ham, London, for CBS.

10. *Éclat* (Bursts) for Fifteen Instruments (March 1965), premiere for the inauguration of the Los Angeles County Museum and Boulez's fortieth birthday, conducted by the composer. Continued in *Multiples* for Orchestra (1966–70), first performed 21 October 1970 in London by the BBC Symphony Orchestra, again conducted by Boulez.

11. "It is obvious that the proper tempo of a musical work can only be determined in relation to the specific character of its interpretation. We cannot determine the former unless we are certain of the latter. The demands of the interpretation, its propensity for continuity of sound (song) or rhythmic movement (representation) will determine what kind of tempo the orchestra will have to observe." (Richard Wagner, 1869, "On Conducting," in Georges Liebert, ed., *L'art du chef d'orchestre*. Boulez had just read this essay.)

12. *Symphonie fantastique* by Hector Berlioz: Charles Munch and the Boston Symphony Orchestra; André Cluytens and the Orchestre Philharmonique; Sir Georg Solti and the Chicago Symphony Orchestra; Charles Dutoit and the Montreal Symphony Orchestra; Igor Markevitch and the Orchestre des Concerts Lamoureux; Pierre Boulez and the London Symphony Orchestra (1973). Roger Norrington uses no baton to conduct the London Classical Players, an orchestra of period instruments.

13. Recorded December 1968 in London; issued in France for the bicentennial of Beethoven's birth in 1970. Boulez had recently replaced an ailing Otto Klemperer (1885–1973) in a performance of the Fifth Symphony, as part of the Beethoven cycle given at the Royal Festival Hall, London.

14. First Chamber Symphony, Op. 9 (1906).

15. Recorded by CBS on 16 September 1979 with the Ensemble InterContemporain at IRCAM, Paris. Also recorded for Adès in 1959 with the Domaine Musical.

16. Boulez's conducting calmed down in other ways. Consider Paul Griffiths's analysis of the 1956, 1965, and 1972 versions of *Le marteau sans maître* as compared to the 1985 version (Ensemble InterContemporain, recorded by CBS, 1989, sponsored by the Total Foundation for Music). The length of the work's nine segments is indicated; pauses are given in parentheses except where the record side is changed:

> 1956: 1'26 (5")/ 3'50 (5")/ 2'02 (9")/ 4'12 (6")/ 3'08/ 4'06 (5") 46" (1")/
>   4'46 (6")/ 6"57.
> Around 1965: 1'24 (4")/ 3'33 (6")/ 1'59 (8")/ 4'04 (10")/ 3'17/ 4'16 (5")
>   46" (1")/ 4'44 (8")/ 7'07.

1972: 1'47 (9")/ 4'04 (5")/ 2'27 (8")/ 4'36 (4")/ 3'52 (7")/ 4'13 (5")/ 1'00/
  5'48 (8")/ 8'03.
1985: 1'46 (5"30)/ 4'28 (5"30)/ 2'29 (5"30)/ 3'58 (7")/ 3'49 (5"30)/ 4'37
  (5")/ 1'01 (5"30)/ 5'56 (5")/ 8'26.

From *Pierre Boulez: Eine Festchrift zum 60 Geburtstag am 26 Marz 1985*. J.
Hausler, ed. Vienna: Universal Edition, 1985.

17. In favor: Boulez has been called the

> professional musician's conductor. He knows instruments better than the
> others. He can tell the cimbalom player how to restring his box of wires to
> facilitate complexities, or show the violist a more effective fingering for a
> harmonic. Second, he is most fastidious about articulation. Third, he has
> the keenest ear for balance in the equilibrating of the various components of
> an orchestra. Finally, he draws the most refined colors from the orchestra. It
> follows that his performances are clean, clear, intelligent, and supremely
> controlled. (Robert Craft, quoted in Peyser, *Boulez*, p. 256.)

Against: "To be sure, I pay tribute to the authoritative precision Boulez displayed in leading his remarkable performers." (Jacques Feshotte, *Réforme*, 6
January 1962.)

18. A subtle distinction. As Boulez commented, above, "I simply play it as I
like to hear it, as I think it should be heard. Which doesn't mean I turn it into
something wholly personal." Harriet Johnson wrote in the *New York Post* in
1974, concerning a performance of Handel's *Water Music* and Schumann's First
Symphony: "These joyous works were played but not really interpreted. They
were not played with style. The result was prosaic." (Quoted in Peyser, *Boulez*,
p. 256.)

19. From Stravinsky's autobiography, in translation:

> This preoccupation with the subject of tone material manifested itself also
> in my instrumentation of *Les noces*, which, after long delays, was at last to
> be produced by Diaghilev.
>   While still at Morges I had tried out various forms of instrumentation,
> first of all for a large orchestra, which I gave up almost at once in view of the
> elaborate apparatus that the complexity of that form demanded. I next
> sought for a solution in a smaller ensemble. I began a score which required
> massed polyphonic effects: a mechanical piano and an electrically driven
> harmonium, a section of percussion instruments, and two Hungarian cim-
> baloms. But there I was balked by a fresh obstacle, namely, the great diffi-
> culty for the conductor of synchronizing the parts executed by the instru-
> mentalists and singers with those rendered by the mechanical players. I was
> thus compelled to abandon this idea also, although I had already orches-
> trated the first two scenes. . . .
>   I saw clearly that the sustained, that is to say *soufflé [breathed]* ele-
> ments in my work would be best supported by an ensemble consisting
> exclusively of instruments that are struck. I thus found my solution in the

form of an orchestra comprising piano, timbals [timpani], bells, and xylophones—none of which instruments gives a precise note.

Such a sound combination in *Les noces* was the necessary outcome of the music itself, and it was in nowise suggested by a desire to imitate the sounds of popular fetes of this kind, which I had, indeed, neither seen nor heard. (Igor Stravinsky, *An Autobiography*. New York: Simon and Schuster, Inc., 1936. Originally *Chroniques de ma vie*. Paris: 1935.

20. France.

21. Recall the funeral elegy for Dimitri Mitropoulos, quoted above. Another southern European who migrated to the north, Mitropoulos "possessed an essentially Greek mind, conditioned by German discipline, a mind that had adapted to the realities of life in America (but without their commercial flavor)." (*Melos*, April 1961.)

22. "For me, the Latin countries are countries for vacationing and tourism. . . . The only countries in which I can henceforth do serious work are the Anglo-Saxon and Germanic ones." (Pierre Boulez, *Lectures pour tous*, July 1969.)

23. Professor of composition at the Berlin Academy of Arts from 1925 until Hitler's arrival in power. Schoenberg fled to Paris where he formally converted back to Judaism on 30 July 1933, with Marc Chagall as witness.

24. Henri Sauguet (1901–1989) observed at the age of eighty-six:

I came to Paris in 1921 to hear Schoenberg's *Pierrot lunaire*, having been invited by Darius Milhaud who was conducting it. I was not particularly impressed. I found its esthetics rather out of date; the *Mariés de la tour Eiffel*, created that same year by the group called Les Six, seemed more contemporary.

Even so, the Viennese composers have become our Gurus now.

I almost choked when they turned them into Scriptures in 1945. They wanted people to start writing like Schoenberg. And then Boulez at their head: we'd just emerged from one Occupation, only to fall into another! To think that even this morning, I heard someone say that a Beethoven sonata was close to Schoenberg! Composers have dazzled themselves with a few lucky inventions they thought they were the first to find. When I was young, one could just as easily get carried away by muted trumpets or glissandi played by harps. Debussy knew how to use all that, he knew how to write. But for everyone else, it turned into a recipe. Didn't Schoenberg himself say of his imitators, "They're killing my music?" He was an exceptional thinker, a master. But I prefer young people to be interested in Xenakis—that's important for them. Boulez's whole life has been nothing but bluff, invective, impertinence, and conceit.

He's grown much gentler with *Répons*.

Well, well! He's joined the old men now. But this warmth of his you speak of, I don't feel it at all. He's exercised a bad influence over an entire generation that's wasted its energies in following him. ("Henri Sauguet, so gay," interview by Jean Vermeil in *Gai pied hebdo*, 19 December 1987.)

25. See chapter 1, note 4.

26. Henri Sauguet:

> We used to meet at the Boeuf sur le toit, the café that lent its name to that era. It was founded by a friend of Jean Cocteau, and Cocteau thought of the name. What a talented and driving force he was, Cocteau!
>
> Was Edgar Varèse one of you?
>
> Not really, although Cocteau had discovered him and was originally responsible for his music being heard. It didn't work out, however, and Varèse left for America (December 1915). He was more in contact with the American public. That's why, when Cocteau launched Satie and the Group of Six, nobody believed him. Everyone said it was the Varèse business all over again! (From Vermeil, "Henri Sauguet, so gay" in *Gai pied hebdo*, 19 December 1987.)

27. End of 1949. A private recital on prepared piano ensued, sponsored by Suzanne Tézenas whom Boulez had just met, as well as three months of exchanges in Paris, a common publisher, and a lengthy correspondence. The two men were brought together by their quest for a common absolute, albeit by opposite paths, and by Boulez's acoustic interest in prepared piano (although he soon rejected its "necessary misappropriation of instrumental integrity"). According to Jameux, "it has been suggested that . . . Boulez's involvement with Cage was both pleasurable and stimulating, since it offered a valuable opportunity for exchanging ideas with an avant-garde musical culture completely divorced from his own European heritage." (Dominique Jameux, *Pierre Boulez*, p. 54.)

28. "A book neither begins nor ends; at most, it pretends to do so." (Mallarmé, quoted by Boulez in connection with his Third Sonata, in *Méditations*, no. 7, Spring 1964.) See also his two *Improvisations sur Mallarmé* for Soprano and Instrumental Ensemble (1957), combined with *Pli selon pli* (1960). The Boulez-Mallarmé combination is a commonplace of Boulezian exegesis. Boulez contributed to it with the concert he gave at the Royal Festival Hall on 16 March 1966: *Trois poèmes de Stéphane Mallarmé* (1913) by Ravel and Debussy, followed by *Pli selon pli*.

29. Boulez's villa in Baden-Baden is entirely furnished in Knoll's International Design style of the 1970s, the time when the house was decorated. Few furnishings were added subsequently. On the other hand, Boulez's newer apartment in Paris was decorated in 1989 by Andrée Putnam, famous for her re-creations of furniture dating from between the two world wars.

30. Fraternity can extend back through time. Pressed by the Concertgebouw to answer a rumor that he detested conducting Schubert, Boulez replied:

> What I may have said is that what I most admired in Schubert was his prodigious spontaneity of invention, a spontaneity I myself was far from possessing, since our era scarcely encourages it, and that I admired him all the more for that.
>
> On the subject of spontaneity, I recently conducted his *Gesang der Geister über den Wassern*, an absolutely extraordinary work, as you know.

But even Schubert reworked it several times before deciding on the admirable and profound definitive version, so worthy of the poem. . . .

I've never changed my opinion of him as a composer—and if, like everyone else since Schumann, I find him guilty of *himmlische Länge* [heavenly lengths], I must admit that they are heavenly before all else! (When I was in New York I even resurrected his *Lazarus*!) (Boulez to Flothuis, 5 July 1989, for subsequent publication in *Preludium*, November 1989.)

31. Robert Craft, quoted in note 17, above: "he has the keenest ear for balance in the equilibrating of the various components of an orchestra." (Peyser, *Boulez*, p. 256.)

32. Goethe again.

33. Hans Keller, an associate of Sir William Glock and subsequently chief new music assistant at the BBC, scathingly maintains:

Boulez is incapable of phrasing. It's as simple as that. The number of examples proving he doesn't know what phrasing is are legion. That's why he conducts Bach, Beethoven, or Webern in exactly the same way: for with all the precision and lucidity of which he's capable, with his supposed rhythm which is actually metrical, he is in fact incapable of forming a phrase correctly, and that's because he ignores the harmonic implications of every musical structure, paying no attention to harmonic rhythm or therefore of any rhythm characterizing his tonal music. . . . People who can't phrase properly . . . don't even replace phrasing with space (everything's too fast), or rhythm with the mechanical pseudo-excitement of beats. As a result, in places where one would like to hear what should be heard—especially in rich, tonal or partly tonal structures—the music shoots by before one's had time to say Phew! (Hans Keller in *1975, 1984 minus nine*. London, 1977.)

34. This idea is found in the work of Jean-Louis Barrault, whom Boulez had assisted with stage music: "To get up again, I shall use one muscle after another, being careful to see that the rest of my body remains relaxed. . . . The proper economy of energy is the basic principle and secret governing acting." (J.-L. Barrault, "Le corps magnétique," in *Cahiers Renaud-Barrault*, no. 99, 1979.)

SIX **Rehearsing** (pages 90–103)

1. New version, 26 January 1988, London.

2. "Since the appointment of Michel Guy, secretary of state at the Ministry of Culture, there has been much talk about the departure of Marcel Landowski, director of the departments of music and opera from May 1966. . . . His place in cultural affairs will be taken by M. Jean Maheu, aged 43, referendary counsel to the Court of Accounts, director of young people's educational and social activities at the State Bureau of Youth and Sports from 1967. . . . This appointment would be a vindication for the French composer, who was passed over in favor

of Marcel Landowski in 1966 and left France in high dudgeon, refusing all official jobs." (Unsigned article, *L'Aurore*, 11 November 1974.)

Jean Maheu is the son of a former president of UNESCO. He was nominated general director of the Centre Georges Pompidou (of which IRCAM is one of four main elements) on 23 February 1983. In February 1989 he became president and general director of Radio France.

3. The metaphor is a play on words involving the verb *conduire*, "to drive," an international neologism Boulez uses in the sense of "to conduct." Boulez frequently says *conduire* instead of the more usual *diriger*, which the Germans borrowed in the verb *dirigieren*.

4. In 1966, in Florence.

5. The German concept of *die Routine* was borrowed from the French *routine* at a time when the French word did not have its present pejorative connotations. The German word never acquired them, and the related adjective *routiniert* means "experienced, an old hand at the job, skillful."

6. "I have just as many rights as the conductor," declared director Jean Vilar, who planned a national popular opera with Boulez and Maurice Béjart. (*Paris-Express*, 20 February 1964.)

7. Second version for soprano, alto, female chorus, and large orchestra (1951–52).

8. Rehearsals paired with *Le soleil des eaux*. On Thursday 22 October there were four sessions: percussion minus keyboard; first and second violins; harp, celesta, timpani, xylophone, vibraphone, glockenspiel; violas, cellos, double basses. On Friday 23 October 1981, five sessions: harp, celesta, etc.; woodwinds; brass. The work was replaced by Stravinsky's *Song of the Nightingale*.

9. Revised version, parts 1, 2, 4, and 5. World premiere concert on Monday 25 January 1988, in London, with the BBC Symphony Orchestra.

10. Boulez has said:

> A further example: the Strasbourg Percussion Group. Being able to work outside the normal orchestral sessions, being able to express their artistic personality in a more individual way, and then having the opportunity to travel and participate in international musical events—all that has quickened their vocation as instrumentalists, besides greatly enhancing their abilities as virtuosos and whetting their musical gifts. The benefits are thus threefold, and the example is typical because the group in question initially had no repertoire, unlike the classical groups. This group could never have come into being if the principle of exclusive rights had been strictly applied. (Interview with Boulez and Émile Biasini, *Journal de l'Artiste Musicien*, April 1966.)

11. The players of the Ensemble InterContemporain founded the Brass and Percussion Ensemble of the Ensemble InterContemporain, the Ensemble Inter-Contemporain Wind Quintet (1982), the InterContemporain Quartet (1986), and the String Trio.

12. Boulez has also said:

> All the same, we should not rely entirely on the judgment of musicians. I've been around them enough to know that they usually follow the path of least resistance. If some of them enthusiastically accept the more demanding challenges required of them, others are distinctly disturbed. The fact is, if you begin by giving each of them a more individual and therefore harder task to perform, there are two ways to get results. You can stimulate their curiosity, skill, or their professional capacity for inventiveness. Or—and this is a formula as old as the hills—you can pay them. If you pay them you arouse their interest, but the best thing is to arouse it without paying them too much. Such is the dilemma of the artistic director in regard to the manager of the organization. (Boulez, Conference on the Future of Radio Symphony Orchestras, European Broadcasting Union, Frankfurt, 2–4 April 1984.)

SEVEN   **Recording** (pages 104–108)

1. Andrew Kazdin, a freelance American producer, worked part-time for the former CBS Records.

2. Schoenberg's *Gurrelieder*, recorded on 26 October and 7–8 November 1974 at the West Ham Central Mission, London, with *Moses und Aron*; BBC Symphony Orchestra. During this period Boulez recorded primarily for Columbia (CBS), in the United Kingdom from January 1966 and with the U.S. division beginning in 1969. Recent recordings are with Deutsche Grammophon.

    According to CBS-France, Boulez's best-selling recordings have been Stravinsky's *Rite of Spring*, Debussy's *La mer*, Ravel's *La valse*, and Bartók's *Miraculous Mandarin*. Highest sales of his own recorded works were achieved by *Le marteau sans maître* and *Éclat/Multiples* as of 1989.

    Boulez never asked to make recordings of the Mahler symphonies, judging that "there are quite enough as it is." His live recording of the *Ring* cycle was issued by Philips; that of *Lulu*, by Deutsche Grammophon. Two French companies have shared the remaining crumbs: La Guilde du Disque (his earliest recordings, partly reissued by Adès) and Erato (some coproduced with the Ensemble InterContemporain).

3. On 18 April 1978 with the Ensemble InterContemporain. A similar situation occurred 26 August 1984 with Berg's Op. 6. The recording began in the BBC's studio no. 1, but when the studio proved unable to absorb the work's climax, it was necessary to move to St. John's Church, Smith Square. Thus the full sound range was preserved, but at the cost of some reverberation.

4. A Hungarian by birth, Georges Kadar was a student of Messiaen—"Which of us was not?" he inquires—and began working for CBS late in 1957. Assigned ("for want of someone better") to work with Boulez, he began a fruitful collaboration with the composer by recording *Éclat/Multiples* on 8–9 December 1981 at IRCAM in Paris.

5. Boulez's recording of the *Ring* cycle took place on the Bayreuth stage, but without a live audience. *Lulu* was recorded in a studio at IRCAM. Both recordings contain a few slight imperfections, appealing rather than annoying. The recordings of *Pelleas und Melisande*, *Wozzeck*, and *Moses und Aron* were carried out in a studio shortly after live performances.

EIGHT Settings (pages 109–112)

1. Jerzy Grotowski (b. 1933), author of *Towards a Poor Theatre* (Touchstone Books, 1970).

2. Performances on 11, 12, 13, 16, 17, 18, 19 July 1988 at ten o'clock in the evening in the Callet Quarry at Boulbon, with a vast display of electronic equipment. Program: *Dialogue de l'ombre double* (Dialogue of the Double Shadow) for clarinet, and *Répons*. With its conductor occupying the place of honor amid a double circle of musicians themselves surrounded by the audience, *Répons* is a perfect example of the spectacular type of composition.

On 15 July 1988, from ten at night until dawn, the same quarry was the setting for a well-attended IRCAM Night, with performances of works by Harvey, Vinao, Manoury, Stroppa, and Boulez. The Callet Quarry was inaugurated by Peter Brook for the production of his spectacular *Mahabharata* in 1987.

3. Music city of La Villette, east side. Egg-shaped in form and capable of being reconfigured, the auditorium of La Villette seats between eight hundred and twelve hundred spectators. It welcomes the Ensemble InterContemporain whose administrative offices and rehearsal rooms are situated nearby. Its architect was Christian de Portzamparc.

The Bastille Opera House, intended for use by "the people," was the first of the grandiose constructions called for by President François Mitterand after his election in 1981. Its small auditorium, the variable auditorium dear to Boulez, was threatened by the liberal-conservative coalition that governed France from March 1986 to May 1988 in conjunction with the socialist president. There was even talk of transforming it into a hotel. In July 1986, approximately one hundred personalities from the international operatic community issued a joint declaration calling for its completion.

> After 1986, work on the construction of the building's "shell"' was continued, but all decisions as to its definitive purpose . . . had been put off. The variable auditorium is an indispensable complement to the main auditorium. It allows for a wide repertoire to be performed, a repertoire otherwise unsuited to the architecture and constrictions of the main auditorium. . . . It meets the expectations of composers, directors, and dramatists who wish to introduce new forms of entertainment (often ill-adapted to the simple frontal stage-audience relationship). . . . Certain musical genres are performed far too infrequently, and under unacceptable conditions. For example, polyphonic and baroque music, chamber music in general, or even the evolution of instrumental music throughout the twentieth century (until the appear-

ance of computers) require variable configurations and acoustic space. (Official statement on the Public Establishment of the Bastille Opera House, March 1988.)

4. The Berlin Philharmonic auditorium was designed in 1963 by the architect Hans Scharoun. Some of his sketches inspired the adjoining chamber music hall of 1987, which employs the same principle just as effectively.

NINE   **Audiences** (pages 113–117)

1. From Paul Claudel's *L'échange* (first version):

> Lechy Elbernon: As for me, I know the world. I've been everywhere. I'm an actress, you know. I act in theater. Theater. Don't you know what that is?
> Martha: No.
> L. E.: There's the stage and there's the house. When everything's closed, people come there in the evening and sit in rows, one behind another, and they watch.
> Martha: How is that? What do they watch, since everything is closed?
> L. E.: They watch the curtain on the stage. They watch what's behind it when the curtain's raised. And something happens on the stage, as if it were real. . . . I watch the audience and the house is nothing but a mass of living flesh, dressed in clothes. And they decorate the walls like flies, right up to the ceiling.

L'échange was performed in November and December 1951 by the Renaud-Barrault Company at the Théâtre Marigny.

2. The public's infatuation with the Domaine Musical after the Second World War results from this phenomenon of worldliness, which Boulez manipulated brilliantly. The active support of Madame Suzanne Tézenas constitutes a rare recent example of a committed patron at once perspicacious and disinterested, unconcerned with her own image. The presence of numerous aristocrats—many of them women—among the Domaine Musical's supporters may further constitute the final spark of cultural effulgence in the nobility, already weakened by the First World War, as Marcel Proust has observed.

3. Boulez has commented:

> In my opinion, there are certainly people in this audience who want Bayreuth to be protected. They've barely digested the reforms introduced by Wieland Wagner in 1951 and already they're being asked to accept something else. After twenty-five years, they still think that's too soon. Much has been said about the hostile reactions to Chéreau's staging of the *Ring* and to the production in general, but that ignores the many favorable reactions. And it ended up with the people who wanted to prove they were right . . . who were determined not to go on watching, but to protest right away. Such systematic opposition indicates not only narrowmindedness but a

complete absence of intelligence. I won't even call them the audience—they're simply a small part of the audience who showed themselves to be extremely intolerant, but, thank God, they're not the whole audience. (Boulez on the scandal of the French *Ring* cycle at the centennial performance, radio broadcast, 31 July 1976.)

4. Dominique Jameux:

> Nine performances barely sufficed to quench the thirst of Parisian audiences, after the event had given rise to one of the most astonishing influences of fashion to be witnessed in the recent history of French musical life. One would like to dwell on this influence of fashion, because it is so dependent on the personality and stature of Boulez. . . . Berg had not yet really become fashionable. But the Bayreuth team had—and justifiably. . . . What can one say about that production now? It belongs not to history, but to news reports. . . . What remains of that hugely effervescent moment is . . . the dramatic encounter that took place, for the first time up to that point, between Boulez and the French musical establishment.

TEN   **France and Its Orchestras** (pages 118–119)

1. Lorin Maazel took over as musical director of the Orchestre National de France on 1 September 1988, with Boulez commissioned to be in charge of special events. Jeffrey Tate became principal guest conductor on 1 September 1989.

2. Radio France's New Philharmonic Orchestra (Nouvel Orchestre Philharmonique de Radio France) was founded 1 January 1976 by Gilbert Amy (Boulez's successor at the Domaine Musical). Since 1 February 1989, it has been known as the Orchestre Philharmonique de Radio France. Marek Janowski, the orchestra's principal conductor since 1984, was appointed musical director. Walter Coomans replaced Yon Kapp as artistic delegate.

3. In London and New York, Boulez negotiated contracts requiring four months in residence with the BBC Symphony and the New York Philharmonic, respectively.

4. Boulez was named principal guest conductor of the Chicago Symphony Orchestra on 30 March 1995.

ELEVEN   **The Future** (pages 120–127)

1. This was at the time of *Éclat* for fifteen instruments (1964), first performed in March 1965 at the Los Angeles County Museum.

2. Wagner:

> As to the general effect of a work and its tempos, I have only this to say: if the conductor and the singers have only the metronomic markings to guide them in their choice of tempos, then they will have a very poor understand-

ing of the work they must interpret. Conductors and singers will only find the right tempo if their comprehension of the dramatic and musical situations, and the keen sense they acquire of them, enable them to find the right speed as if it were self-evident, with no other goal. (Richard Wagner, note on the performance of *Tannhäuser*, 1852.)

3. Debussy to his publisher Jacques Durand, in 1915: "You know what I think of metronomic markings. They mark a bar about as accurately as roses do the space of a morning." Yet in his letter of 22 July 1915: "I wasn't able to give the metronomic markings. Monsieur Maelzel has no representative in the country since the war. So do as you please." (Maelzel, from the German firm of the same name, was descended from the Viennese J. N. Maelzel who in 1816 took out a patent in Paris for the "first" metronome, a copy of a Dutch device.)

Schoenberg was far more categorical:

> One has to admit that too detailed indications can make life hard for conductors, just as Draconian laws make life hard for the people they govern. But one must also admit that the person who has no intention of becoming a thief doesn't bother much about laws that punish theft. . . . One hears a lot about the rights of the interpreter: why don't we hear more about the rights of the composer! . . . I can't understand why conductors commit such mayhem with the metronomic markings. . . . Once one has learned at one's own expense what conductors of genius are capable of doing, despite the precise idea one has of one's own work, one tends to refuse them the tiniest liberty thereafter. (Arnold Schoenberg, *Style and Idea*, 1926; New York, 1950.)

4. Boulez:

> Musical activities are becoming increasingly compartmentalized. If, a few years ago, one could still entertain the utopian vision of a culture encompassing all periods of music, how can we expect a musician of today to perform in all these specialized fields? Records have made the public very demanding; and radio broadcasts, in which the musicians play either live or on tape, can't afford a standard inferior to that we've grown used to in records. From now on we can't just say we're going to bring some work to light, create a new breed of musicians, and worry about accuracy later. It isn't possible. Some needs are imperative. Even if it seems extremely pretentious to try to reach the level of a few exceptional orchestras in all we do, nevertheless we cannot sink below a certain level of proficiency, of specialization.
>
> Diversity or specialization, that's the dilemma. Besides, musicians as a group have developed too. . . . Individuals need to express themselves by giving full rein to their personalities, and it seems to me we should turn that to good account. And to do so, naturally, we should be able to split up the orchestra . . . and reconstitute it at will. . . . You can't divide up the orchestral body without some problems. It's been tried several times. I did so at the BBC and I know it's been tried at Radio France's New Philharmonic Orchestra, but at the cost of huge difficulties—stupid problems of seating, marriages, education! (Boulez, Conference on the Future of Radio Sym-

phony Orchestras, European Broadcasting Union, Frankfurt, 2–4 April 1984.)

5. On this special tuning:

> The second movement of the Fourth Symphony takes the place of a scherzo and bears the epigraph "Freund Hein spielt auf," which has been cut from the score. It is hard to ignore this, for the strangeness of the piece demands some explanation. It was conceived to some extent in terms of its unusual instrumentation. First, there's the solo violin playing without a mute and tuned a full tone higher. The legendary character is an image of death in the form of a fiddler, scraping away to invite the others to join in the dance. (Jean Matter, *Connaissance de Mahler*, Lausanne 1974.)

6. Provisions for decentralized activity were included in the statutes of eight regional French orchestras when they were founded (1969–79), at the instigation of Marcel Landowski.

TWELVE **Education of Conductors and the Changing of the Guard** (pages 128–130)

1. In Basel during July 1965 and June/July 1969; at the Charterhouse of Villeneuve-lès-Avignon, July 1988; and at the Juilliard School of Music and the Conservatoire National Supérieur de Musique in Paris.
Courses at the Conservatoire National Supérieur de Musique:
• Festival of the Grange de Meslay, 1985, with musicians from the two national conservatories of Paris and Lyons, at the University of Tours (general rehearsals conducted by Boulez, rehearsals for individual sections conducted by the principal players of the EIC). Program: Schoenberg, Second Chamber Symphony, Op. 38 (fifty-six instrumentalists, four instructors); York Hoeller, *Resonances* (twenty-seven instrumentalists, seven instructors).
• December 1986, with a concert on 14 December 1986 at the Salle Pleyel in Paris, in the context of the Autumn Festival. Two orchestras of students from the conservatory worked intensively with Boulez from the beginning of December. Program: Boulez, *Rituel*; Varèse, *Octandre* and *Intégrales*; Messiaen, *Les couleurs de la cité céleste*; Debussy, *Nocturnes*.
• December 1987, master classes in musical analysis and conducting. For two days, Boulez taught analysis to young composers and conducting to young conductors from the conservatory, accompanied by Orchestra C. Program: Webern, Variations for Orchestra, Op. 30; Six Pieces, Op. 6, nos. 1, 2, 3, and 4.
• March 1989, concert in the studio of Radio France during the conservatory's Hommage to Messiaen. Boulez conducted one of two student orchestras at the conservatory following several rehearsals. (Olivier Messiaen attended this concert. Program: Stravinsky, *The Song of the Nightingale*; Grisey, *Modulation*; Webern, Five Movements for String Quartet, Op. 5; Messiaen, *Chronochromie*.
See also: Paul Griffiths, "Body Language."

2. Claudio Abbado (b. 1933) studied conducting at the Giuseppe Verdi Conservatory in Milan until 1955. He worked with Hans Swarowsky in Vienna in 1957. Giuseppe Sinopoli (b. 1947) studied at the Venice Conservatory. He, too, worked with Hans Swarowsky in Vienna between 1971 and 1975. Riccardo Chailly (b. 1953) studied at the Giuseppe Verdi Conservatory in Milan; Riccardo Muti (b. 1941) studied at the Naples Conservatory and at the Giuseppe Verdi Conservatory in Milan. Chailly and Muti did not become expatriates.

3. Boulez uses the German word *Spritze*, "injection" or "squirt." On the related topic of composition:

> I think that continuing education, especially in conservatories, should be entrusted to young people aged thirty to thirty-five. In composition, for example, that's really the age when one is able to step outside oneself and stir up a class, instead of turning it into a basin of warm water as is usually the case. It's absurd to wait until composers have been crowned with laurels before appointing them professors—posts they occupy until retirement age. In my view, education doesn't mean conservation; it means waking people up. And how do you expect a man of sixty to awaken anyone at all, when he can't even wake himself? (Interview with Louis Dandrel, *Le Monde*, 12 September 1970.)

4. Boulez's first assistant was chosen from the students in the course he taught at Villeneuve-lès-Avignon in July 1988. A competition was arranged for fall 1989.

THIRTEEN **Colleagues** (pages 131–135)

1. Barenboim wrote:

> My dear Pierre,
>   We have been making music together for twenty-two years, ever since our first concert together with the Berlin Philharmonic Orchestra in 1963. During these years you have opened my eyes and ears to music I was not always familiar with. I have always tried to play and conduct the great works of the standard repertoire, not as museum pieces, but by reinvesting them with the shock one feels on hearing a contemporary work. Conversely, you have shown me that the music of our time can and should be approached with the same clarity, precision, and freedom as the traditional repertoire. Inspired and influenced by you, I had the privilege of conducting the first performance of *Notations*, which you are going to conduct this evening, and which we commissioned from you some years ago. Neither the Orchestre (de Paris) nor I played them with any feeling of obligation toward a contemporary French composer; on the contrary, we played them with all the goodwill, enthusiasm, and, I trust, learning that any true symphonic creation is entitled to. (Daniel Barenboim, program dedication for the concert given on the occasion of Boulez's sixtieth birthday, 3 October 1985.)

2. Herbert von Karajan died on 16 July 1989.

3. Boulez conducted them in the first performance of *Soleil des eaux* (fourth version), October 1965, with soprano Catherine Gayer.

4. "When a recording's finished, Boulez forgets it like a telephone number one no longer needs," says Georges Kadar. In 1988, however, Boulez expressed the intention to install a studio full of listening equipment in the basement of his villa in Baden-Baden.

5. On 14 November 1958, a performance of Stravinsky's *Threni*, conducted by the composer himself, turned out calamitously. Although they had been rehearsed by Robert Craft, the singers had been badly chosen and proved unsatisfactory. Boulez was present at a piano rehearsal: "I told Stravinsky that he should be stronger with them. But Stravinsky was fatherly and supported them. He refused to be strong. He was not a good conductor; he was a terribly lousy conductor." (Quoted in Peyser, *Boulez*, p. 172.)

Boulez had turned to Stravinsky the preceding year to lead the Southwest German Radio Orchestra in the European premiere of *Agon* on 11 October 1957. The program declared: "Through our indelible feelings of solidarity, we address our warmest wishes to Igor Stravinsky on the occasion of his seventy-fifth birthday. May he know how deeply touched we are that he has come to celebrate it with us."

In 1958, the program notes for *Threni id est Lamentationes Jeremiae Prophetae* are in the same vein: "Once again Igor Stravinsky manifests his solidarity with our endeavors by coming to conduct the Paris premiere of his new work, *Threni*."

Selection of Programs Conducted by Boulez

Compiled by Paul Griffiths

What follows is a fairly comprehensive record of Boulez's work as a conductor, except that, of the productions he conducted for the Renaud-Barrault company, only two, with scores of his own, are listed. Pieces not conducted by Boulez are shown in square brackets; an asterisk indicates a world premiere; a question mark in square brackets draws attention to a lacuna in the information; Roman numerals are used in place of dates to distinguish programs given several times.

6 January 1955   Paris (Marigny: Compagnie Renaud-Barrault)
    Tchaikovsky/Boulez: Music for Chekhov: *The Cherry Orchard*

[?] 1955   Bordeaux (Compagnie Renaud-Barrault)
    Boulez: Music for Aeschylus/Obey: *Orestie*

21–22 March 1956   Paris (Petit-Marigny)
(concert-conducting debut, in the series called "Domaine Musical" from the next season)
    Webern: Symphony
    Nono: *Incontri*
    Stockhausen: *Kontra-Punkte*
    Webern: Two Songs op. 8, Four Songs op. 13 (Jeanne Héricard)
    Boulez: *Le marteau sans maître* (Marie-Thérèse Cahn)

16 June 1956   Caracas (Orquestra Sinfonica Venezuela)
(debut with a symphony orchestra)
    Debussy: *Jeux*
    Prokofiev: Symphony no. 1 "Classical"

Stravinsky: Symphonies of Wind Instruments
Debussy: *Ibéria*

15 December 1956   Paris (Domaine Musical)
Stockhausen: *Zeitmasze**

11 March 1957   Los Angeles (Monday Evening Concerts)
Boulez: *Le marteau sans maître*

30 March 1957   Paris (Salle Gaveau: Domaine Musical)
Philippot: *Variations* for ten instruments*
Berio: *Serenata I** (Severino Gazzelloni)
Nilsson: *Frekvenser**
[Boulez: Sonatina (Gazzelloni, Boulez)]
[Messiaen: Seven pieces* (? from *Catalogue d'oiseaux*, Loriod)]

6 May 1957   London (BBC: Domaine Musical)
Nono: *Canti per tredici*
Webern: Concerto
Stockhausen: *Zeitmasze*
Boulez: *Le marteau sans maître*

28 September 1957   Berlin
[Boulez: Piano Sonata no. 3 (Boulez)]
Debussy: *Danse sacrée et danse profane*
Boulez: *Le marteau sans maître*

4 December 1957   Cologne (Westdeutscher Rundfunk SO)
(official debut with a symphony orchestra)
[Berg: Three Pieces from the *Lyric Suite* (Hermann Scherchen)]
[Hauer: *Wandlungen* (Scherchen)]
Boulez: *Le visage nuptial**

16 March 1958   Paris (Lamoureux)
Boulez: *Doubles**

24 March 1958   Cologne (Rheinsaal)
Stockhausen: *Gruppen** (with Stockhausen and Maderna)
[Boulez: Piano Sonata no. 3 (Boulez)]
Stockhausen: *Gruppen*

9 June 1958   Naples (Orchestra Scarlatti)
Dallapiccola: *Cinque canti* (Teodoro Rovetta)

23 July 1958   Aix-en-Provence (Südwestfunk SO)
Stravinsky: Symphonies of Wind Instruments
Stockhausen: *Kontra-Punkte*

Webern: Symphony
Wildberger: *Intensio-Centrum-Remissio**
Boulez: *Improvisations sur Mallarmé I–II*

11 September 1958   Darmstadt
    Matsudaira: *U-mai**

18–19 October 1958   Donaueschingen (Südwestfunk SO)
18: Stockhausen: *Gruppen* (with Hans Rosbaud and Stockhausen)
19: Boulez: *Poésie pour pouvoir** (with Rosbaud)

21 January 1959   Freiburg (Südwestfunk SO)
    Berg: *Der Wein* (Helga Pilarczyk)
    Webern: Five Movements op. 5
    Berg: *Altenberglieder* (Pilarczyk)
    [Boulez: Piano Sonata no. 3 (Boulez)]
    Debussy: *Ibéria*

30 January 1959   Cologne (Westdeutscher Rundfunk SO)
    Webern: Symphony, Two Songs op. 19, Four Songs op. 13 (Josephine
    Nendick), *Das Augenlicht*
    Schoenberg: *Incidental Music to a Motion Picture Scene* op. 34
    Boulez: *Le soleil des eaux*
    Stravinsky: *Renard*

6 March 1959   Munich (Herkulessaal: Bayrischer Rundfunk SO)
    Stravinsky: *Threni*
    Varèse: *Intégrales*
    Boulez: *Le soleil des eaux*
    Debussy: *Rondes de printemps*

14 March 1959   Paris (Salle Gaveau: Domaine Musical)
    Stockhausen: *Zeitmasze*
    Berio: *Différences**

21 March 1959   Milan (Incontri Musicali)
    Castiglioni: *Movimento continuato**

11 May 1959   Hamburg (Domaine Musical)
    Boulez: [Piano Sonata no. 3 (Boulez)], *Le marteau sans maître*

14 June 1959   Rome (Orchestra della RAI di Roma)
    Boulez: *Improvisations sur Mallarmé I–II* (Eva Maria Rogner)

15/17 June 1959   Vienna (Westdeutscher Rundfunk SO)
15: Boulez: *Le visage nuptial* (Steingruber, Cahn)
17: Stockhausen: *Gruppen* (with Maderna and Stockhausen)

25 July 1959   Aix-en-Provence (Südwestfunk SO)
    Webern: Six Pieces op. 6
    Berg: Three Fragments from *Wozzeck* (Pilarczyk)
    Pousseur: *Rimes pour différentes sources sonores*
    Hindemith: Concerto for Orchestra

17 October 1959   Donaueschingen (Domaine Musical)
    Boulez: *Tombeau**
    Kagel: String Sextet
    Amy: *Mouvements*
    Schoenberg: Suite op. 29
    Pousseur: *Rimes pour différentes sources sonores*
    Kotoński: Chamber Music for twenty-one instruments and percussion
    Varèse: *Intégrales*

18 October 1959   Donaueschingen (Südwestfunk SO)
    Fortner: *Parergon zur den Impromptus**
    Petrassi: *Invenzione concertata*
    Bäck: *A Game around a Game**
    Berio: *Allelujah II* (with Berio)
    Haubenstock-Ramati: *Petite musique de nuit**
    Bartók: Suite from *The Miraculous Mandarin*
*(repeated on 6 November in Paris with first three works replaced by
Stravinsky:* Chant du rossignol *and Schoenberg: Variations op. 31)*

18 January 1960   Freiburg (Südwestfunk SO)
    Górecki: Concerto for five instruments and string quartet
    Schoenberg: Variations op. 31

26 January 1960   Paris (Odéon: Domaine Musical)
    [Kagel: *Transición II* (Aloys Kontarsky, Christoph Caskel)]
    Barraqué: *. . . au delà du hasard**
    [Stockhausen: *Zyklus* (Caskel)]
    Varèse: *Hyperprism, Ionisation*

24–25 February 1960   Amsterdam (Concertgebouw)
    Haydn: Symphony no. 92
    Stravinsky: *Chant du rossignol*
    Debussy: *Danse sacrée et danse profane*
    Bartók: Suite from *The Miraculous Mandarin*
*(repeated on 27 February with Debussy replaced by the Ravel Piano
Concerto in G played by Monique Haas)*

13 June 1960   Cologne (Südwestfunk SO)
    Boulez: *Pli selon pli** (Rogner)

10 July 1960   Darmstadt (Stadthalle: Südwestfunk SO)
    Boulez: *Pli selon pli* (Rogner)

9 August 1960   Salzburg (Westdeutscher Rundfunk SO)
Stockhausen: *Kontra-Punkte*
Webern: Songs op. 15, 14, 17 (Rogner), Concerto
Boulez: *Improvisations sur Mallarmé I–II* (Rogner)

21 October 1960   Basle (Casino: Südwestfunk SO)
Berg: Three Pieces op. 6
Boulez: *Pli selon pli* (Rogner)

28 November 1960   Munich (Herkulessaal: Bayrischer Rundfunk SO)
anon.: *Mass of Tournai*
Boulez: *Pli selon pli* (Rogner)
Debussy: *Le martyre de Saint-Sébastien* (Barrault)

29 November 1960   Baden-Baden (Südwestfunk SO)
Debussy: *Gigues, Rondes de printemps*
Bach: Brandenburg Concerto no. 6
Stravinsky: *Petrushka*

14 January 1961   Berlin (Berlin Philharmonic)
Boulez: *Improvisations sur Mallarmé I–II, Tombeau* (Rogner)
Webern: Six Pieces op. 6
Debussy: *Ibéria*

24 January 1961   Hamburg (Norddeutscher Rundfunk SO)
Boulez: *Pli selon pli* (Rogner)

15 March 1961   Paris (Odéon: Südwestfunk SO)
Webern: Five Pieces op. 10, Six Songs op. 14 (Rogner)
Boulez: *Pli selon pli* (Rogner)

28 April 1961   Cologne (Westdeutscher Rundfunk SO)
Calonne: *Pages**
Berio: *Tempi concertati*
Webern: Five Pieces op. 10
Schoenberg: *Die glückliche Hand*

7 June 1961   Vienna (Südwestfunk SO)
Boulez: *Pli selon pli* (Rogner)

6 July 1961   Amsterdam (Concertgebouw)
Schoenberg: Chamber Symphony no. 1
Debussy: *Jeux*
Webern: Five Movements op. 5
Schubert: Symphony no. 6

17 January 1962   The Hague (Residentie Orkest)
Mozart: Symphony no. 29 K. 201

Schoenberg: Piano Concerto (Theo Bruins)
Petrassi: Flute Concerto (Koos Verheul)
Debussy: *Images*

2 March 1962   Baden-Baden (Südwestfunk SO)
Schoenberg: Chamber Symphony no. 1
Beethoven: Symphony no. 3

30 March 1962   Munich (Bayrischer Rundfunk SO)
anon.: *Mass of Barcelona*
Messiaen: *Chronochromie*
Berio: *Allelujah II* (with Francis Travis)
Stravinsky: *Renard*

4 April 1962   Paris (Odéon: Domaine Musical)
[Stockhausen: Piano Pieces I–IV; Berg: Four Pieces op. 5; Boulez: Piano
Sonata no. 1]
Varèse: *Octandre*
Webern: Concerto
[Webern: Piano Variations, Quartet op. 22]
Webern: Five Pieces op. 10

5–6 July 1962   Amsterdam/Scheveningen (Südwestfunk SO)
Boulez: *Pli selon pli* (Rogner)

15/19 July 1962   Darmstadt
15: Pousseur: *Madrigal III**; Maderna: Oboe Concerto no. 1* (Lothar
Faber); Schoenberg: *Pierrot lunaire* (Pilarczyk)
19: Castiglioni: *Consonante** (Gazzelloni); Webern: Symphony; Debussy:
Danse sacrée et danse profane; Boulez: *Le marteau sans maître* (Jeanne
Deroubaix)

20 October 1962   Donaueschingen (Südwestfunk SO)
Boulez: *Pli selon pli* (Rogner)

31 October 1962   Paris (Odéon: Domaine Musical)
Stockhausen: *Kontra-Punkte*
Berio: *Serenata I* (Gazzelloni)
Messiaen: *Oiseaux exotiques* (Loriod)
Boulez: *Le marteau sans maître* (Deroubaix)

8 January 1963   Baden-Baden (Südwestfunk SO)
Debussy: *Jeux, Première rapsodie*
Schubert: Symphony no. 6
Berlioz: Overture *Le carnaval romain*

17 January 1963   Baden-Baden (Südwestfunk SO)
(concert in memory of Rosbaud, whom Boulez replaced in ensuing Concertgebouw engagements)
    Mozart: Adagio and Fugue in C minor K. 546
    Haydn: Symphony no. 102
    Hartmann: Concerto for viola and piano with wind and percussion
    (Ulrich Koch, Maria Bergmann)
    Schoenberg: Variations op. 31

2–10 February 1963   Amsterdam (Concertgebouw)
(six concerts with the following repertory)
    Debussy: *Berceuse héroïque, Danse sacrée et danse profane, Jeux, Marche écossaise*; Mendelssohn: Overture, Nocturne, and Scherzo for *A Midsummer Night's Dream*; Mozart: Symphony no. 41 K. 551; Schat: *Entelechie no. 1*; Schoenberg: Piano Concerto (Bruins); Webern: Piece op. 6 no. 4 *(played in memory of Rosbaud)*

3 April 1963   Los Angeles (Monday Evening Concerts)
    [Debussy: *Trois poèmes de Mallarmé*]
    Ravel: *Trois poèmes de Mallarmé*
    Stravinsky: Three Japanese Lyrics
    Boulez: *Improvisations sur Mallarmé I–II*, [*Structures II* (Karl Kohn, Boulez)]
    Webern: Concerto

24 May 1963   New York
    Boulez: *Le marteau sans maître*

18 June 1963   Paris (Champs-Elysées: Orchestre National)
(to celebrate the fiftieth anniversary of The Rite of Spring*)*
    Stravinsky: Four Etudes, *Zvezdoliki*, Symphonies of Wind Instruments, *A Sermon, a Narrative, and a Prayer, The Rite of Spring*

20 July 1963   Darmstadt
    Eloy: *Equivalences**
    Boehmer: *Zeitläufe*
    Lehmann: *Quanti** (Gazzelloni)
    Schoenberg: Serenade (Heinz Rehfuss)

14 September 1963   Baden-Baden (Südwestfunk SO)
    Berg: Three Pieces from the *Lyric Suite*, Three Fragments from *Wozzeck* (Halina Lukomska)
    Webern: *Das Augenlicht*, Cantata no. 2, Cantata no. 1 (Lukomska, Barry McDaniel)

20 October 1963   Donaueschingen (Südwestfunk SO)
    Webern: Piece op. 6 no. 4 *(played in memory of Rosbaud)*

Wildberger: Oboe Concerto* (Holliger)
Eloy: *Equivalences*
Amy: *Diaphonies*
Stockhausen: *Punkte* (1962 version)*

30 October 1963   Paris (Odéon: Domaine Musical)
Messiaen: *Sept haïkaï** (Loriod)

9–16 November 1963   The Netherlands (Concertgebouw)
(six concerts with the following repertory)
Bach: Double Violin Concerto; Debussy: *Prélude à "L'après-midi d'un faune," Première rapsodie*; Haydn: Symphony no. 104; Schubert: Symphony no. 5; Stravinsky: *Chant du rossignol*; Van Vlijmen: *Gruppi*; Webern: Variations op. 30

27 November 1963   Paris (Opéra)
(opera debut; nine subsequent performances)
Berg: *Wozzeck* (Barrault production)

[?] 1964   Paris
Rameau: *Hippolyte et Aricie* (in concert)

9–10 January 1964   Basle/Strasbourg (Südwestfunk SO)
Berg: Three Pieces from the *Lyric Suite*
Messiaen: *Sept haïkaï* (Loriod)
Boulez: *Figures-Doubles-Prismes**
Debussy: *Jeux*
(Messiaen also recorded by Südwestfunk on 14 January)

23 February 1964   Worthing (BBC SO)
(debut with the orchestra)
Mozart: Overture to *Die Zauberflöte*
Chopin: Piano Concerto no. 2 (Ashkenazy)
Schubert: Symphony no. 5
Debussy: *La mer*

4 March 1964   London (BBC SO)
Webern: Six Pieces op. 6
Bach/Webern: Ricercare
Stravinsky: Symphonies of Wind Instruments
Boulez: *Le soleil des eaux* (Nendick)
Mozart: Adagio and Fugue in C minor K. 546
Debussy: *Images*

10 March 1964   Paris (Orchestre National)
Varèse: *Arcana*

13 April 1964   Munich (Herkulessaal: Südwestfunk SO)
Boulez: *Figures-Doubles-Prismes*
Berg: Three Pieces from the *Lyric Suite*
Debussy: *Images*

17 April 1964   Munich (Herkulessaal: Bayrischer Rundfunk SO)
anon.: Coronation music of the thirteenth and fourteenth centuries
Stravinsky: *The Flood*
Messiaen: *Oiseaux exotiques* (Loriod)
Bartók: *Cantata profana*

13 May 1964   Paris (Odéon: Percussions de Strasbourg, Domaine
                Musical)
Schat: *Signalement*
Amy: *Alpha-Beth I–II**
Shinohara: *Alternance**
Xenakis: *Eonta** (Yuji Takahashi)
Schoenberg: Three Pieces op. posth., Chamber Symphony no. 1

27 May 1964   Frankfurt (Hessischer Rundfunk SO)
Debussy: *Jeux*
Stravinsky: *Zvezdoliki*
Webern: Cantata no. 2, Cantata no. 1 (Lukomska, McDaniel)
Boulez: *Don*

9 June 1964   Hamburg (Norddeutscher Rundfunk SO)
Eloy: *Etude III*
Webern: Six Pieces op. 6
Boulez: *Don* (Rogner)
Messiaen: *Sept haïkaï* (Loriod)

20 June 1964   Berlin (Berlin Philharmonic)
Schoenberg: *Incidental Music to a Motion Picture Scene* op. 34
Stravinsky: Four Etudes
Bartók: Piano Concerto no. 1 (Barenboim)
Boulez: *Doubles*

18–20 September 1964   Ulm (Ulm Festival musicians)
18: Bach/Webern: Ricercare; Stravinsky: Concertino; Webern: Concerto;
Stravinsky: Two Balmont Poems, Three Japanese Lyrics; [Boulez:
Structures]
20: Vivaldi: *The Four Seasons*; Albinoni: Oboe Concerto in C; Bach: Suite
no. 2 Bach: Cantata no. 207a "Auf, schmetternde Töne der munteren
Trompeten"

17 October 1964   Donaueschingen (Domaine Musical)
Messiaen: *Couleurs de la Cité Céleste** (Loriod)
Holliger: *Glühende Rätsel** (Deroubaix)

13 December 1964   Brussels (Radio Belge SO)
Boulez: *Figures-Doubles-Prismes*

16 December 1964   Paris (Odéon: Percussions de Strasbourg, Domaine Musical)
Eloy: *Polychronies I–II*
Xenakis: *Eonta* (Takahashi)
Holliger: *Glühende Rätsel* (Deroubaix)
Messiaen: *Couleurs de la Cité Céleste* (Loriod)

8–30 January 1965   The Netherlands (Concertgebouw)
(fourteen concerts with the following repertory)
Bartók: Piano Concerto no. 2 (Theo Bruins); Debussy: *Images, Trois nocturnes*; Mendelssohn: Violin Concerto (Hermann Krebbers); Mozart: Bassoon Concerto K. 191 (Thom de Klerk), Concerto for Flute and Harp K. 299 (Jan Visser, Vera Badings), Symphony no. 38 K. 504; Nono: *Il canto sospeso*; Purcell: Four Fantasias; Ravel: *Rapsodie espagnole*; Saint-Saëns: Cello Concerto no. 1 (Tibor de Maenula); Schat: Dances from *Labyrinth*; Schubert: Symphony no. 7; Schumann: Overture to *Manfred*; Van Vlijmen: *Gruppi*; Webern: Symphony

20 February 1965   Baden-Baden (Südwestfunk SO)
Schoenberg: Chamber Symphony no. 2
Stravinsky: Two Balmont Poems, Three Japanese Lyrics (Dorothy Dorow), Four Etudes
Berg: Suite from *Lulu* (Dorow)

4 March 1965   Rome (Orchestra Filarmonica Romana)
Stravinsky: *Elegy for J. F. K., Abraham and Isaac*

11/13 March 1965   Cleveland (Cleveland Orchestra)
(American orchestral debut)
Rameau: *Concerts en sextuor* nos. 3 and 6
Boulez: *Figures-Doubles-Prismes*
Debussy: *Gigues, Rondes de printemps, Jeux*
Stravinsky: *Chant du rossignol*

26 March 1965   Los Angeles (Bing Center)
Machaut: *Messe de Nostre Dame*
Eloy: *Equivalences*
Boulez: *Eclat*,* [*Structures I–II*]

April 1965   Paris (Opéra)
Stravinsky: *Les noces, Renard, The Rite of Spring* (all Béjart productions)

28 April 1965   Stanford (Palmer Auditorium: BBC SO)
Stravinsky: Symphonies of Wind Instruments
Beethoven: Piano Concerto no. 5
Webern: Six Pieces op. 6
Debussy: *Images*

2 May 1965   New York (BBC SO)
Boulez: *Doubles*
Webern: Six Pieces op. 6
Berg: [?]
Debussy: *Images*

15 July 1965   Holland Festival (Residentie Orkest)
Ives: *Three Places in New England*
Schat: Dances from *Labyrinth*
Obrecht: *Missa Maria Zart*
(repeated on the 18th in Darmstadt with Webern: op. 10 and Boulez: Figures-
Doubles-Prismes *in place of the Obrecht)*

31 July 1965   Darmstadt
Calonne: *Métalepses**
Miroglio: *Réseaux** (Francis Pierre)
De Pablo: *Modulos I*
Wyttenbach: *Divisions*

[?] 1965   Edinburgh (BBC SO)
Boulez: *Pli selon pli* (Lukomska)

7 September 1965   London (Albert Hall: BBC SO)
(Promenade Concert debut)
Stravinsky: Symphonies of Wind Instruments
Berg: Three Fragments from *Wozzeck* (Heather Harper)
Webern: Six Pieces op. 6
Stravinsky: Four Etudes
Boulez: *Le soleil des eaux* (Nendick)
Debussy: *Images*

12 January 1966   Paris (Odéon: Percussions de Strasbourg, Domaine
                       Musical)
Silvestrov: *Mystère* for alto flute and six percussionists* (Gazzelloni)
Messiaen: *Et exspecto resurrectionem mortuorum*
[Brown: *From here* (conducted by Brown)]
Porena: *Cadenze* for alto flute and ensemble (Gazzelloni)*
Fukushima: *Kada 4**
De Pablo: *Modulos I*

30 January 1966   Paris (Champs-Elysées: Conservatoire)
  Debussy: *Jeux*
  Bartók: Piano Concerto no. 2 (Pommier)
  Berg: Three Pieces op. 6

2 February 1966   Paris (Odéon: Domaine Musical)
  [Haubenstock-Ramati: *Séquences* for violin and orchestra (Wanda
  Wilkomirska/Amy)]
  [Schoenberg: Piano Pieces op. 19 and 11 (Barenboim)]
  Berg: Chamber Concerto (Barenboim, Wilkomirska)

8 February 1966   Paris (Champs-Elysées: Orchestre National)
  Berg: Suite from *Lulu* (Halina Lukomska)
  Boulez: *Le soleil des eaux* (Lukomska)
  Webern: Variations op. 30, *Das Augenlicht*, Cantata no. 2, Cantata no. 1
  (Lukomska, Barry McDaniel)

16 March 1966   London (Festival Hall: BBC SO)
  Stravinsky: *Chant du rossignol*
  Webern: Five Pieces op. 10, Symphony
  [Debussy: *Trois poèmes de Mallarmé* (Dorow, Boulez)]
  Ravel: *Trois poèmes de Mallarmé*
  Boulez: *Don, Improvisations sur Mallarmé I–II* (Lukomska)

April 1966   Frankfurt
  Berg: *Wozzeck* (Wieland Wagner production)

[?] 1966   Paris (Opéra)
  Berg: *Wozzeck* (Barrault production)

9 May 1966   London (BBC: BBC SO)
  Boulez: *Eclat*
  Berg: Three Pieces op. 6
(also BBC recording on 13 May of Debussy with the New Philharmonia)

August 1966   Bayreuth
  Wagner: *Parsifal* (Wieland Wagner production)

30 August–2 September 1966   London (Albert Hall: BBC SO)
30: Haydn: Symphony no. 104; Webern: Cantata no. 2, Variations op. 30,
    Cantata no. 1 (Lukomska, McDaniel); Schoenberg: Four Songs op. 22
    (Yvonne Minton); Debussy: *La mer*
31: Debussy: *Trois nocturnes*; Beethoven: Piano Concerto no. 4
    (Barenboim); Webern: Six Pieces op. 6; Stravinsky: *The Rite of Spring*
2: Bach: Brandenburg Concerto no. 6; Berg: Suite from *Lulu* (Lukomska);
    Boulez: *Eclat*; Debussy: *Images*

24 September 1966   Baden-Baden (Südwestfunk SO)
Debussy: *Prélude à "L'après-midi d'un faune"*
Berg: Violin Concerto (Saschko Gawriloff)
Schoenberg: *Pierrot lunaire* (Marie-Thérèse Escribano)

27 September 1966   London (Festival Hall: New Philharmonia)
Beethoven: Symphony no. 2, Piano Concerto no. 3 (Firkusny),
Symphony no. 5

15 October 1966   Hamburg (Norddeutscher Rundfunk SO)
Kayn: *Signals**

30 October/1 November 1966   London (Festival Hall: New
                                                Philharmonia)
Beethoven: Symphony no. 1, Symphony no. 9

2 December 1966   Baden-Baden (Südwestfunk SO)
Berio: *Allelujah II*
Messiaen: *Oiseaux exotiques* (Loriod)
Schubert/Webern: *Deutsche Tänze*
Schoenberg: Variations op. 31
(repeated the next day in Karlsruhe with Debussy: La mer *in place of the
Berio and a changed order)*

11–18 December 1966   Brussels (Reconnaissances des Musiques
                                                Modernes)
11: Messiaen: *Chronochromie*; Webern: Symphony; Schoenberg: *Die
        glückliche Hand*; Varèse: *Arcana*
15: Denisov: *Le soleil des Incas* (Berthe Kal); Berg: Chamber Concerto
        (Diane Andersen, André Gertler)
18: Boulez: *Figures-Doubles-Prismes*; Amy: *Strophes** (Liliane Poli); Berio:
        Chemins I (Pierre); Berg: Three Pieces op. 6

January 1967   Prague/Berlin/Russia (BBC SO)
(tour with the following repertory)
        Bartók: Piano Concerto no. 2 (John Ogdon); Debussy: *Jeux*; Stravinsky:
        Chant du rossignol; Volkonsky: *The Lament of Shchazï* (Catherine
        Gayer); Webern: Six Pieces op. 6, Variations op. 30

21 January–13 February 1967   The Netherlands (Concertgebouw)
(fourteen concerts with the following repertory)
        Bartók: Piano Concerto no. 2 (Bruins); Berg: Violin Concerto
        (Grumiaux); Boulez: *Doubles, Eclat*; Debussy: *Jeux, Prélude à
        "L'après-midi d'un faune," Le martyre de Saint-Sébastien*; Haydn:
        Symphony no. 13; Mozart: Violin Concerto in A K. 219 (Jo Juda); Schat:
        Signalement; Schoenberg: Variations op. 31; Schumann: Symphony no.
        2; Stockhausen: *Kontra-Punkte*

15/20/29 March 1967   London (Festival Hall: BBC SO)
15: Stravinsky: *Zvezdoliki, Les noces, The Rite of Spring*
20: Berg: *Altenberglieder*, Three Fragments from *Wozzeck*, Chamber
    Concerto, Three Pieces op. 6
29: Debussy: *Prélude à "L'après-midi d'un faune," Nocturnes, Le martyre
    de Saint-Sébastien*

10 April 1967   Osaka
Wagner: *Tristan und Isolde* (in concert)

3 May 1967   Frankfurt (Hessischer Rundfunk SO)
Boulez: *Eclat, Figures-Doubles-Prismes*

19–21 May 1967   Ojai (Ojai Festival Orchestra)
19: Schoenberg: String Quartet no. 2 (orchestral version); Debussy: *Danse
    sacrée et danse profane*; Bartók: Music for Strings, Percussion, and
    Celesta
20: Varèse: *Ecuatorial, Octandre, Offrandes, Intégrales*; Webern: Concerto;
    Stravinsky: *Les noces*
21: Stockhausen: *Zeitmasze*; Haydn: Sinfonia Concertante in B-flat; Ives:
    Three Places in New England; Boulez: *Eclat*; Schubert: Symphony no. 6

11 June 1967   London (Festival Hall: London SO)
Webern: Passacaglia, Six Pieces op. 6, Five Pieces op. 10
Debussy: *La mer*
Schoenberg: *Erwartung* (Annamaria Bessel)

August 1967   Bayreuth
Wagner: *Parsifal* (Wieland Wagner production)

28 August/5 September 1967   London (Albert Hall: BBC SO)
28: Debussy: *Jeux*; Mozart: Piano Concerto in B-flat K. 595 (Curzon);
    Volkonsky: *The Lament of Shchazï* (Lukomska); Stravinsky: *Les noces*
5: Berg: Three Fragments from *Wozzeck, Altenberglieder* (Harper);
    Stockhausen: *Gruppen* (with Michael Tabachnik and Edward Downes);
    Stravinsky: *The Rite of Spring*

2 September 1967   Edinburgh (Usher Hall: BBC SO)
Stravinsky: *Chant du rossignol*, Requiem Canticles (Minton, Günther
Reich), Symphonies of Wind Instruments

26/31 October 1967   London (Festival Hall: London SO)
26: Berlioz: *Symphonie fantastique, Lélio*
31: Berg: Three Pieces from the *Lyric Suite*; Webern: Five Movements op. 5;
    Berg: Seven Early Songs (Evelyn Lear); Webern: Symphony; Berg:
    Suite from *Lulu* (Lear)

9–25 November 1967   Cleveland (Cleveland Orchestra)
I: Schubert: Symphony no. 6; Debussy: *Danse sacrée et danse profane*;
      Stravinsky: *The Rite of Spring*
II: Haydn: Sinfonia Concertante in B-flat; Berlioz: *Nuits d'été* (Judith
      Raskin); Debussy: *Images*
III: Handel: Suite no. 1 from the *Water Music*; Berg: Three Pieces op. 6;
      Beethoven: Symphony no. 2

16 December 1967   Baden-Baden (Südwestfunk SO)
      Wagner: Prelude to *Parsifal*
      Debussy: *Nocturnes*
      Schoenberg: Chamber Symphony no. 1
      Bartók: Music for Strings, Percussion, and Celesta

7 February 1968   London (BBC: BBC SO)
      Wagner: *Wesendoncklieder*
      Varèse: *Intégrales*

14/21 February 1968   London (Festival Hall: BBC SO)
14:   Messiaen: *Chronochromie*; Varèse: *Arcana*; Boulez: *Le marteau sans
      maître* (Minton)
21:   Schoenberg: Four Songs op. 22 (Minton); Stravinsky: *Pulcinella*;
      Stockhausen: *Gruppen* (with Tabachnik and Downes)

[?] 1968   London (BBC: BBC SO)
      Schoenberg: *Incidental Music to a Motion Picture Scene* op. 34
      Pieces op. 16, Piano Concerto (Ogdon), Variations op. 31

27–28 February 1968   Leyden/The Hague (Residentie Orkest)
      Perotin: *Sederunt principes*
      Webern: Symphony
      Boulez: *Eclat*
      Bartók: Music for Strings, Percussion, and Celesta

8 March 1968   Amsterdam (Concertgebouw)
      Purcell: Four Fantasias
      Webern: Symphony
      Shinohara: *Alternance*
      Klaus Huber: *Alveare vernat* (Paul Verhey)

7 June 1968   Basle (Casino)
      Stravinsky: *Agon*, Capriccio, *The Rite of Spring*

June 1968   Holland Festival
      Schoenberg-Berg-Webern cycle

1 August–5 September 1968   London (Albert Hall: BBC SO)
1: Varèse: *Arcana, Ionisation*; Stravinsky: *Zvezdoliki, Requiem Canticles* (Minton, Reich), *The Rite of Spring*
28: Mozart: Piano Concerto in D K. 537 (Curzon); Mahler: Symphony no. 5
3: Messiaen: *Chronochromie*; Boulez: *Le marteau sans maître* (Deroubaix); [Stockhausen: Piano Piece X (Kontarsky)]; Berg: Three Pieces op. 6
5: Bartók: Music for Strings, Percussion, and Celesta; Boulez: *Pli selon pli* (Lukomska)

August 1968   Bayreuth
Wagner: *Parsifal* (Wieland Wagner production)

August 1968   Bayreuth (International Youth Meeting)
Schoenberg: Five Pieces op. 16
Berg: *Altenberglieder*
Bartók: Music for Strings, Percussion, and Celesta
Stravinsky: Symphonies of Wind Instruments

26 November–8 December 1968   London/Croydon/Brighton (New Philharmonia)
(four concerts with the following repertory)
Beethoven: Symphony no. 5, Overture *Leonora* no. 3, Piano Concerto no. 5 (Misha Dichter); Boulez: *Livre pour cordes I**; Debussy: *Prélude à "L'après-midi d'un faune," Jeux*; Mozart: Serenade in C minor K. 388; Schumann: Cello Concerto (Fournier); Stravinsky: *The Rite of Spring*

13/20 December 1968   Brussels (Reconnaissances des Musiques Modernes)
13: Stravinsky: Symphonies of Wind Instruments; Berg: *Altenberglieder* (Harper); Webern: Six Pieces op. 6; Schoenberg: Five Pieces op. 16; Bartók: Music for Strings, Percussion, and Celesta
20: De Pablo: *Imaginario II*; Pousseur: *Couleurs croisées**; Boulez: *Domaines** (Walter Boeykens), *Livre pour cordes I*

30 December 1968   Baden-Baden (Südwestfunk SO)
Schumann: Symphony no. 2
Stravinsky: *Chant du rossignol*
Berlioz: Overture *Le carnaval romain*

7/8/11 February 1969   Boston (Boston Symphony)
Haydn: Sinfonia Concertante in B-flat
Debussy: *Jeux*
Stravinsky: Symphonies of Wind Instruments, Four Etudes
Berg: Three Pieces op. 6

20/21/22 February 1969   Chicago (Chicago Symphony)
Debussy: *Jeux*

Bartók: Piano Concerto no. 1 (Barenboim)
Webern: Passacaglia, Six Pieces op. 6
Messiaen: *Et exspecto resurrectionem mortuorum*

13 March–7 April 1969   New York (Philharmonic Hall: New York PO)
(debut with the orchestra)
I: Debussy:*Jeux*; Berg: Violin Concerto (Leonid Kogan); Varèse:
     Intégrales; Debussy: *La mer*
II: Haydn: Symphony no. [?]; Bartók: Piano Concerto no. 1 (Malcolm
     Frager), Music for Strings, Percussion, and Celesta
III: Haydn: Symphony no. 91; Ravel: *Shéhérazade* (Raskin); Schoenberg:
     Five Pieces op. 16; Ives: *Three Places in New England*
IV: Purcell: Fantasias; Stravinsky: Symphonies of Wind Instruments;
     Webern: Six Pieces op. 6; Stravinsky: *The Rite of Spring*

10/12 April 1969   Cleveland (Cleveland Orchestra)
     Mozart: Adagio and Fugue in C minor K. 546
     Berg: Violin Concerto (Rafael Druian)
     Debussy: *Première rapsodie*
     Webern: Six Pieces op. 6
     Ravel: *Rapsodie espagnole*

7 May 1969   London (Festival Hall: BBC SO)
     Varèse: *Intégrales*, *Offrandes* (Lukomska)
     Boulez: *Pli selon pli* (Lukomska)
(repeated in Paris)

15 May–1 June 1969   London (South Bank: London SO)
(Second Viennese School cycle in five programs)
15: Berg: Three Fragments from *Wozzeck* (Lukomska); Webern: *Das
    Augenlicht*, Cantata no. 2, Cantata no. 1 (Lukomska, McDaniel);
    Schoenberg: Four Songs op. 22 (Minton); Berg: Three Pieces op. 6
22: Schoenberg: *Incidental Music to a Motion Picture Scene* op. 34; Five
    Pieces op. 16; Webern: Symphony, Three Pieces op. posth., Variations
    op. 30; Berg: Violin Concerto (Stern)
25: Webern: Concerto, *Entflieht auf leichten Kähnen*, Two Songs op. 19;
    Schoenberg: Three Pieces op. posth.; Berg: Chamber Concerto (Kitchin,
    Gawriloff)
29: Mahler: Adagio from Symphony no. 10, *Lieder eines fahrenden Gesellen*
    (Lear), *Das klagende Lied*
1: Webern: Five Movements op. 5; Berg: Seven Early Songs (Lear);
    Webern: Six Pieces op. 6; Schoenberg: *Erwartung* (Lear)
(partially repeated in two concerts on 12 and 13 June in Vienna)

17 July–3 August 1969   Blossom Music Center (Cleveland Orchestra)
17: Berlioz: Overture *Le carnaval romain*, *Nuits d'été* (Raskin); Ravel:
    Shéhérazade (Raskin), *Alborada del gracioso*, *Rapsodie espagnole*

19: Schubert: Symphony no. 5; Beethoven: Piano Concerto no. 3 (Grant Johannesen); Debussy: *La mer*
[?]: Boulez: *Pli selon pli* (Carole Farley)
26: Mozart: Serenade in D K. 320; Schumann: Cello Concerto (Leonard Rose); Stravinsky: *The Rite of Spring*
31: Beethoven: Overture to *Prometheus*, Violin Concerto (Perlman); Bartók: Concerto for Orchestra
3: Beethoven: Symphony no. 5; Mozart: Piano Concerto in A K. 488 (De Larrocha); Stravinsky: Suite from *The Firebird* (1911 version)

2 August 1969   Tanglewood (Boston Symphony)
    Haydn: Sinfonia Concertante in B-flat
    Debussy: *Jeux*
    Bartók: Two Rhapsodies
    Debussy: *La mer*

5 September 1969   London (Albert Hall: BBC SO)
    Bartók: Music for Strings, Percussion, and Celesta
    Boulez: *Pli selon pli* (Lukomska)

18 October 1969   Donaueschingen (Südwestfunk SO)
    Boulez: *Domaines* (Boeykens)

2 November 1969   London (Festival Hall: New Philharmonia)
    Handel: Concerto Grosso no. 7 in C
    Schoenberg: Violin Concerto (Wolfgang Marschner)
    Schumann: Symphony no. 2

1 December 1969   London (Covent Garden)
(seven subsequent performances)
    Debussy: *Pelléas et Mélisande* (Václav Kašlík production)

18 December 1969   London (Festival Hall: New Philharmonia)
    Boulez: *Livre pour cordes I*
    Bartók: Piano Concerto no. 2 (Vladimir Krainov), *The Miraculous Mandarin*

3 January 1970   Croydon (National Youth Orchestra)
    Debussy: *La mer, Première rapsodie*
    Stravinsky: *The Rite of Spring*

8 February 1970   Ipswich (Gaumont: BBC SO)
    anon.: "God Save the Queen"
    Schubert: Symphony no. 5
    Bartók: Piano Concerto no. 1 (Peter Frankl)
    Stravinsky: Symphonies of Wind Instruments
    Debussy: *La mer*

18 February 1970   London (Festival Hall: BBC SO)
Bartók: Music for Strings, Percussion, and Celesta
Mahler: Seven Songs from *Des Knaben Wunderhorn* (John Shirley-Quirk)
Stravinsky: *The Rite of Spring*

5 March–4 April 1970   Cleveland (Cleveland Orchestra)
I: Bartók: Piano Concerto no. 1 (Barenboim); Mahler: Symphony no. 5
II: Schubert: Symphony no. 5;Berg: Three Fragments from *Wozzeck*
      (Lukomska); Ives: *Three Places in New England*; Stravinsky: Suite from
      The Firebird (1911)
III: Wagner: Prelude to *Parsifal*; Bartók: Violin Concerto no. 2 (Daniel
      Majeske); Debussy: *Images*
IV: Haydn: Mass in D minor "Nelson"; Ravel: *Daphnis et Chloé*

15 April 1970   London (Festival Hall: BBC SO)
Stravinsky: Suite from *The Firebird* (1911)
Messiaen: *Oiseaux exotiques* (Michel Béroff)
Ravel: *Daphnis et Chloé*

21 April 1970   London (Festival Hall: London SO)
Mahler: *Waldmärchen*
Webern: Passacaglia
Berg: *Altenberglieder* (Söderström), Three Pieces op. 6

April–May 1970   Bratislava/Vienna/Budapest/Perugia/Florence (BBC
                   SO)
(tour with the following repertory)
Bartók: Music for Strings, Percussion, and Celesta; Beethoven: Piano
Concerto no. 4 (Curzon), Piano Concerto no. 1 (Charles Rosen); Berg:
Three Fragments from *Wozzeck* (Harper); Debussy: *Jeux*; Mahler:
Symphony no. 5; Messiaen: *Et exspecto resurrectionem mortuorum*;
Stockhausen: *Punkte*; Stravinsky: *The Rite of Spring*

31 May 1970   Los Angeles (Royce Hall: Los Angeles PO)
Schoenberg: Chamber Symphony no. 1
Webern: Five Movements op. 5, Variations op. 30
Stravinsky: Symphonies of Wind Instruments, Suite from *The Firebird*
(1911)

5–7 June 1970   Ojai (Los Angeles PO)
5:    Stravinsky: Concertino, *Pribaoutki* (Jayne Proppe); Stockhausen:
      Kontra-Punkte; Boulez: *Domaines* (Mitchell Lurie); Stravinsky: *Renard*
6:    Berg: Chamber Concerto; Schoenberg: *Verklärte Nacht*; Webern: Five
      Movements op. 5; Boulez: *Livre pour cordes I*; Bartók: Divertimento
7:    Schoenberg: Chamber Symphony no. 1; Mahler: *Lieder eines fahrenden
      Gesellen*; Webern: Variations op. 30, Six Pieces op. 6; Stravinsky: Suite
      from *The Firebird* (1919)

June 1970   London (BBC: BBC SO)
Schumann: Overture to *Manfred*
Ravel: *Shéhérazade* (Margaret Price)
Bartók: *The Miraculous Mandarin*

18–30 July 1970   Blossom Music Center (Cleveland Orchestra)
18: Mozart: Overture to *Die Zauberflöte*; Beethoven: Piano Concerto no. 5 in
E-flat (John Browning); Stravinsky: *Petrushka*
19: Wagner: Prelude to *Parsifal*; Berg: Violin Concerto (Edith Peinemann);
Berlioz: *Symphonie fantastique*
23: Gabrieli: *Sacrae symphoniae*; Debussy: *Nocturnes*; Mozart: Piano
Concerto in D K. 537 (Christoph Eschenbach); Prokofiev: *Scythian Suite*
25: Debussy: *Printemps*; Bartók: Piano Concerto no. 1 (Nelson Freire);
Ravel: *Daphnis et Chloé*
30: Handel: Concerto Grosso; Brahms: Piano Concerto no. 1 (Dichter);
Bartók: *Cantata profana*

4 August–4 September 1970   London (Albert Hall: BBC SO)
4: Schoenberg: *Pierrot lunaire* (Escribano); Mahler: Symphony no. 5
10: Stravinsky: Suite from *The Firebird* (1911); Bartók: Piano Concerto no.
2 (Geza Anda); Ravel: *Daphnis et Chloé*
4: Debussy: *Nocturnes*; Messiaen: *Et exspecto resurrectionem mortuorum*;
Stravinsky: *The Rite of Spring*

August 1970   Bayreuth
Wagner: *Parsifal* (Wieland Wagner production)

August 1970   Bayreuth (International Youth Meeting)
Debussy: *Jeux*
Varèse: *Intégrales*
Messiaen: *Oiseaux exotiques* (Istvan Lantos)
Boulez: *Eclat*
Stravinsky: *Les noces*

18–20 September 1970   Ulm (Ulm Festival musicians)
18: Andrea Gabrieli: *Canzon da sonar no. XII*; Schütz: *Die sieben Worte
unseres lieben Erlösers*; Giovanni Gabrieli: *Canzon no. 2 duodecimi
toni*; Bach: Magnificat
19: Schoenberg: Serenade; Boulez: *Cummings ist der Dichter**; Stravinsky:
Renard
20: Purcell: Ode for St. Cecilia's Day (? 1692); Handel: *Alexander's Feast*

25 September 1970   Stuttgart (Süddeutscher Rundfunk SO)
Boulez: *Domaines* (Hans Deinzer), *Cummings ist der Dichter*

21 October 1970   London (Festival Hall: BBC SO)
Stravinsky: Symphonies of Wind Instruments

Boulez: *Eclat/multiples**
Bartók: *Bluebeard's Castle* (Lear, Ward)

9–10 November 1970   Paris (Théâtre National Populaire)
9   (BBC SO):   Bartók: Music for Strings, Percussion, and Celesta; Boulez: *Eclat/multiples*; Berg: Three Pieces op. 6
10   (Musique Vivante):   Boulez: *Le marteau sans maître, Domaines* (Michel Portal)

19–28 November 1970   Cleveland (Cleveland Orchestra)
I: Stravinsky: *Chant du rossignol*; Ravel: Piano Concerto for the Left Hand (Philippe Entremont); Messiaen: *Oiseaux exotiques*; Bartók: *The Miraculous Mandarin*
II: Berlioz: *Roméo et Juliette* (Anna Reynolds, George Shirley, Thomas Paul)

5 December 1970   Cleveland (Cleveland Orchestra)
informal evening on Messiaen: *Oiseaux exotiques* (Paul Jacobs), *Et exspecto resurrectionem mortuorum*

10 December 1970   Brussels (Conservatoire Royal: Radio Belge CO)
Birtwistle: *Verses for Ensembles*
Boucourechliev: *Ombres**
Boulez: *Cummings ist der Dichter* (Schola Cantorum Stuttgart), *Domaines* (Boeykens)

30 December 1970   Baden-Baden (Südwestfunk SO)
Boulez/Gottwald: *Über das, über ein Verschwinden*
Mozart: Adagio and Fugue in C minor K. 546
Schumann: Cello Concerto (Fournier)
Boulez: *Eclat*
Berg: Three Pieces op. 6

7 January 1971   London (BBC: BBC SO)
Ravel: *Le tombeau de Couperin*
Schoenberg: Chamber Symphony no. 1
Bartók: *The Miraculous Mandarin*

14–23 January 1971   Cleveland (Cleveland Orchestra)
I: Bach: Brandenburg Concerto no. 1; Mozart: Piano Concerto in C K. 467 (Robert Casadesus); Berg: Three Pieces from the *Lyric Suite*; Liszt: *Mazeppa*
II: Handel: Overture to *Alcina*; Carter: Concerto for Orchestra; Beethoven: Piano Concerto no. 1 (Eschenbach); Prokofiev: *Scythian Suite*

8 February 1971   London (BBC: BBC SO)
Mahler: Symphony no. 9

17 February 1971   London (Festival Hall: BBC SO)
Schumann: Overture to *Manfred*
Beethoven: Piano Concerto no. 5 (Curzon)
Schoenberg: *Pelleas und Melisande*

February–March 1971   Hamburg/Hanover/Wiesbaden/Munich/Berne
(BBC SO)
(tour with the following repertory)
Bartók: *The Miraculous Mandarin*; Berg: Seven Early Songs (Harper);
Boulez: *Eclat/multiples*; Debussy: *Images*, *La mer*; Messiaen: *Oiseaux
exotiques* (Béroff); Ravel: *Shéhérazade* (Harper); Schoenberg: Chamber
Symphony no. 1; Stravinsky: *The Rite of Spring*, *Chant du rossignol*;
Webern: Six Pieces op. 6

18 March–10 April 1971   Cleveland (Cleveland Orchestra)
I: Schubert: Symphony no. 3; Schoenberg: Piano Concerto (Brendel);
Mozart: Piano Concerto in G K. 453 (Brendel); Schoenberg: Variations
op. 31
II: Debussy: *Trois nocturnes*; Schoenberg: *Erwartung* (Pilarczyk), Chamber
Symphony no. 1; Varèse: *Arcana*
III: Schoenberg: *Incidental Music to a Motion Picture Scene* op. 34; Mahler:
Lieder eines fahrenden Gesellen (McDaniel); Stravinsky: Suite from *The
Firebird*; Bartók: Music for Strings, Percussion, and Celesta

26 March 1971   Cleveland (Cleveland Orchestra)
informal evening on Varèse: *Arcana*, *Ionisation*, [*Poème électronique*]

15 April–15 May 1971   New York (Philharmonic Hall: New York PO)
I: Webern: Passacaglia; Schoenberg: *Verklärte Nacht*; Berg:
Altenberglieder, Seven Early Songs (Harper), Three Pieces op. 6
II: Berlioz: Overture and Scenes from *Béatrice et Bénédict*; Messiaen:
Oiseaux exotiques (Jacobs); Varèse: *Ionisation*; Ravel: *Le tombeau de
Couperin*
III: Stravinsky: *Pulcinella*, Requiem Canticles, *Petrushka*
IV: Schubert: Symphony no. 6; Schoenberg: Four Songs op. 22 (Minton);
Mahler: *Lieder eines fahrenden Gesellen* (Minton); Bartók: *The
Miraculous Mandarin*
V: Gabrieli: *Canzon duodecimi toni a 8*, *Sonata pian e forte*, *Canzon
septimi toni a 8*; Pousseur: *Couleurs croisées*; Debussy: *Première
rapsodie*, *Images*

25–26 May 1971   Brussels/Paris (BBC SO)
Berg: Three Pieces from the *Lyric Suite*
Schoenberg: Variations op. 31
Boulez: *Livre pour cordes I*
Bartók: *The Miraculous Mandarin*

27 May 1971   Paris (Salle Pleyel: BBC SO)
Schumann: Symphony no. 3
Mahler: Symphony no. 5

2 June 1971   London (Festival Hall: BBC SO)
Birtwistle: *An Imaginary Landscape**
Bartók: Piano Concerto no. 2 (Claude Helffer)
Holliger: *Siebengesang* (Holliger)
Schoenberg: Variations op. 31

18 June 1971   London (Queen Elizabeth Hall: London Sinfonietta)
Boulez: *Domaines* (Alan Hacker)
Stockhausen: *Zeitmasze*
Schoenberg: *Pierrot lunaire* (Escribano)
(Domaines *recorded the previous day by the BBC with the Berg Chamber*
Concerto)

20 June–3 July 1971   Vienna/Florence/Perugia/Rome/ Amsterdam/The
                            Hague/Tours (London Sinfonietta)
(tour with the following repertory)
Berg: Chamber Concerto (Béroff, Gawriloff); Birtwistle: *Verses for*
Ensembles; Boulez: *Domaines* (Hacker), *Improvisations sur Mallarmé*
I–II (Lukomska); Davies: *Alma redemptoris mater*; Schoenberg: *Pierrot*
lunaire (Escribano), Chamber Symphony no. 1; Stockhausen: *Zeitmasze*;
Stravinsky: Three Japanese Lyrics (Lukomska); Webern: Concerto

4 July 1971   Tours (Grange de Meslay: London Sinfonietta)
Purcell: Fantasias
Mozart: Piano Concerto in C minor K. 491 (Richter), Horn Concerto no.
3 K. 447 (Tuckwell)
Haydn: Symphony no. 99

12–24 July 1971   Filene/Blossom Centers (Cleveland Orchestra)
12: Stravinsky: *Chant du rossignol*; Debussy: *La mer, Prélude à "L'après-*
    midi d'un faune"; Bartók: Suite from *The Miraculous Mandarin*
13: Berlioz: Overture *Le carnaval romain*, Excerpts from *Roméo et Juliette*,
    Symphonie fantastique
17: Schumann: Overture to *Manfred*; Wagner: *Wesendoncklieder* (Horne);
    Mahler: *Rückertlieder* (Horne); Schumann: Symphony no. 3
23: Berlioz: *Symphonie fantastique, Lélio*
24: Bartók: Dance Suite; Ravel: Piano Concerto for the Left Hand, Piano
    Concerto in G (Entremont); Stravinsky: Suite from *Pulcinella*

3–31 August 1971   London (Albert Hall)
3 (BBC SO):   Debussy: *Ibéria*; Boulez: *Eclat/multiples* (Rosen); Ravel:
    Shéhérazade (Söderström); Stravinsky: *Petrushka*
5 (BBC SO):   Schumann: Overture to *Manfred*; Berlioz: *Nuits d'été* (Janet
    Baker); Mahler: Symphony no. 9

23 (NYO):   Stravinsky: Symphonies of Wind Instruments; Bartók: Music
   for Strings, Percussion, and Celesta; Berg: Seven Early Songs (Harper);
   Webern: Six Pieces op. 6; Debussy: *La mer*
31 (BBC SO):   Stravinsky: *Chant du rossignol*; Schoenberg: Piano Concerto
   (Brendel); Bartók: *Bluebeard's Castle* (Lear, Stewart)

6 September 1971   London (Round House: BBC SO)
(first Round House concert)
   [Connolly: *Cinquepaces**]
   Ligeti: *Aventures, Nouvelles aventures*
   George Newson: *Arena**

21 September 1971   New York (Philharmonic Hall: New York PO)
(first concert as music director of the orchestra)
   Wagner: Overture *Faust*
   Berlioz: *Chasse royale et orage* from *Les troyens*
   Liszt: *Totentanz* (Jorge Bolet)
   Debussy: *Prélude à "L'après-midi d'un faune"*
   Stravinsky: *The Rite of Spring*

23 September–4 October 1971   New York (Philharmonic Hall: New
                                 York PO)
I: Ives: Overture *Robert Browning*; Liszt: *Malédiction* (David Bar-Illan);
     Mahler: Adagio from Symphony no. 10; Prokofiev: *Scythian Suite*
II: Liszt: *The Legend of St. Elizabeth*

1 October 1971   New York (Public Theater: New York PO)
(first downtown concert)
   [Davidovsky: *Synchronisms no. 6* (Jacobs)]
   Wuorinen: *The Politics of Harmony*

13 October 1971   London (Festival Hall: BBC SO)
   Stravinsky: *Petrushka*
   Varèse: *Nocturnal*
   Bartók: *Cantata profana*
   Varèse: *Amériques*

18 October 1971   Graz (Stephaniensaal: BBC SO)
   Stravinsky: Symphonies of Wind Instruments
   Birtwistle: *An Imaginary Landscape*
   Carter: Concerto for Orchestra
   Boulez: *Eclat/multiples*

19–21 October 1971   Vienna (BBC SO)
19:   Haydn: Symphony no. 104; Mahler: Symphony no. 9
21:   Debussy: *Nocturnes*; Bartók: Piano Concerto no. 2 (Béroff); Schoenberg:
      Variations op. 31; Debussy: *La mer*

27 October 1971   London (Festival Hall: BBC SO)
Schubert: *Gesang der Geister über den Wassern*
Brahms: Piano Concerto no. 1 (Bruno-Leonardo Gelber)
Schumann: Symphony no. 1

26 November–4 December 1971   Cleveland (Cleveland Orchestra)
I: Debussy: *Jeux*; Ravel: Piano Concerto in G (Entremont), Suite from *Ma mère l'oye*; Debussy: *La mer*
II: Haydn: Symphony no. 26; Webern: Passacaglia; Berg: Seven Early Songs, *Altenberglieder* (Lukomska); Schubert: Symphony no. 4

3 December 1971   Cleveland (Cleveland Orchestra)
informal evening on Berg: Seven Early Songs, *Altenberglieder* (Lukomska)

3–19 January 1972   London (BBC: BBC SO)
3:   Messiaen: *Poèmes pour Mi* (Felicity Palmer); Stravinsky: Violin Concerto (Szymon Goldberg); Bartók: Concerto for Orchestra
7:   Mahler: Symphony no. 6
19: Berg: Violin Concerto (György Pauk); Schoenberg: *Verklärte Nacht*

10 January 1972   London (St. John's Smith Square: BBC SO)
Haydn: Te Deum in C; Symphony no. 92; Mass in B-flat "Theresienmesse"

13–29 January 1972   London (Covent Garden)
(six performances)
Debussy: *Pelléas et Mélisande* (Václav Kašlík production)

17/31 January 1972   London (Round House: BBC SO)
17: Maderna: *Juilliard Serenade*; Connolly: *Tetramorph**; Stockhausen: *Mixtur*
31: Ligeti: *Ramifications*; Rands: *Mésalliance**; Salzman: *Foxes and Hedgehogs*

26 January 1972   London (Festival Hall: BBC SO)
Preconcert program of Stravinsky: Symphonies of Wind Instruments, *Berceuses du chat, Pribaoutki*
Stravinsky: *The Nightingale, Renard, Les noces*

3 February–6 March 1972   New York (Philharmonic Hall: New York PO)
I: Liszt: *Via Crucis*; Ravel: *Daphnis et Chloé*
II: Schubert: Symphony no. 4; Liszt: Three Songs (Christa Ludwig); Bartók: Dance Suite; Berg: Three Fragments from *Wozzeck* (Ludwig)
III: Telemann: Excerpts from *Tafelmusik III*; Berg: Three Pieces from the *Lyric Suite*; Mozart: Piano Concerto in B-flat K. 595 (De Larrocha); Varèse: *Arcana*

IV: Stravinsky: *Chant du rossignol*; Bartók: Divertimento; Mozart: Violin
Concerto in A K. 219 (Druian); Ravel: *Rapsodie espagnole*
V: Berg: Chamber Concerto (Barenboim, Zukerman); Schumann: Overture
to *Manfred*, Symphony no. 3

8/29 February 1972   New York (Juilliard Theater: New York PO)
(informal evenings)
8: Berg: [Songs (Ludwig, Boulez)], Three Fragments from *Wozzeck*
(Ludwig)
29: Berg: Chamber Concerto (Barenboim, Zukerman)

18 February 1972   New York (Public Theater: New York PO)
Crumb: *Ancient Voices of Children*
Silverman: *Planh*
Salzman: *Ecologue*

9 March–8 April 1972   Cleveland (Cleveland Orchestra)
I: Stravinsky: *Agon*, Symphonies of Wind Instruments, Four Russian Songs
for women's choir, *Les noces*
II: Bartók: Divertimento, *Bluebeard's Castle* (Tatiana Troyanos, Zoltán
Kélémen)
III: Schoenberg: *Pelleas und Melisande*, *Pierrot lunaire* (Bethany Beardslee)
IV: Mahler: Adagio from Symphony no. 10, *Das klagende Lied*

31 March 1972   Cleveland (Cleveland Orchestra)
Informal evening of Stravinsky: Symphonies of Wind Instruments, *The Rite
of Spring*

19 April 1972   London (Festival Hall: BBC SO)
Preconcert program of Stravinsky: *Ragtime*, Concertino, Two Balmont
Poems, Three Japanese Lyrics (Jill Gomez), Four Russian Songs for
women's choir
Stravinsky: *A Sermon, a Narrative, and a Prayer*
Boulez: *Cummings ist der Dichter*
Schoenberg: *Die Jakobsleiter* (Reich)

3–12 May 1972   Nice/Grenoble/Strasbourg/Paris (BBC SO)
(tour with the following repertory)
Bartók: Piano Concerto no. 2 (Béroff); Berg: Three Fragments from
Wozzeck (Wendy Fine); Berio: *Epifanie* (Berberian); Boulez:
Eclat/multiples; Debussy: *Prélude à "L'après-midi d'un faune"*; Mahler:
Symphony no. 9; Schumann: Symphony no. 1 in B-flat; Stravinsky:
Petrushka, Symphonies of Wind Instruments; Varèse: *Amériques*;
Wagner: Overture *Faust*; Webern: Six Pieces op. 6, Five Movements op.
5; Wood: Cello Concerto (Zara Nelsova)

20 May 1972   London (BBC Concert Hall: BBC SO)
    Bach: Brandenburg Concerto no. 3
    Haydn: Symphony no. 92
    Brahms: Serenade no. 2

29 May 1972   London (Round House: BBC SO)
    [Globokar: *Discours II* (Vinko Globokar and others)]
    Schafer: *Requiems for the Party Girl*
    Davies: *Blind Man's Buff**

2 June 1972   Bristol (Colston Hall: BBC SO)
    Berg: Three Pieces from the *Lyric Suite*
    Webern: Five Pieces op. 10
    Bartók: Piano Concerto no. 1 (Roger Woodward)
    Stravinsky: *Petrushka*

21 July–30 August 1972   London (Albert Hall: BBC SO)
    21: Beethoven: *Missa solemnis*
    4: Messiaen: *Poèmes pour Mi* (Palmer); Mahler: Symphony no. 6
    10: Cage: *First Construction (in Metal)*; Carter: Concerto for Orchestra;
        Messiaen: *Sept haïkaï* (Jean-Rodolphe Kars); Stravinsky: *Petrushka*
    25: Stravinsky: Symphonies of Wind Instruments, *The Firebird*, *The
        Nightingale*
    28: Wagner: *Parsifal* Act I
    30: Wagner: *Parsifal* Acts II–III

7 August 1972   London (Round House: BBC SO)
    Davies: *Blind Man's Buff*
    Boulez: *Cummings ist der Dichter*
    Holliger: *Siebengesang* (Holliger)

8 September 1972   Bloomington
    Berlioz: Overture to *Benvenuto Cellini*
    Haydn: Symphony no. 31
    Schumann: Symphony no. 4
    Ravel: Suite no. 2 from *Daphnis et Chloé*

20 September–17 October 1972   New York (Philharmonic Hall: New
                                 York PO)
    I: Berlioz: Overture to *Benvenuto Cellini*; Dvořák: Cello Concerto
       (Piatigorsky)
    II: Haydn: Symphony no. 31; Stravinsky: Symphonies of Wind Instruments,
        Four Etudes; Ravel: Piano Concerto for the Left Hand (Leon Fleischer);
        Wagner: Suite from *Die Meistersinger*
    III: Mozart: Sinfonia Concertante in E-flat K. 364 (Druian, Sol Greitzer);
         Mahler: Symphony no. 6
    IV: Schütz: *Fili mi, Absalom*; Bartók: *Cantata profana*; Berlioz: Te Deum

V: Bach: Brandenburg Concerto no. 1; Bartók: Piano Concerto no. 2
(Béroff); Kirchner: Music for Orchestra; Scriabin: *Le poème d'extase*

6 October 1972   New York (Loeb Center: New York PO)
Druckman: *Incenters*
Davies: *Eight Songs for a Mad King*

22 October 1972   Brighton (Dome: BBC SO)
Bartók: Divertimento
Mahler: Symphony no. 9

25 October 1972   London (Festival Hall: BBC SO)
Schumann: Overture, Scherzo, and Finale
Mahler: Symphony no. 6

1 November 1972   London (St. John's Smith Square: BBC SO)
Schubert: *Ständchen* D. 920, *Nur wer die Sehnsucht kennt* D. 656,
Nachtgesang D. 913
Schoenberg: *Herzgewächse* (Mady Mesplé), Three Pieces op. posth.,
Herzgewächse
Nono: *Canti per tredici, Ha venido*
Webern: *Entflieht auf leichten Kähnen*, Two Songs op. 19, *Das
Augenlicht*

2 November 1972   Croydon (Fairfield Hall: BBC SO)
Wagner: Overture *Faust*
Schumann: Symphony no. 1
Debussy: *Prélude à "L'après-midi d'un faune"*
Stravinsky: *The Rite of Spring*

8 November 1972   London (Festival Hall: BBC SO)
Stravinsky: Symphony of Psalms
Berg: Violin Concerto (Perlman)
Ravel: *Daphnis et Chloé*

14 November 1972   London (Albert Hall: BBC SO)
Ravel: *Shéhérazade* (Harper)
Berlioz: Excerpts from *Roméo et Juliette*
*(Berlioz also recorded by BBC on 11 November with Mendelssohn: Concerto
for Piano and Violin in D minor)*

27 November 1972   London (Round House: BBC SO)
Messiaen: *Couleurs de la Cité Céleste* (Kars)
Xenakis: *Aroura*
Alsina: *Funktionen*

3 December 1972   London (BBC: BBC SO)
   Schumann: Symphony no. 4
   Mahler: Symphony no. 4

6 December 1972   London (Festival Hall: BBC SO)
   Berg: Suite from *Lulu* (Farley)
   Mozart: Piano Concerto in A K. 488 (De Larrocha)
   Schumann: Symphony no. 4

14 December 1972–2 January 1973   New York (Philharmonic Hall: New York PO)
I: Bach: Cantata no. 48 "Ich elender Mensch"; Stravinsky: *A Sermon, a Narrative, and a Prayer*, *Zvezdoliki*; Bartók: Concerto for Orchestra
II: Mozart: Serenade in D K. 320; Schumann: Cello Concerto (Lorne Munroe); Stockhausen: *Kontra-Punkte*; Prokofiev: Suite from *Chout*

29/31 December 1972   London (Albert Hall: BBC SO)
29: Stravinsky: Suite from *The Firebird* (1911), *The Faun and the Shepherdess*, Symphony of Psalms, *Zvezdoliki*, *The Rite of Spring*
31: Berlioz: *La damnation de Faust*

[?] 1973   London (BBC: BBC SO)
   Ravel: *L'heure espagnole*, *L'enfant et les sortilèges*

4 January–6 February 1973   New York (Philharmonic Hall: New York PO)
I: Schumann: Overture, Scherzo, and Finale; Beethoven: Piano Concerto no. 4 (André Watts); Ravel: *Valses nobles et sentimentales*; Mozart: Symphony no. 36 in C K. 425
(on 5 January this program included, in place of the Ravel Valses, *that composer's* Une barque sur l'océan *and in addition Boulez:* . . . explosante-fixe . . . *performed in Tully Hall)*
II: Haydn: Mass in B-flat "Theresienmesse"; Stravinsky: *The Nightingale*
(on 12 January this program included in addition Bolcom: Morning and Evening Poems*)*
III: Telemann: Suite in A minor for flute and strings (Julius Baker); Crumb: *Ancient Voices of Children* (Jan de Gaetani); Stravinsky: *Ragtime*, *Renard*; Strauss: *Till Eulenspiegel*
IV: Wagner: Overture to *Tannhäuser*; Schumann: Piano Concerto (Rudolf Serkin); Webern: Five Movements op. 5; Beethoven: Symphony no. 2
(on 27 January the concerto was one of Mozart's for horn, played by John Cerminaro)
V: Schubert: Overture and Ballet Music from *Rosamunde*; Mahler: *Rückertlieder* (Siegmund Nimsgern); Webern: Variations op. 30, Six Pieces op. 6; Wagner: Prelude and Liebestod from *Tristan und Isolde*
(on 6 February the Mahler was replaced by Till Eulenspiegel, *and the order changed)*

23 January 1973   New York (Juilliard Theater: New York PO)
informal evening on Webern: Five Movements op. 5 [plus quartet version]

9–15 February 1973   Philadelphia/New York (Philadelphia Orchestra)
Debussy: *Jeux*
Ravel: *Shéhérazade* (Harper)
Webern: Six Pieces op. 6
Berg: *Altenberglieder* (Harper)
Bartók: *The Miraculous Mandarin*

19 February 1973   London (Round House: BBC SO)
Webern: *Entflieht auf leichten Kähnen, Das Augenlicht*
Stockhausen: *Kreuzspiel*
[Smalley: *Strata* (conducted by Smalley)]

28 February/7 March 1973   London (Festival Hall: BBC SO)
28: Schubert/Webern: *Deutsche Tänze*; Webern: Five Pieces op. 10;
Bach/Webern: Ricercare; Messiaen: *Poèmes pour Mi* (Palmer); Berlioz:
Harold en Italie (Peter Schidlof)
7:   Schumann: *Scenes from Goethe's Faust*

15 March–3 April 1973   New York (Philharmonic Hall: New York PO)
I: Schumann: Overture *Julius Caesar*; Haydn: Symphony no. 49; Berio:
Concerto for Two Pianos* (Bruno Cannino, Antonio Ballista);
Mendelssohn: Symphony no. 4
II: *Children's concert with movements from* Bartók: Concerto for Orchestra;
Mozart: Horn Concerto in E-flat K. 417; Schubert: *Rosamunde*;
Schumann: Cello Concerto; Telemann: Suite in A; Webern: Five
Movements op. 5
III: Brahms: Serenade no. 2; Schoenberg: Variations op. 31; Schumann:
Symphony no. 4
IV: Haydn: *L'incontro improvviso*
V: Babbitt: [*Occasional Variations*], *Correspondences*; Ligeti: *Aventures,
Nouvelles aventures*

7 April 1973   London (BBC: BBC SO)
Mozart: Symphony no. 36 in C K. 425
Mahler: Symphony no. 5

11 April 1973   London (Festival Hall: BBC SO)
Webern: Cantata no. 2, Variations op. 30, Cantata no. 1
Berio: Concerto for Two Pianos (Cannino, Ballista)
Bartók: Concerto for Orchestra
(Bartók also recorded by BBC with Birtwistle: Nenia on the Death of
Orpheus*)*

25 April 1973   London (St. John's Smith Square: BBC SO)
Mozart: Serenade in C minor K. 388
Webern: Four Songs op. 13, Six Songs op. 14 (Lukomska)
Stockhausen: *Kreuzspiel*
Webern: Three Sacred Folksongs op. 17, Three Songs op. 18
(Lukomska)
Stockhausen: *Kontra-Punkte*

5–23 May 1973   Bologna/Brescia/Bergamo/Turin/Perugia/Rome/
                                Florence/Venice/Vienna (BBC SO)
(tour with the following repertory)
Bartók: Piano Concerto no. 2 (Anda), *The Miraculous Mandarin*,
Concerto for Orchestra; Berlioz: *Harold en Italie* (Schidlof); Birtwistle:
Nenia on the Death of Orpheus (Jane Manning); Boulez: . . . *explosante-
fixe* . . .; Debussy: *Ibéria*; Mahler: Symphony no. 4 (Palmer), Symphony
no. 5; Messiaen: *Poèmes pour Mi* (Palmer); Mozart: Sinfonia
Concertante in E-flat K. 364 (Norbert Brainin, Schidlof), Symphony no.
36 in C K. 425, Piano Concerto in B-flat K. 456, "Bella mia fiamma" K.
528 (Palmer); Ravel: *Valses nobles et sentimentales*; Stravinsky: Suite
from *The Firebird* (1911)

12–17 June 1973   New York (Philharmonic Hall: New York PO)
(Rug Concerts)
12: Weber: Overture to *Der Freischütz*; Brahms: Serenade no. 2 in A; Ives:
    Three Places in New England; Stravinsky: Suite from *The Firebird*
    (1919 version)
13: Bach: Brandenburg Concerto no. 1; Webern: Five Movements op. 5;
    Crumb: *Ancient Voices of Children*; Haydn: Symphony no. 49
14: Haydn: Symphony no. 31; Webern: Six Pieces op. 6 (1928 version);
    Stravinsky: Four Etudes; Debussy: *Prélude à "L'après-midi d'un
    faune"*; Schumann: Symphony no. 4
15: Purcell: Fantasias nos. 1, 8, 4, and 5; Stravinsky: Concertino; Webern:
    Variations op. 30; Ravel: Introduction and Allegro; Mozart: Serenade in
    D K. 320
16: Gluck: Overture to *Alceste*; Beethoven: Symphony no. 2; Bartók:
    Concerto for Orchestra
17: Telemann: Suite in A minor for flute and strings; Stockhausen: *Kontra-
    Punkte*; Debussy: *Danse sacrée et danse profane*; Haydn: Overture and
    Arias from *L'incontro improvviso*; Stravinsky: *Ragtime, Renard*

20 July–29 August 1973   London (Albert Hall: BBC SO)
20: Stravinsky: Symphony of Psalms; Brahms: *Ein deutsches Requiem*
    (Harper, Prey)
25: Webern: Passacaglia, Six Pieces op. 6; Schumann: Piano Concerto
    (Michael Roll); Mahler: Symphony no. 4 (Palmer)
27: Birtwistle: *The Triumph of Time*; Berio: Concerto for Two Pianos
    (Cannino, Ballista); Berlioz: *Symphonie fantastique*

10: Schoenberg: *Gurrelieder*
15: Mahler: Symphony no. 3
17: Ravel: Suite from *Ma mère l'oye*; Berlioz: *Nuits d'été* (Minton); Boulez:
   . . . *explosante-fixe* . . .; Messiaen: "Turangalîla II–III–I" from the
   Turangalîla Symphony
20: Stravinsky: *Agon, Renard, Les noces, The Rite of Spring*
29: Schumann: Overture, Scherzo, and Finale; Brahms: Piano Concerto no. 1
   in D minor (Gelber); Bartók: Concerto for Orchestra

25–26 August 1973   Edinburgh (Usher Hall: BBC SO)
25: Ravel: *Valses nobles et sentimentales*; Berlioz: *Nuits d'été* (Minton);
   Bartók: Concerto for Orchestra
26: Stravinsky: *Chant du rossignol*; Boulez: *Cummings ist der Dichter*;
   Holliger: *Siebengesang* (Holliger); Berg: Three Pieces op. 6

18 September 1973   New York (Philharmonic Hall: New York PO)
   Brahms: Piano Concerto no. 2 (Van Cliburn)
   Bartók: Concerto for Orchestra

20/21/22/25 September 1973   New York (Philharmonic Hall: New
                                          York PO)
   Strauss: *Also sprach Zarathustra*
   Schoenberg: *Verklärte Nacht*
   Debussy: *La mer*
(other fall concerts canceled due to musicians' union strike)

5 October 1973   Bordeaux (Entrepôts Lainé: Musique Vivante)
   Boulez: . . . *explosante-fixe* . . ., *Domaines*, [*Eclat/multiples* (conducted
   by Diego Masson)]

10 October 1973   London (Festival Hall: BBC SO)
   Bartók: Music for Strings, Percussion, and Celesta
   Zimmermann: *Photoptosis*
   Mahler: Symphony no. 4 (Palmer)
(Bartók also recorded by BBC on 7 October with Haydn: Symphony no. 99)

19 October 1973   Hemel Hempstead (Pavilion: BBC SO)
   Schumann: Overture to *Manfred*
   Bartók: Violin Concerto no. 2 (Pauk)
   Ravel: Suite from *Ma mère l'oye*
   Debussy: *La mer*

21 October 1973   Donaueschingen (Stadthalle: BBC SO)
   Boulez: . . . *explosante-fixe* . . .

25 November 1973   London (BBC: BBC SO)
   Berlioz: Overture to *Benvenuto Cellini*

Mendelssohn: Overture, Nocturne, and Scherzo for *A Midsummer Night's Dream*
Schumann: Symphony no. 3

28 November 1973   London (St. John's Smith Square: BBC SO)
   Webern: Symphony
   Boulez: *Cummings ist der Dichter*
   Haydn: Mass in B-flat "Harmoniemesse"

5 December 1973   London (Festival Hall: BBC SO)
   Bartók: Suite from *The Wooden Prince*, Piano Concerto no. 2 (Anda),
   Village Scenes, *The Miraculous Mandarin*

13–22 December 1973   New York (Philharmonic Hall: New York PO)
I: Schumann: *Scenes from Goethe's Faust*
II: Handel: Suite from the *Royal Fireworks Music*; Mozart: Piano Concerto
      in F K. 459 (Peter Serkin); Copland: *Connotations*; Janáček: *Lachian
      Dances*

11–12 January 1974   Paris (Champs-Elysées: BBC SO)
11:   Messiaen: *Poèmes pour Mi* (Palmer); Mahler: Symphony no. 4
12:   Birtwistle: *The Triumph of Time*; Boulez: *Cummings ist der Dichter*;
      Bartók: Concerto for Orchestra

16/23 January 1974   London (Festival Hall: BBC SO)
16:   Schoenberg: *Incidental Music to a Motion Picture Scene* op. 34; Mozart:
      Piano Concerto in D K. 537 (Curzon); Birtwistle: *The Triumph of Time*;
      Debussy: *La mer*
23:   Webern: Passacaglia; Berg: Three Fragments from *Wozzeck* (Harper);
      Brahms: *Ein deutsches Requiem* (Harper, Shirley-Quirk)

21 January 1974   London (Round House: BBC SO)
   Eloy: *Faisceaux-diffractions*
   Ligeti: *Ramifications*
   Schoenberg: *Pierrot lunaire* (Manning)

31 January–5 March 1974   New York (Fisher Hall: New York PO)
I: Ravel: *Une barque sur l'océan*, *Alborada del gracioso*; Chabrier: *Ode à
      la musique*; Debussy: *Nocturnes*; Webern: Symphony; Bartók: Music for
      Strings, Percussion, and Celesta
II: Wagner: *Siegfried Idyll*; Mozart: Piano Concerto in D minor K. 466
      (Rudolf Serkin); Beethoven: Piano Concerto no. 5 (Serkin)
III: Boyce: Concerto Grosso in B-flat; Mozart: Piano Concerto in C minor K.
      491 (Eschenbach); Carter: Concerto for Orchestra; Debussy: *Ibéria*
IV: Mahler: Symphony no. 8
V: Ravel: *La valse*, *Menuet antique*, *Ma mère l'oye*; Schoenberg: *Incidental
      Music to a Motion Picture Scene* op. 34; Brahms: Symphony no. 4

VI: Schubert: Overture in the Italian Style; Bartók: Piano Concerto no. 1 (Pollini); Berg: Three Pieces from the *Lyric Suite*; Ravel: Suites nos. 1 and 2 from *Daphnis et Chloé*

11 February 1974   New York (Juilliard Theater: New York PO)
Informal evening on Carter: Concerto for Orchestra

11/18 March 1974   London (Round House: BBC SO)
11: Varèse: *Ionisation*; Souster: *Song of an Average City**; [Berio: *Circles* (Berberian and BBC SO musicians)]
18: Stockhausen: *Kontra-Punkte*; Rands: *Aum*; Berg: Chamber Concerto (Frankl, Pauk)

20 March 1974   London (Festival Hall: BBC SO)
Schoenberg: *Verklärte Nacht*
Maderna: *Aura*
Bartók: Concerto for Orchestra

3 April 1974   London (St. John's Smith Square: BBC SO)
Schoenberg: Serenade (Michael Rippon)
Schubert: *Lazarus*

13–14 April 1974   Leeds (Town Hall: BBC SO)
13: Berlioz: *Grande messe des morts*
14: Berg: Three Fragments from *Wozzeck* (Fine); Webern: Six Pieces op. 6; Mahler: Symphony no. 4

25/26/27/30 April 1974   New York (Fisher Hall: New York PO)
Handel: Suites nos. 2 and 3 from the *Water Music*
Beethoven: Symphony no. 1
Reimann: *Zyklus* (Fischer-Dieskau, *25 and 27 July only*)
Hindemith: Symphony *Mathis der Maler*

26 April/3 May 1974   New York (Loeb Center: New York PO)
26: Webern: Concerto; Ives: Songs (De Gaetani); Sollberger: Chamber Variations
3: Varèse: *Octandre*; Wolpe: [Piece for Trumpet], Piece for Trumpet and Seven Players; Ligeti: Chamber Concerto

2 May 1974   New York (Juilliard Theater: New York PO)
Informal evening on Varèse: *Ecuatorial*

3/7 May 1974   New York (Fisher Hall: New York PO)
Schubert: Three Choruses
Varèse: *Ecuatorial*
Schoenberg: *A Survivor from Warsaw*
Berlioz: *Harold en Italie* (Sol Greitzer)

6 May 1974   New York (Whitney Museum)
        Boulez: *Eclat, Le marteau sans maître*

May–June 1974   Hanover/Vienna/Innsbruck/Munich/Zurich/Berne/
        Basle/Baden-Baden/Stuttgart/Düsseldorf/Berlin/
        Hamburg (BBC SO)
(tour with the following repertory)
        Bartók: Music for Strings, Percussion, and Celesta; Berg: Three Pieces
        op. 6; Berio: *Allelujah II*; Berlioz: *Nuits d'été* (Minton, Robert Tear);
        Boulez: *Figures-Doubles-Prismes, . . . explosante-fixe . . .*; Debussy:
        Ibéria; Goehr: Three Pieces from *Arden must die*; Haubenstock-Ramati:
        Petite musique de nuit; Mahler: Symphony no. 6, *Rückertlieder*
        (Minton); Mozart: Piano Concerto in D K. 537 (Curzon), Piano Concerto
        in A K. 488 (Eschenbach); Rands: *Wildtrack 1*; Ravel: *Ma mère l'oye*;
        Schoenberg: Five Pieces op. 16, *Incidental Music to a Motion Picture
        Scene* op. 34; Schubert: Symphony no. 3; Stockhausen: *Kontra-Punkte*;
        Stravinsky: *Petrushka*

11–16 June 1974   New York (Fisher Hall: New York PO)
(Rug Concerts)
        11: Brahms: Symphony no. 4; Debussy: *Ibéria*; Bartók: Music for Strings,
        Percussion, and Celesta
        12: Handel: *Royal Fireworks Music*; Mozart: Flute Concerto; Webern:
        Concerto; Varèse: *Octandre*; Ligeti: *Aventures, Nouvelles aventures*
        13: Schumann: Symphony no. 2; Berg: Three Pieces from the *Lyric Suite*;
        Ravel: Suites nos. 1 and 2 from *Daphnis et Chloé*
        14: Bach: Brandenburg Concerto no. 3; Schubert: Symphony no. 2; Webern:
        Symphony; Boulez: *Improvisations sur Mallarmé I–II* (Bryn-Julson);
        Stravinsky: Suite from *Histoire du soldat*
        15: Schoenberg: Serenade, *Ode to Napoleon* (Richard Frisch), *Pierrot
        lunaire* (De Gaetani)
        16: Schoenberg: *Verklärte Nacht*; Berg: Three Fragments from *Wozzeck*
        (Marahiu Niska); Stravinsky: *The Rite of Spring*

6 July 1974   La Rochelle (Oratoire)
        Boulez: *. . . explosante-fixe . . .* (two performances)

6 July 1974   La Rochelle (Théâtre Municipal: Musique Vivante)
        Boulez: *Eclat,* [*Le marteau sans maître* (De Gaetani, conducted by
        Masson)], *Eclat/multiples*

19 July–27 Aug 1974   London (Albert Hall: BBC SO)
        19: Haydn: Mass in B-flat "Harmoniemesse"; [Schubert: Symphony no. 9
        (Boult)]
        21: Schoenberg: *Gurrelieder*
        23: Schubert: Symphony no. 3; Mozart: Clarinet Concerto K. 622 (Hacker);
        Schoenberg: *Incidental Music to a Motion Picture Scene* op. 34;
        Debussy: *Images*

26: Wagner: Overture to *Die Meistersinger, Wesendoncklieder* (Norman);
    Stockhausen: *Gruppen* (with Elgar Howarth and Masson); Berg: *Der
    Wein* (Norman), Three Pieces op. 6
14: Berio: *Allelujah II* (with Berio); Mozart: Piano Concerto in D K. 537
    (Curzon); Bartók: Concerto for Orchestra
21: Ravel: *L'heure espagnole*; Stravinsky: Suites nos. 1 and 2, *Petrushka*
24: Ravel: *Valses nobles et sentimentales*; Debussy: *Danse sacrée et danse
    profane*; Messiaen: *Poèmes pour Mi* (Palmer); Bartók: *Village Scenes*;
    Stravinsky: *Les noces*
27: [Mozart: Piano Quartet in E-flat K. 493], Mahler: Symphony no. 2

18 September 1974   New York (Fisher Hall: New York PO)
    Mozart: Overture to *Così fan tutte*, Piano Concerto in E-flat K. 271
    (Watts)
    Liszt: Piano Concerto no. 2 (Watts)
    Stravinsky: *Petrushka*

19 September–15 October 1974   New York (Fisher Hall: New York
                                              PO)
I: Dvořák: Cello Concerto (Starker); Mahler: Symphony no. 4 (Von Stade)
II: Haydn: Trumpet Concerto (Gerard Schwarz); Mahler: Symphony no. 9
III: Rameau: Suite from *Les indes galantes*; Prokofiev: Piano Concerto no. 3
     (Jeffrey Siegel); Zimmermann: *Photoptosis*; Mendelssohn: Symphony
     no. 4

8–12 October 1974   New York (Fisher Hall/Juilliard Theater:
                                   Philharmonic)
(Rug Concerts)
8:   Ives: Overture *Robert Browning*; Copland: Variations; [Ives: String
     Quartet no. 2; Crawford: Study in Mixed Accents]; Webern: Six Pieces
     op. 6; Stravinsky: *Scherzo fantastique*
9:   [Bartók: Violin Sonata no. 1; Schoenberg: Five Pieces op. 23; Ives:
     Violin Sonata no. 4]; Ruggles: *Portals*; Ives: *Tone Roads no. 3*; Cowell:
     Ensemble for Strings
10: [Debussy: Sonata for flute, viola, and harp; Ives: Piano Trio; Crawford:
     String Quartet]; Ives: *Decoration Day*; Hindemith: Dances from *Nusch-
     Nuschi*; Prokofiev: Suite from *The Love for Three Oranges*
11: [Janáček: *By an Overgrown Path*; Rudhyar: *Three Paeans*; Bartók:
     Three Etudes; Ives: Songs; Varèse: *Density 21.5*]; Varèse: *Octandre*;
     [Stravinsky: Three Pieces for clarinet]; Stravinsky: Suite from *Histoire
     du soldat*
12: [Bartók: Sonata for two pianos and percussion; Ravel: Sonata for violin
     and cello]; Berg: *Altenberglieder*; Ives: Symphony no. 4

23 October 1974   Paris (Théâtre d'Orsay)
(first IRCAM event)
    Boulez: . . . *explosante-fixe* . . . (two performances)

30 October 1974　　　London (St. John's Smith Square: BBC SO)
Schoenberg: Suite op. 29, *Dreimal tausend Jahre*, *De profundis*, Four
Pieces op. 27; Brahms: Serenade no. 2

3 November 1974　　　Leeds (University Great Hall: BBC SO)
(on the occasion of receiving an honorary doctorate from Leeds University)
Bach/Stravinsky: Chorale Variations on *Vom Himmel hoch*
Bartók: Divertimento
Goehr: Chaconne for wind*
Boulez: *Eclat*
Webern: Five Pieces op. 10
Haydn: Symphony no. 76

6 November–4 December 1974　　　London (Festival Hall: BBC SO)
6:　Mozart: Symphony no. 29 in A K. 201; Schoenberg: Violin Concerto
　　(Zvi Zeitlin); Stravinsky: *The Firebird*
13:　Berlioz: *Roméo et Juliette*
20:　Mahler: Symphony no. 3
4:　Schoenberg: *Moses und Aron* (Reich, Richard Cassilly)

25 November 1974　　　London (Round House: BBC SO)
Guy: *D**
Maderna: *Amanda*
Boulez: *Le marteau sans maître* (Minton)

12 December 1974–25 March 1975　　　New York (Fisher Hall: New York
　　　　　　　　　　　　　　　　　　PO)
I:　Mozart: Symphony no. 40 in G minor K. 550; Berg: Three Pieces from
　　the *Lyric Suite*; Ravel: Piano Concerto in G (Ruth Laredo); Janáček:
　　Sinfonietta
II:　Handel: Suite no. 1 from the *Water Music*; Schumann: Symphony no. 1;
　　Szymanowski: Violin Concerto no. 2 (Eliot Chapo); Ravel: *Boléro*
III:　Bach: Brandenburg Concerto no. 5; Falla: Harpsichord Concerto (Igor
　　Kipnis); Bartók: Concerto for Orchestra
IV:　Birtwistle: *The Triumph of Time*; Debussy: *Fantaisie* (Nerine Barrett);
　　Mozart: Rondo in D K. 382 (Barrett); Mendelssohn: Symphony no. 3
V:　Gluck: Overture to *Iphigénie en Aulide*; Druckman: *Windows*;
　　Stravinsky: *The Firebird*
VI:　Stravinsky: *Chant du rossignol*; Mozart: Flute and Harp Concerto K.
　　299; Carman Moore: *Wildfires and Field Songs*; Falla: Suite from *El
　　sombrero de tres picos*
VII:　C. P. E. Bach: Symphony no. 1; Beethoven: Piano Concerto no. 3 (Gina
　　Bachauer); Bartók: Suite from *The Wooden Prince*
VIII:　Borodin: Symphony no. 3; Kodály: *Marosszek Dances*; Ravel:
　　Daphnis et Chloé
IX:　Frescobaldi: *Ricercari e canzoni*; Boulez: *Improvisations sur Mallarmé
　　I–II* (Bryn-Julson); Liszt: Piano Concerto no. 2 (Martha Argerich);
　　Berlioz: Scenes from *Roméo et Juliette*

4–8 March 1975   New York (Fisher Hall: New York PO)
(Rug Concerts)
4: [Beethoven: Septet]; Dvořák: Serenade for strings; Schubert: Symphony no. 4
5: [Schubert: String Quintet in C; Piano Duet Fantasy in F minor]; Symphony no. 5
6: Salieri: Overture to *Axur, re d'Ormus*; Wolf: Italian Serenade; [Haydn: Songs; Mozart: Songs]; Mahler: *Lieder eines fahrenden Gesellen*; Schubert: Overture to *Rosamunde*
7: [Schumann: Andante and Variations in B-flat for two pianos; Mozart: String Quartet in F K. 590]; Schubert: *Lazarus*
8: Ravel: *Valses nobles et sentimentales*; [Liszt: Piano transcriptions of Schubert and Schumann songs; Voříšek: Impromptu]; Schubert: Symphony no. 9

2/16 April 1975   London (Festival Hall: BBC SO)
2: Bartók: *Cantata profana*; Rands: *Aum*; Boulez: *Rituel**; Bartók: *The Miraculous Mandarin*
16: Stravinsky: *The Nightingale*; Ravel: *L'enfant et les sortilèges*

7 April 1975   London (Round House: BBC SO)
Scherchen-Hsiao: *Khouang*
Rands: *Mésalliance*
Messiaen: *Sept haïkaï* (Howard Shelley)

9 April 1975   London (St. John's Smith Square: BBC SO)
Schumann: *Der Rose Pilgerfahrt*

11/20/24 April 1975   London (BBC: BBC SO)
11: Debussy: *Jeux*; Stravinsky: *The Firebird*
20: Webern: Passacaglia; Schoenberg: Five Pieces op. 16; Ravel: *Daphnis et Chloé*
24: Berlioz: Scenes from *Roméo et Juliette*; Bartók: Concerto for Orchestra

8–24 May 1975   Tokyo/Koriyama/Osaka (BBC SO)
(tour with the following repertory)
Bartók: Concerto for Orchestra; Berg: Three Fragments from *Wozzeck* (De Gaetani); Berlioz: Scenes from *Roméo et Juliette*; Birtwistle: *Nenia on the Death of Orpheus* (De Gaetani); Boulez: *Rituel*; Davies: *Stone Litany* (De Gaetani); Debussy: *Jeux*; Mahler: Symphony no. 4 (De Gaetani); Ravel: *Daphnis et Chloé*; Schoenberg: Five Pieces op. 16; Stravinsky: *The Firebird*; Webern: Passacaglia

4–6 July 1975   Tours (Grange de Meslay: Musique Vivante)
4: Brahms: Serenade no. 2; Wagner: *Siegfried Idyll*; Berg: Chamber Concerto
5: Schubert: Choruses; Stravinsky; Berio
6: Schoenberg; Webern; Boulez; Stravinsky

25–30 July 1975　　　London (Albert Hall: BBC SO)
25: Mahler: Symphony no. 8
27: Schoenberg: *Moses und Aron* (Reich, Cassilly)
30: Berio: *Ora*; Stockhausen: *Kontra-Punkte*; Boulez: *Pli selon pli*

28 August–19 September 1975　　　Edinburgh/London/Berlin/Paris/
　　　　　　　　　　　　　　　　　　　　Chartres (NYPO)
(tour with the following repertory)
　　Bartók: *The Miraculous Mandarin*; Beethoven: Symphony no. 7;
　　Berlioz: Scenes from *Roméo et Juliette*; Carter: Concerto for Orchestra;
　　Ligeti: *Lontano*; Mahler: Adagio from Symphony no. 10, Symphony no.
　　9; Stravinsky: *Petrushka*

25 September–21 October 1975　　　New York (Fisher Hall: New York
　　　　　　　　　　　　　　　　　　　　PO)
I:　　Brahms: Variations on the "St. Anthony" Chorale; Mozart: Clarinet
　　　Concerto K. 622 (Stanley Drucker); Copland: Variations; Stravinsky:
　　　The Rite of Spring
II:　 Wagner: *Das Liebesmahl der Apostel*; Beethoven: Symphony no. 9
III:　Debussy:: *Prélude à "L'après-midi d'un faune"*; Mozart: Piano
　　　Concerto in B-flat K. 595 (Peter Serkin); Bartók: *The Wooden Prince*
IV:　Stravinsky: Suite from *Pulcinella*; Druckman: *Lamia* (De Gaetani);
　　　Falla: *El sombrero de tres picos*

5/12 November 1975　　　London (Festival Hall: BBC SO)
5:　 Schoenberg: *Verklärte Nacht*; Mahler: *Das klagende Lied*
12: Messiaen: *Des canyons aux étoiles . . .* (Loriod)

10 November 1975　　　London (Round House: BBC SO)
　　Sandström: *Utmost*
　　Boulez: *Eclat*
　　Webern: Concerto, Songs op. 13, 16 (Gomez), Five Pieces op. 10

20 November–16 December 1975　　　New York (Fisher Hall: New York
　　　　　　　　　　　　　　　　　　　　　PO)
I:　　Stravinsky: Symphonies of Wind Instruments, Violin Concerto
　　　(Menuhin); Taxin: *Saba*; Dukas: *La péri*
II:　 Mozart: Overture to *Die Zauberflöte*; Beethoven: Piano Concerto no. 5
　　　(Watts); Stravinsky: *Scherzo fantastique*; Varèse: *Amériques*
III:　Schumann: Overture to *Genoveva*, Introduction and Allegro
　　　appassionato; Strauss: *Burleske* (Natalie Hinderas); Davidovsky:
　　　Synchronisms no. 7; Musorgsky/Ravel: *Pictures at an Exhibition*
IV:　Brahms: Academic Festival Overture; Saint-Saëns: Violin Concerto no.
　　　3 (Zino Francescatti); Kolb: *Soundings*; Roussel: Symphony no. 3

5 January 1976　　　Paris (Palais des Congrès: Orchestre de Paris)
　　Beethoven: Piano Concerto no. 5 (Barenboim)
　　Stravinsky: *The Firebird*

6 February 1976   London (Festival Hall: BBC SO)
Bálassa: *Iris*
Ligeti: *San Francisco Polyphony*
Bartók: *Bluebeard's Castle* (Troyanos, Nimsgern)

4–23 March 1976   New York (Fisher Hall: New York PO)
I: Brahms: Double Concerto (Chapo, Munroe); Sessions: Symphony no. 3;
     Debussy: *La mer*
II: Schubert: Symphony no. 9; Schoenberg: Five Pieces op. 16; Prokofiev:
     Piano Concerto no. 5 (Ashkenazy)

5–13 March 1976   New York (Juilliard Theater: New York PO)
5:   Sessions: Symphony no. 3; Druckman: *Lamia*; [Maderna: *Quadrivium*
     (James Levine)]
12: Schuller: *Gala Music*; Blackwood: Piano Concerto (Ursula Oppens);
     Davies: *Stone Litany* (De Gaetani)
13: Xenakis: *Aroura*; Babbitt: *Correspondences*; Brown: *Centering* (Paul
     Zukofsky); Lieberson: Cello Concerto (Paul Tobias); Carter: Double
     Concerto (Jacobs, Oppens)

23 April 1976   Basle (Casino: Basel Kammerorchester)
Boulez: *Le marteau sans maître* (Minton), . . . *explosante-fixe* . . .

29 April–15 May 1976   New York (Fisher Hall: New York PO)
I: Bach: Brandenburg Concerto no. 4; Berg: Suite from *Lulu*; Mozart:
     "Vorrei spiegarvi" K. 418 (Judith Blegen); Wagner: Excerpts from
     Götterdämmerung
II: Mendelssohn: Overture to *A Midsummer Night's Dream*, Violin
     Concerto (Stern); Beethoven: Symphony no. 4
III: Webern: Passacaglia, Five Movements op. 5; Mahler: Symphony no. 7

July–August 1976   Bayreuth
Wagner: *Der Ring des Nibelungen* (Chéreau production)

1/3 September 1976   London (Albert Hall: BBC SO)
1:   Debussy: *Prélude à "L'après-midi d'un faune," La mer*; Bartók:
     Bluebeard's Castle (Troyanos, Nimsgern)
3:   Stravinsky: Symphony of Psalms; Mahler: *Das klagende Lied*

16–25 October 1976   New York (Carnegie Hall: New York PO)
16: Mahler: Symphony no. 7
17: Mahler: Symphony no. 9
25: Mahler: Symphony no. 3

21 October–9 November 1976   New York (Fisher Hall: New York PO)
I: Mahler: Symphony no. 3
II: Handel: Concerto for two wind choirs and strings; Berg: Violin Concerto

(Kogan); Messiaen: *Et exspecto resurrectionem mortuorum*
III: Cage: *Renga with Apartment House 1776*; Martinů: Cello Concerto no. 1
(Fournier); Ravel: Overture *Shéhérazade, Fanfare, Rapsodie espagnole*

29 October 1976   New York (Cooper Union Great Hall: New York
     PO)
David Gilbert: *Centering II, Poem VI*
Stephen Jablonsky: *Wisconsin Death Trip**
Loren Rush: *Nexus 16**

15/29 November 1976   London (Round House: BBC SO)
15: Finnissy: *Pathways of Sun and Stars**; [Boulez: *Structures II*
(Labèques)]; Varèse: *Octandre, Hyperprism, Intégrales*
29: Sinopoli: Three Pieces from *Souvenirs à la mémoire*; Carter: *A Mirror
on Which to Dwell* (Gomez); Schoenberg: Serenade (Rippon)

18 November 1976   Oxford (New Theatre: BBC SO)
Berlioz: Scenes from *Roméo et Juliette*
Ravel: *Daphnis e Chloé*

24 November 1976   London (Festival Hall: BBC SO)
Boulez: *Rituel*
Debussy: *Trois ballades de Villon*
Ravel: *Don Quichotte à Dulcinée* (Shirley-Quirk), *Daphnis et Chloé*

5 January–22 February 1977   New York (Fisher Hall: New York PO)
I: Haydn: Symphony no. 104; Takemitsu: *Arc* (Peter Serkin); Beethoven:
Symphony no. 5
II: Boulez: *Rituel*; Debussy: Suite from *Le martyre de Saint-Sébastien*;
Stravinsky: *The Firebird*
III: Bartók: Four Pieces op. 12; Berg: *Der Wein*; Wagner: *Wesendoncklieder*
(Norman), Excerpts from *Die Meistersinger*
IV: Bach: Suite no. 2 (Roland Kohloff); Mozart: Two Piano Concerto K. 365
(Anthony and Joseph Parratore); Donatoni: Concertino for strings, brass,
and timpani; Strauss: *Till Eulenspiegel*
V: Debussy: *Nocturnes*; Bartók: Piano Concerto no. 2 (Pollini), *Village
Scenes*; Stravinsky: Symphony of Psalms
VI: Wagner: *Siegfried Idyll*; Mozart: Violin Concerto in G K. K. 216
(Perlman); Varèse: *Ionisation, Arcana*
VII: Schubert: Symphony no. 8; Carter: A Symphony of Three Orchestras*;
Mozart: Piano Concerto in B-flat K. 450 (Garrick Ohlsson); Beethoven:
Overture *Leonora* no. 3

4 February 1977   New York (Cooper Union Great Hall, New York PO)
Albright: *Marginal Worlds*
Berio: *Chemins II* (Greitzer)
Daniel Plante: *Love in the Asylum** (Sanford Sylvan)

23 March 1977   Paris (Salle Pleyel: Orchestre de Paris)
Holliger: *Atembogen*
Berio: *Laborintus II* (Berio narrating)
Boulez: *Rituel*

13 April 1977   London (Festival Hall: BBC SO)
Wagner: Prelude and Liebestod from *Tristan und Isolde*
Schoenberg: *Erwartung* (Martin)
Ravel: *Le tombeau de Couperin*
Stravinsky: Symphony of Psalms

21/23/24 April 1977   London/Paris/Le Havre (National Youth
                        Orchestra)
Bartók: Music for Strings, Percussion, and Celesta
Berg: Violin Concerto (Perlman)
Stravinsky: *The Rite of Spring*

28 April–14 May 1977   New York (Fisher Hall: New York PO)
(final concerts as music director of the orchestra)
I: Bach: Brandenburg Concerto no. 3, Concerto for Oboe d'Amore
       (Thomas Stacy), Suite no. 3; Webern: Symphony; Bartók: Divertimento
II: Crumb: *Star-Child**; Mendelssohn: Symphony no. 4; Ravel: *Le tombeau
       de Couperin*; Stravinsky: Suites nos. 1 and 2
III: Berlioz: *La damnation de Faust*

13 May 1977   New York (Cooper Union Great Hall: New York PO)
Harley Gaber: *The Winds Rise in the North*
Sydney Hodkinson: *The Edge of the Olde One* for electric cor anglais,
strings, and percussion* (Stacy)
Jeffrey Levine: Divertimento*

12–19 June 1977   Paris (Champs-Elysées/de la Ville: EIC)
12:    [Berg: Piano Sonata; Schoenberg: Phantasy; Webern: Four Pieces op. 7;
       Berg: Four Pieces op. 5 (Barenboim, Zukerman, Pay)]; Berg: Chamber
       Concerto (Barenboim, Zukerman)
16:    [Berg: String Quartet (Alban Berg)]; Webern: Five Pieces op. 10;
       Concerto; [String Quartet]; Schoenberg: Three Pieces op. posth.,
       Chamber Symphony no. 1
17:    Schoenberg: Chamber Symphony no. 1, *Herzgewächse*; Webern: Songs
       op. 15, 16 (Bryn-Julson); [Six Bagatelles (Alban Berg)]; Songs op. 18,
       17; [Berg: *Lyric Suite*]
19:    Berg: Chamber Concerto (Barenboim, Zukerman); Schoenberg: *Pierrot
       lunaire* (Minton)

26 July–22 August 1977   Bayreuth
Wagner: *Der Ring des Nibelungen* (Chéreau production)

9–15 September 1977   London (Albert Hall: BBC SO)
9:   Wagner: Prelude and Liebestod from *Tristan und Isolde*; Berg: *Der Wein* (Norman); Ravel: *Daphnis et Chloé*
12: Boulez: *Rituel*; Mahler: Symphony no. 7
15: Ligeti: *San Francisco Polyphony*; Bartók: Piano Concerto no. 2 (Béroff); Stravinsky: *The Firebird*

10/11 October 1977   Paris (Opéra: Orchestre National de l'Opéra)
10: Carter: A Symphony of Three Orchestras; Messiaen: *Oiseaux exotiques* (Aimard); Bartók: *Bluebeard's Castle* (Minton, Nimsgern, Barrault)
11: Zimmermann: Symphony *Die Soldaten*; Bartók: *Bluebeard's Castle* (Minton, Nimsgern, Barrault)

26 October 1977   Paris (Champs-Elysées: Orchestre de Paris)
      Webern: Five Movements op. 5, Variations op. 30, Six Pieces op. 6
      Schoenberg: Four Songs op. 22 (Minton)
      Davies: *Worldes Blis*

3–4 November 1977   Paris/Lyon (BBC SO)
      Crumb: *Star-Child* (Deborah Cook)
      Sinopoli: *Tombeau d'armor II*
      Bartók: Piano Concerto no. 1 (Barenboim)

23 November 1977   London (Festival Hall: BBC SO)
      Debussy: *Jeux*
      Boulez: *Le soleil des eaux* (Manning)
      Schoenberg: Variations op. 31
      Stravinsky: *The Firebird*

30 November/1 December 1977   Paris (Salle Pleyel: BBC SO)
30: Debussy: *Jeux*; Ives: Symphony no. 4 (with Lionel Friend); Berg: *Altenberglieder* (Bryn-Julson); Schoenberg: Variations op. 31
1:   Ligeti: *San Francisco Polyphony*; Lumsdaine: *Hagoromo*; Boulez: *Le soleil des eaux* (Bryn-Julson); Nono: *Il canto sospeso*

7 December 1977   London (Festival Hall: BBC SO)
      Wagner: *Das Liebesmahl der Apostel*
      Schoenberg: Prelude to *Genesis*, *Die Jakobsleiter* (Nimsgern)

19 January 1978   Paris (Théâtre de la Ville: EIC)
      Scherchen-Hsiao: *L'invitation au voyage**

15 February 1978   London (Festival Hall: BBC SO)
      Bartók: Four Pieces op. 12
      Sinopoli: *Tombeau d'armor II*
      Schoenberg: *Von heute auf morgen*

12–20 May 1978   Vienna/Lausanne (BBC SO)
12: Webern: Passacaglia; Bartók: Four Pieces op. 12; Birtwistle: *An Imaginary Landscape*; Boulez: *Rituel*
13: Bartók: Music for Strings, Percussion, and Celesta; Berg: Seven Early Songs (Palmer); Stravinsky: *The Firebird*
20: Schoenberg: *Verklärte Nacht*; Ravel: *Daphnis et Chloé*

July–August 1978   Bayreuth
Wagner: *Der Ring des Nibelungen* (Chéreau production)

2/3 September 1978   Edinburgh (Usher Hall: BBC SO)
2: Schoenberg: *Verklärte Nacht*; Mahler: *Das Lied von der Erde* (Minton, Jung)
3: Boulez: *Rituel*; Stravinsky: *The Nightingale*
(Mahler repeated on the 6th in London with Amoyal in the Berg Violin Concerto)

6 November 1978   Paris (Palais des Congrès: Orchestre de Paris)
Ravel: *Valses nobles et sentimentales*
Berg: Three Pieces op. 6
Mahler: Symphony no. 1

10 December 1978   Paris (Opéra: EIC)
(celebration of Messiaen's seventieth birthday)
Messiaen: *Des canyons aux étoiles . . .* (Loriod)

2 March 1979   Paris (Opéra)
Berg: *Lulu* with Act III* (Chéreau production)

9/12 April 1979   Paris (Théâtre de la Ville: EIC)
9: Birtwistle: *. . . agm . . .**; Grisey: *Modulations*; Stravinsky: *Ragtime, Renard*
12: Schoenberg: Serenade (Shirley-Quirk); Janáček: Capriccio (Alain Planès); Ives: *The Unanswered Question*; Stravinsky: *Ragtime, Renard*

July–August 1979   Bayreuth
Wagner: *Der Ring des Nibelungen* (Chéreau production)

12 September 1979   London (Albert Hall: EIC)
Varèse: *Déserts, Intégrales*
Bartók: *Village Scenes*
Stravinsky: Four Russian Songs for women's choir
Schoenberg: "Lied der Waldtaube" (Elizabeth Connell), Chamber Symphony no. 1, Three Pieces op. posth.

24 October 1979   London (Festival Hall: BBC SO)
Boulez: *Eclat/multiples* (Béroff)

Schoenberg: Piano Concerto (Brendel)
Berg: Three Pieces op. 6

8 November 1979   Paris (Théâtre de la Ville: EIC)
Ligeti: Cello Concerto (Philippe Mullcr)
Ives: *Three Places in New England*
Dufourt: *Antiphysis* for flute and ensemble (István Matúz)
Varèse: *Déserts*

27/28 March 1980   Paris (Théâtre de la Ville: EIC)
27: Schoenberg: Chamber Symphony no. 2, [Two Ballads op. 14], *Ode to Napoleon* (David Wilson-Johnson), Suite op. 29
28: Lenot: *Allégories d'exil IV "Dolcezze ignote all'estasi"**; Carter: *Syringa* (Creffield, Wilson-Johnson); Schoenberg: *Ode to Napoleon*

23–28 April 1980   Paris (Théâtre d'Orsay: EIC)
Educational projects including Eclat/multiples *and movements from Webern: Cantata no. 1*

4 May 1980   Milan (Scala: EIC)
Schoenberg: Suite op. 29
Boulez: *Eclat/multiples*

July–August 1980   Bayreuth
Wagner: *Der Ring des Nibelungen* (Chéreau production)

8/13 October 1980   Paris (Théâtre de la Ville: EIC)
8: Stravinsky: Pastorale, Two Balmont Poems, Three Japanese Lyrics, Four Songs (1953–54), Suites nos. 1 and 2, Three Little Songs, "Tilimbom" (Bryn-Julson); Ravel: *Trois poèmes de Mallarmé*; Webern: Five Pieces op. 10; Boulez: *Improvisations sur Mallarmé I–II*
13: Stravinsky: Concertino, Eight Instrumental Miniatures, *Pribaoutki*, In memoriam Dylan Thomas (Tear), Pastorale, Two Verlaine Songs (Shirley-Quirk); [Scriabin; Roslavets; Debussy]

1 December 1980   Brussels (Palais des Beaux Arts: EIC)
Boulez: *Eclat/multiples*

8/15 December 1980   Paris (Théâtre de la Ville/Châtelet: EIC)
8: Stravinsky: Three Shakespeare Songs, *Berceuses du chat* (Murray); Webern: Concerto; Stockhausen: *Kreuzspiel*
15: Stravinsky: *Pulcinella, Renard, Histoire du soldat* (Chéreau, Planchon, Vitez)

11 March 1981   London (Festival Hall: BBC SO)
Bartók: Four Pieces op. 12, Piano Concerto no. 1 (Barenboim)
Schoenberg: *Die glückliche Hand* (Nimsgern)
Varèse: *Amériques*

29 March 1981   Paris (Opéra)
Ligeti: *Melodien, Ramifications*, Chamber Concerto, *Aventures, Nouvelles aventures*

12 May 1981   Paris (Radio France Grand Auditorium: EIC)
Webern: Concerto, Symphony
Ferneyhough: *Funérailles I*
Berg: Chamber Concerto (Leonskaya, Fried)

26 May 1981   Paris (Champs-Elysées: Orchestre National)
Bartók: Music for Strings, Percussion, and Celesta
Stockhausen: *Punkte*
Berio: *Sinfonia*

10 June 1981   Paris (RF Grand Auditorium: Orchestre National)
Stravinsky: Four Russian Songs for women's choir (two versions), *Les noces* (three versions)

21 September 1981   Paris (Champs-Elysées: EIC)
[Fénelon: *Latitude* for clarinet and ensemble* (Michel Arrignon, Eötvös)]
[Dufourt: *Antiphysis* (Matúz, Eötvös)]
Boulez: *Le marteau sans maître* (Murray)

18 October 1981   Donaueschingen (EIC)
Boulez: *Répons**

29 October 1981   Paris (Champs-Elysées: Orchestre National)
Boulez: *Le soleil des eaux, Le visage nuptial* (Bryn-Julson, Penelope Walker)
Schoenberg: *Pelleas und Melisande*

31 October 1981   Paris (RF Grand Auditorium: EIC)
[Wagner: *Siegfried Idyll* (conducted by Hubert Soudant)]
Boulez: *Messagesquisse*
Liszt: *Via Crucis*
Boulez: *Cummings ist der Dichter*

25/27 November 1981   London/Paris (BBC SO)
Webern: Five Movements op. 5
Boulez: *Livre pour cordes I, Pli selon pli* (Bryn-Julson)

7 December 1981   Paris (Odéon: EIC)
Barraqué: *Séquence* (Manning)
[Kagel: *Transición II* (Aimard, Cerutti)]
Boucourechliev: *Grodek*
Boulez: *Eclat/multiples*

15–17 December 1981   Bobigny (Maison de la Culture: EIC)
Boulez: *Répons*

10 June 1982   Paris (Châtelet: EIC)
Schocnberg: Suite op. 29
Stockhausen: *Mixtur*

6 September 1982   London (Royal Horticultural Hall: EIC)
Boulez: *Répons*

13 February 1983   Bayreuth (Bayreuth Festival Orchestra)
(celebration of the centenary of Wagner's death)
Liszt: *Von der Wiege bis zum Grabe*
Wagner: *Siegfried Idyll*

11 April 1983   Paris (EIC)
Varèse: *Hyperprism, Offrandes, Ecuatorial*
Grisey: *Modulations*
Kurtág: *Messages of the Late Miss R. V. Trusova*

9 October 1983   Strasbourg (EIC, Percussions de Strasbourg)
Varèse: *Intégrales, Octandre, Ecuatorial, Déserts, Hyperprism,
Offrandes, Ionisation*

18–22 October 1983   Paris (Châtelet: EIC)
(four performances)
Davies: *Eight Songs for a Mad King* (David Freeman production)
Ligeti: *Aventures, Nouvelles aventures* (Freeman production)

28 November 1983   Nanterre (Amandiers: EIC)
Webern: Op. 2, 19, 13, 14, 15, 16 (Bryn-Julson), Eight Fragments
[Berg: Piano Sonata, Four Pieces op. 5]
Schoenberg: Four Pieces op. 27, Three Satires (Choeurs de Radio
France)

6–15 December 1983   Vienna/London/Nanterre/Geneva (EIC)
(tour with the following repertory)
Boulez: *Le marteau sans maître* (Bryn-Julson); Ravel: *Trois poèmes de
Mallarmé* (Bryn-Julson); Schoenberg: *Pierrot lunaire* (Laurence), Four
Pieces op. 27, Three Satires; Stravinsky: Two Balmont Poems, Three
Japanese Lyrics (Bryn-Julson); Varèse: *Octandre*; Webern: Op. 8, 10,
14–18, 21, 24; Schoenberg: Chamber Symphony no. 1

9 January 1984   Paris (Théâtre de la Ville: EIC)
Ives: *Three Places in New England*
Zappa: *The Perfect Stranger,* Naval Aviation in Art?* Duprée's
Paradise**

Ruggles: *Vox clamans in deserto* (Lucia Meeuwsen)
Carter: *A Mirror on Which to Dwell* (Meeuwsen)

10 February 1984   Zurich (Collegium Musicum)
Webern: Five Movements op. 5
Schoenberg: String Quartet no. 2 (orchestral version)
Boulez: *Improvisations sur Mallarmé I–II* (Bryn-Julson)

24 February 1984   Festival Hall (BBC SO)
Webern: Six Pieces op. 6, Five Pieces op. 10
Boulez: *Improvisation sur Mallarmé III* (new version),* *Le soleil des eaux* (Bryn-Julson)
Bartók: *The Miraculous Mandarin*

6–20 May 1984   Los Angeles (Royce Hall: Los Angeles PO)
6:   Bartók: *The Miraculous Mandarin*; Boulez: *Notations I–IV*
13: Boulez: *Improvisations sur Mallarmé I–III* (Bryn-Julson)
20: Webern: Five Pieces op. 10; Schoenberg: *Erwartung* (Bryn-Julson); Berg: Three Pieces op. 6; Boulez: *Rituel*

2/3 June 1984   Ojai (Los Angeles PO)
2:   Schoenberg: "Lied der Waldtaube" (Claudine Carlson), Chamber Symphony no. 1; Boulez: *Eclat/multiples*
3:   Berg: Three Pieces from the *Lyric Suite*; Webern: Symphony; Boulez: *Messagesquisse*

22 August 1984   Edinburgh (Usher Hall: BBC SO)
Bartók: *The Miraculous Mandarin*
Berg: *Altenberglieder* (Norman)
Boulez: *Notations I–IV*
Debussy: *Trois ballades de Villon*
Berg: Three Pieces op. 6
(repeated the next day in London and on 18 September in Turin)

20 September 1984   Turin (EIC)
Boulez: *Le marteau sans maître, Domaines*

22 September–19 October 1984   Turin/Basle/Metz/Paris (EIC)
Boulez: *Répons*

10 December 1984   Paris (Champs-Elysées: Orchestre National)
Amy: *Adagio et stretto*

5/8 March 1985   London (BBC/Festival Hall: BBC SO)
5:   Boulez: *Figures-Doubles-Prismes, Cummings ist der Dichter, Rituel*
8:   Boulez: *Rituel*; Stravinsky: Symphonies of Wind Instruments; Webern: Passacaglia, Variations op. 30; Berg: Three Pieces op. 6

29 March–1 April 1985   Baden-Baden (Südwestfunk SO/EIC)
(celebration of Boulez's sixtieth birthday)
29: Boulez: *Répons*
31: Boulez: *Le marteau sans maître* (Laurence)
1:    Boulez: *Rituel, Cummings ist der Dichter, Improvisation sur Mallarmé III, Le soleil des eaux* (Bryn-Julson)

13 May 1985   Paris (Rond-Point: EIC)
    Ferneyhough: *Carceri d'invenzione III*
    Carter: *Penthode**
    Boulez: *Domaines* (André Trouttet)

31 May 1985   Copenhagen (Odd-Fellow Palast: Det Konglige Kapel)
    Berg: *Altenberglieder* (Bryn-Julson)
    Boulez: *Notations I–IV*

29 June–7 July 1985   Tours (Grange de Meslay: EIC)
29: Stravinsky: Symphonies of Wind Instruments, Movements (Richter), Capriccio, *Pulcinella*
30: Ligeti: Chamber Concerto; Berio: *Corale* (Maryvonne Le Dizès-Richard); Boulez: *Eclat/multiples*
5:    Schoenberg: Chamber Symphony no. 2; Höller: *Résonance*)
6:    Carter: *Penthode*; [Berg: Four Songs op. 2, Seven Early Songs; Bartók: *Out of Doors*]; Höller: *Résonance*
7:    [Messiaen: *Poèmes pour Mi*]; Donatoni: *Cadeau**; Schoenberg: Three Pieces op. posth., Chamber Symphony no. 1

26 July 1985   London (Albert Hall: EIC)
    Höller: *Résonance*
    Carter: *Penthode*
    Berio: *Corale* (Le Dizès-Richard)
    Boulez: *Eclat/multiples*

2/4 September 1985   Lucerne (EIC/Basle SO)

20/23 September 1985   Berlin/Venice (Südwestfunk SO)

24 September 1985   Venice (EIC)

3 October 1985   Paris (Salle Pleyel: Orchestre de Paris, EIC)
    [Boulez: *Rituel* (Barenboim)]
    Berg: Chamber Concerto (Barenboim, Accardo)
    Boulez: *Messagesquisse* (Albert Tétard)
    Boulez: *Notations I–IV*

10 October/1 November 1985   London/Vienna (London SO)
    Schoenberg: *Verklärte Nacht*
    Mahler: *Das Lied von der Erde* (Hanna Schwarz, Walter Raffeiner)

29 November–6 December 1985   Nanterre/Epinal/Geneva/Freiburg
(EIC)
(tour with the following repertory)
Boulez; Donatoni; Ligeti

10 January 1986   Paris (Salle Pleyel: Orchestre de Paris, EIC)
Stravinsky: Symphonies of Wind Instruments, *Berceuses du chat,*
Pribaoutki (Jard van Nes)
Ligeti: Double Concerto (Pierre Roullier, Didier Pateau)
Schoenberg: "Lied der Waldtaube" (Van Nes)
Webern: Variations op. 30
Schoenberg: Chamber Symphony no. 2

20 January 1986   Paris (Rond-Point: Orchestre de Paris, EIC)
Schoenberg: *Verklärte Nacht*
Boulez: *Le marteau sans maître*

25 January 1986   Paris (Salle Pleyel: EIC, Orchestre de Paris)
Messiaen: *Sept haïkaï* (Aimard)
Schnittke: Violin Concerto no. 3 (Jean-Pierre Wallez)
Stravinsky: *Pulcinella*

5 March 1986   New York (Columbia University Gymnasium: EIC)
Boulez: [*Dialogue de l'ombre double*], *Répons*

7/9 March 1986   New York (Fisher Hall: EIC)
7:   Donatoni: *Tema*; Höller: *Résonance*; Carter: *Penthode*; Ligeti: Chamber
Concerto
9:   Varèse: *Octandre*; Ives: *Tone Roads nos.1, 3*; Dufourt: *Antiphysis*;
Stockhausen: *Kreuzspiel*; Boulez: *Dérive I*; Schoenberg: Chamber
Symphony no. 1

13/14/15/18 March 1986   New York (Fisher Hall: New York PO)
Stravinsky; Boulez: *Improvisations sur Mallarmé I–III* (Bryn-Julson);
Debussy

27/28/29 March 1986   Boston (Boston SO)
Stravinsky; Boulez: *Notations I–IV*; Ravel

23–24 April 1986   Paris (Salle Pleyel: Orchestre de Paris)
Stravinsky: *The Nightingale*
Ravel: *L'heure espagnole*

18–21 May 1986   Milan/Perugia/Rome (Scala: EIC)

24 May 1986   Bristol (Clifton Cathedral: EIC)
Stravinsky: Eight Instrumental Miniatures

Boulez: *Improvisations sur Mallarmé I–II* (Bryn-Julson)
Ligeti: Chamber Concerto
Debussy: *Danse sacrée et danse profane*
Stravinsky: Two Balmont Songs, Three Japanese Lyrics (Bryn-Julson)
Messiaen: *Oiseaux exotiques* (Aimard)

26 May 1986   Paris (Théâtre de la Ville: EIC)
Dufourt: [?]
Boulez: *Improvisations sur Mallarmé I–II* (Bryn-Julson)
Grisey: *Modulations*
Messiaen: *Oiseaux exotiques* (Aimard)

2–8 June 1986   Paris/Epinal (EIC)

12 June 1986   Copenhagen (Tivoli)

29 August 1986   Venice (Palazzo Grassi: EIC)

13 September 1986   Strasbourg (Palais des Congrès: Südwestfunk SO)
Boulez: *Pli selon pli* (Christine Whittlesey)

23 September 1986   Strasbourg (Palais des Fêtes: EIC)
[Boulez: Sonatina, *Notations*, *Structures II*, *Dialogue de l'ombre double*]
Boulez: *Cummings ist der Dichter, Eclat/multiples*

2/3 October 1986   Basle/Strasbourg (Basle SO)
Boulez: *Figures-Doubles-Prismes, Rituel, Notations I–IV*

6 October 1986   Paris (Rond-Point: EIC)
Donatoni: *Cadeau*
Holliger: *Turm-Musik* for flute, small orchestra, and tape (Aurèle Nicolet)
Boulez: [*Dialogue de l'ombre double* (Damiens)], *Eclat/multiples*

20–22 November 1986   Cleveland (Cleveland Orchestra)
Stravinsky: *Chant du rossignol*
Ravel: *Valses nobles et sentimentales*
Boulez: *Notations I–IV*
Stravinsky: *Petrushka*

26/28/29 November 1986   Cleveland (Cleveland Orchestra)
Boulez: *Pli selon pli* (Phyllis Bryn-Julson)
Bartók: *The Wooden Prince*

14 December 1986   Paris (Salle Pleyel: Orchestre du Conservatoire)
Boulez: *Rituel*; Varèse; Debussy; Messiaen

26 January 1987   Paris (Théâtre de la Ville: EIC)
    Stockhausen: *Mixtur*
    Berio: *Corale* (Le Dizès-Richard)

March 1987   Los Angeles (Chandler Pavilion: Los Angeles PO)
I: Boulez: *Notations I–IV*; Berio: *Corale*; Bartók: *The Wooden Prince*
II: Boulez: *Le soleil des eaux* (Bryn-Julson), *Messagesquisse, Cummings ist der Dichter*; Stravinsky: *Zvezdoliki, The Rite of Spring*

15 March 1987   Los Angeles (Japan-America: LAPO New Music
    Group)
    Schoenberg: *Pierrot lunaire* (Bryn-Julson)
    Boulez: *Le marteau sans maître* (Bryn-Julson)

20/21 May 1987   Paris (Salle Pleyel: Orchestre de Paris, EIC)
    Stravinsky: *Petrushka*
    Strauss: *Burleske* (Barenboim)
    [Schoenberg: *Pierrot lunaire* (conducted by Barenboim)]

17 June 1987   Paris (Salle Pleyel: Orchestre de Paris, EIC)
    Bartók: Music for Strings, Percussion, and Celesta
    Donatoni: *Tema*
    Berio: *Chemins II*
    Schoenberg: Chamber Symphony no. 1

5–16 July 1987   Rouen/Barcelona/Granada/Rome (Orchestre de Paris)
(tour with the following repertory)
    Bartók: Music for Strings, Percussion, and Celesta; Boulez:
    Messagesquisse, Rituel; Ravel; Stravinsky; Varèse

3 August 1987   London (Albert Hall: National Youth Orchestra)
    Schoenberg: *Gurrelieder*

14 October 1987   Los Angeles (Los Angeles PO)
    Boulez: *Improvisations sur Mallarmé I–II, Eclat*
    Webern: Five Pieces op. 10, Concerto

22 October 1987   Chicago (Chicago SO)
    Boulez: *Notations I–IV*

12–13 November 1987   Paris/Nanterre (EIC)
    Schoenberg: *Pierrot lunaire*, "Lied der Waldtaube" (Laurence)
    Stravinsky: Eight Instrumental Miniatures
    [Roussel: Impromptu (Marie-Claire Jamet)]
    Ravel: Introduction and Allegro

17–22 November 1987   Badenweiler/Bologna/Milan (EIC)
Boulez: *Le marteau sans maître* (Laurence), *Dérive I*
Schoenberg: *Pierrot lunaire* (Laurence)

11 January 1988   (Rond-Point: EIC)
[Stockhausen: Piano Piece IX; Messiaen: *Mode de valeurs*; Boulez:
Structures II (Aimard, Chen)]
Webern: Concerto
[Berio: *Sequenza VII* (Pateau)]
Schoenberg: Chamber Symphony no. 1

25 January 1988   London (Festival Hall: BBC SO)
Benjamin: *Ringed by the Flat Horizon*
Boulez: *Le visage nuptial* (new version,* omitting third movement,
Bryn-Julson, Laurence)
Messiaen: *Chronochromie*
Schoenberg: Variations op. 31

27 January 1988   London (Royal College of Music: BBC SO)
Mozart: Adagio and Fugue in C minor K. 546
Mahler: *Rückertlieder* (Murray)
Stravinsky: Symphonies of Wind Instruments
Berlioz: Scenes from *Roméo et Juliette*

16–25 March 1988   Melbourne/Adelaide/Sydney/Wellington (EIC)
(tour with the following repertory)
Berg: Chamber Concerto; Birtwistle: *Secret Theatre*; Boulez: *Dérive I*,
Le marteau sans maître; Schoenberg; Chamber Symphony no. 1;
Stockhausen: *Kontra-Punkte*; Webern: Concerto, Songs op. 8, 13,
Symphony

4 May 1988   London (Elizabeth Hall: EIC)
(celebration of Sir William Glock's eightieth birthday)
Boulez: *Le marteau sans maître* (Laurence)

1–2 June 1988   Paris (Salle Pleyel: EIC, Orchestre de Paris)
Berio: *Laborintus II*
Schoenberg: *Pelleas und Melisande*

15 June 1988   New York (Museum of Modern Art: EIC)
Boulez: *Le marteau sans maître*

16–17 June 1988   Brooklyn (EIC)
16: Webern: Symphony, Concerto; Messiaen: *Oiseaux exotiques*
17: Boulez: *Dérive, Mémoriale*

3 July 1988   Paris (Cour Napoléon: Orchestre National)
Wagner: Overture to *Die Meistersinger*
Berlioz: "Scène d'amour" from *Roméo et Juliette*
Debussy: *Nuages, Fêtes*
Ravel: Suite no. 2 from *Daphnis et Chloé*

11–19 July 1988   Avignon (Callet Quarry at Boulbon: IRCAM)
[Boulez: *Dialogue de l'ombre double*]
Boulez: *Répons*
[Harvey: *Mortuos plango, vivos voco*; Manoury: *Pluton*; Stroppa: Two
Pieces from *Traettoria*; Viñao: Triple Concerto]

20 July 1988   Avignon (Charterhouse Cemetery Cloister: EIC)
Boulez: *Eclat, Improvisations sur Mallarmé I–II, Le marteau sans
maître* (Bryn-Julson)

25–27 July 1988   Rome (Palazzo Farnese: EIC)
25: Boulez: [*Dialogue de l'ombre double* (Damiens)], *Répons*
27: Boulez: *Eclat, Mémoriale, Dérive I, Le marteau sans maître* (Bryn-
Julson)

14 September 1988   London (Albert Hall: BBC SO)
Mahler: Adagio from Symphony no. 10
Webern: Passacaglia
Berg: Seven Early Songs (Norman)
Bartók: *Bluebeard's Castle*

25 September 1988   Douai (EIC)
Boulez: [*Dialogue de l'ombre double* (Damiens)], *Répons*

30 September/1 October 1988   Ulm (EIC)
30: Boulez: *Improvisations sur Mallarmé I–II*; Messiaen: *Oiseaux exotiques*;
Schoenberg: Chamber Symphony no. 1
1: Boulez: [*Dialogue de l'ombre double*], *Répons*

3–10 November 1988   Paris (Salle Pleyel: EIC, Orchestre de Paris)
3–4:Schoenberg: Suite op. 29; Berio: *Concerto II (Echoing Curves)*
(Barenboim); [Debussy: *La mer* (Barenboim)]
9–10:   Schoenberg: Serenade; Höller: Piano Concerto (Barenboim);
[Debussy: *Images* (Barenboim)]
(Schoenberg op. 29 and Berio repeated on 12 November in London with The
Rite of Spring *under Boulez; both programs repeated and on 18–19
November in Berlin)*

15 November 1988   Vienna (Brahmssaal: EIC)
Schoenberg: Suite op. 29
Boulez: *Mémoriale, Le marteau sans maître* (Laurence)

26 November 1988   Paris (Champs-Elysées: EIC)
(celebration of Messiaen's eightieth birthday)
    Messiaen: *Sept haïkaï, Couleurs de la Cité Céleste, Un vitrail et des oiseaux,* Oiseaux exotiques* (Loriod)

11–12 December 1988   London (Elizabeth Hall: EIC)
11: Hurel: *Pour l'image*; Messiaen: *Un vitrail et des oiseaux* (Loriod);
    [Boulez: *Dialogue de l'ombre double* (Damiens)]; Messiaen: *Oiseaux exotiques*
12: Donatoni: *Cadeau*; Carter: *Penthode*; Boulez: *Dérive I*; Carter: Oboe
    Concerto (Holliger)

19 December 1988   Paris (Renaud-Barrault: EIC)
(celebration of Carter's eightieth birthday)
    Carter: *Penthode, A Mirror on Which to Dwell* (Bryn-Julson), *Esprit rude/Esprit doux*, Oboe Concerto (Holliger)

15–19 January 1989   London (Barbican: BBC SO)
15: Boulez: [Piano Sonata no. 2 (Aimard)], *Pli selon pli* (Whittlesey)
17: Boulez: *Livre pour cordes Ia* (new version),* *Figures-Doubles-Prismes, Rituel*
19: Boulez: *Eclat/multiples, Messagesquisse, Cummings ist der Dichter, Notations I–IV*

17 March 1989   Paris (Maison de la Radio: Conservatoire orchestras)
    Stravinsky: *Chant du rossignol*
    Grisey: *Modulations*
    Webern: Five Movements op. 5
    Messiaen: *Chronochromie*

10/20 April 1989   Paris (Châtelet: EIC)
10: Berio: *Chemins II* (Jean Sulem), *Serenata* (Sophie Cherrier), *Corale* (Le
    Dizès-Richard); Strauss: Suite from *Le bourgeois gentilhomme*
20: Berio: *Points on the Curve to Find . . .* (Aimard), *Chemins IV* (László
    Hadady), *Ritorno degli Snovidenia* (Pierre Strauch); Stravinsky:
    Pulcinella

13 May–4 June 1989   Los Angeles/Ojai (Los Angeles PO)

17 November 1989   Paris (Salle Pleyel: BBC SO)
    Stravinsky: *Zvezdoliki*
    Debussy: *Nocturnes*
    Messiaen: *La Ville d'En-haut** (Loriod)
    Boulez: *Le soleil des eaux, Le visage nuptial* (new version complete,*
    Bryn-Julson, Laurence)
(repeated on 23 November in London)

26 November 1989   Huddersfield (Town Hall: BBC SO)
Boulez: *Eclat/multiples*
Stravinsky: Symphonies of Wind Instruments
Messiaen: *La Ville d'En-haut* (Loriod)
Boulez: *Messagesquisse*
Stravinsky: *Chant du rossignol*

18/20 December 1989   Paris/Milan (EIC)
Berio: *Canticum novum testamentum II**

7–8 February 1990   Paris (Salle Pleyel: EIC)
Varèse: *Intégrales*
Dalbavie: *Diadèmes*
Bartók: Four Pieces op. 12
Varèse: *Amériques*

19–24 February 1990   Moscow/Leningrad (EIC)
(two concerts in each city with the following repertory)
Boulez: *Dérive, Le marteau sans maître*; Dalbavie: *Diadèmes*; Donatoni: *Tema*; Ives: *The Unanswered Question*; Kurtág: *Messages of the Late Miss R.V. Trusova*; Schoenberg: Chamber Symphony no. 1; Varèse: *Octandre*; Webern: Five Pieces op. 10

5/6 April 1990   Stuttgart (Südwestfunk SO)
Debussy: *Prélude à "L'après-midi d'un faune," Nocturnes*
Boulez: *Le visage nuptial, Notations I–IV*

May–June 1990   Prague/Milan/Athens (EIC)
(four concerts with the following repertory)
Benjamin: *At First Light*; Boulez: *Dérive, Improvisations sur Mallarmé I–II, Mémoriale, Répons*; Donatoni: *Tema*; Messiaen: *Oiseaux exotiques*; Ravel: *Trois poèmes de Mallarmé*; Varèse: *Intégrales, Octandre*; Xenakis: *Jalons*

11 June 1990   Paris (Châtelet: EIC)
Schoenberg: *Friede auf Erden*
Webern: *Entflieht auf leichten Kähnen*
Boulez: *Cummings ist der Dichter*
Birtwistle: *Meridian* (Sarah Walker)
Stravinsky: *Les noces*

26–28 July 1990   Avignon/Montpellier/Ravenna (Orchestre National)
Varèse: *Intégrales*
Bartók: *The Miraculous Mandarin*
Boulez: *Le soleil des eaux, Le visage nuptial*

3–9 September 1990   Berlin/Cologne/Lucerne/Frankfurt/London
                          (Junge Deutsche Philharmonie)
Debussy: *Jeux*
Messiaen: *Chronochromie*
Boulez: *Notations I–IV*
Varèse: *Amériques*

September–October 1990   Berlin/Amsterdam/Lisbon (EIC)
(six concerts with the following repertory)
    Boulez: *Répons, Dérive, Mémoriale, Le marteau sans maître,* [*Dialogue
    de l'ombre double*]

9–11 November 1990   Badenweiler (EIC)
(three concerts with the following repertory)
    Benjamin: *At First Light*; Boulez: *Derive*; Donatoni: *Cadeau*; Ives: *The
    Unanswered Question*; Mahler/Schoenberg: *Lieder eines fahrenden
    Gesellen*; Petrassi: *Serenata II*; Ravel: Introduction and Allegro;
    Schoenberg: Three Pieces op. posth., Serenade; Stockhausen: *Kontra-
    Punkte*; Stravinsky: Suite from *Histoire du soldat*, Concertino; Varèse:
    Octandre; Wagner: *Siegfried Idyll*; Webern: Symphony; Xenakis:
    Thallein

21 November 1990   London (Festival Hall: BBC SO)
    Debussy: *Images*
    Stravinsky: *The Nightingale*

18 January 1991   Paris (Châtelet: Orchestre de Paris)
    Ravel: *Valses nobles et sentimentules*
    Debussy: *Première rapsodie, Prélude à "L'après-midi d'un faune,"* Jet
    d'eau (Felicity Lott)
    Ravel: *Shéhérazade* (Lott)
    Debussy: *La mer*

30 January/1 February 1991   Paris/London (EIC, Philharmonia)
    Stravinsky: Eight Instrumental Miniatures, Concertino
    Carter: *A Mirror on Which to Dwell, Anniversary*
    Stravinsky: *The Rite of Spring*

21 February 1991   New York (Carnegie Hall: EIC)
    Boulez: *Dérive*
    Webern: Concerto
    [Webern: Piano Variations, Nono: . . . *sofferte onde serene* . . . (Pollini)]
    Boulez: *Mémoriale, Improvisations sur Mallarmé I–II*
    Ligeti: Chamber Concerto

February–March 1991   Cleveland (Cleveland Orchestra)
I: Debussy: *Images, Première rapsodie*; Stravinsky: *Petrushka*

II: Debussy: *Prélude à "L'après-midi d'un faune," Printemps*; Bartók:
      Violin Concerto no. 2 (Mutter); Stravinsky: *The Rite of Spring*

16/18/21 March 1991   Paris/Montbrison/Rome (EIC)
(three concerts with the following repertory)
      Boulez: *Dérive*; Nono: *Canti per tredici*, [*La fabbrica illuminata*];
      Schoenberg: *Pierrot lunaire* (Laurence); Stravinsky: Eight Instrumental
      Miniatures; Varèse: *Octandre*; Webern: Concerto

4–5 April 1991   Paris (Salle Pleyel: Orchestre de Paris)
      Bartók: Music for Strings, Percussion, and Celesta, Violin Concerto no.
      2, *The Miraculous Mandarin*

26/27/29 April 1991   Paris/Lyon/Bordeaux (EIC)
      Bartók: *Village Scenes*
      Lutosławski: *Trois poèmes d'Henri Michaux*
      Ravel/Boulez: *Frontispice*
      Durieux: *Là au-delà*
      Varèse: *Ecuatorial*

May–June 1991   Toronto/Ottawa/Quebec/Montréal/Halifax (EIC)
(tour with the following repertory)
      Boulez: *Dérive, Le marteau sans maître* (Bryn-Julson); Carter: *A Mirror
      on Which to Dwell*; Dalbavie: *Diadèmes*; Garant: *Circuit III*; Ligeti:
      Chamber Concerto; Messiaen: *Oiseaux exotiques*; Schoenberg: Three
      Pieces op. posth.; Varèse: *Octandre*; Webern: Concerto, [Five
      Movements op. 5, String Quartet]

3/9 June 1991   Halifax, Nova Scotia (Halifax Festival Orchestra)
3:   Haydn: Symphony no. 104; Wagner: *Siegfried Idyll*; Schoenberg:
      Chamber Symphony no. 1
9:   Bartók: *The Miraculous Mandarin*; Debussy: *La mer*; Stravinsky: *The
      Rite of Spring*

22 June 1991   Paris (Châtelet: EIC)
      Ravel: *Le tombeau de Couperin*
      Mahler: Four *Wunderhorn* Songs; Two *Kindertotenlieder*
      Stravinsky: *L'histoire du soldat*

15 July 1991   Avignon (Centre Acanthes: EIC)
      Boulez: *Dérive I*
      Carter: *A Mirror on Which to Dwell*

17–21 July 1991   Rome/Siena/Ravenna (EIC)
(tour with the following repertory)
      Berio: *Ritorno degli Snovidenia*; Boulez: *Le marteau sans maître*
      (Laurence); Donatoni: *Cloches III*; Messiaen: *Couleurs de la Cité
      Céleste*; Petrassi: *Estri*; Varèse: *Intégrales*

5 September 1991   Frankfurt (EIC)
Manoury: *Musique II*
Birtwistle: *Secret Theatre*
Berio: *Calmo*
Messiaen: *Oiseaux exotiques*

14–15 October 1991   Paris/London (EIC, Philharmonia)
Berg: Chamber Concerto (Oleg Maisenberg, Kremer), Violin Concerto
(Kremer), Three Pieces op. 6

November–December 1991   Chicago (Chicago SO)
I: Webern: Passacaglia; Höller: Piano Concerto (Barenboim); Stravinsky:
       Scherzo fantastique; Berio: *Concerto II (Echoing Curves)* (Barenboim)
II: Bach/Schoenberg: Prelude and Fugue in E-flat; Berg: Violin Concerto
       (Midori); Schoenberg: *Pelleas und Melisande*
III: Debussy: *Nocturnes*; Bartók: *Cantata profana*, Schoenberg: Variations
       op. 31
IV: Ravel: *Valses nobles et sentimentales, Une barque sur l'océan*; Bartók:
       The Wooden Prince; Ran: *Chicago Skyline*

February–April 1992   Cardiff/Southampton/Birmingham/
Bristol/Paris (Welsh National Opera)
Debussy: *Pelléas et Mélisande* (Peter Stein production)

26 February 1992   London (Barbican: BBC SO)
Birtwistle: . . . *agm* . . .
Boulez: *Notations I–IV*
[Stockhausen: *Gesang der Jünglinge*]
Berio: *Sinfonia*

20 March 1992   Paris (Châtelet: EIC)
Ives: Set for Theater Orchestra
Crumb: *Ancient Voices of Children*
Berio: *Ritorno degli Snovidenia*
Stravinsky: Concerto in E-flat "Dumbarton Oaks"

May 1992   Los Angeles/Ojai (Los Angeles PO)
(twelve concerts with the following repertory)
Bartók: Music for Strings, Percussion, and Celesta, Four Pieces op. 12;
Berg: Seven Early Songs (Bryn-Julson); Cage: Trio for percussion;
Copland: *Short Symphony*; Debussy: *Trois ballades de Villon* (Bryn-
Julson), *Images, La mer*; Mahler: Symphony no. 5; Manoury: *Musique
II*; Ravel: *Ma mère l'oye, Shéhérazade* (Bryn-Julson); Schoenberg:
Pierrot lunaire op. 21 (Bryn-Julson), Chamber Symphony no. 2 op. 38a;
Stravinsky: Four Etudes, *Petrushka, Pulcinella*; Varèse: *Arcana,
Déserts, Ecuatorial, Ionisation*

15–19 August 1992   Salzburg (EIC)
15/19:   Boulez: [*Dialogue de l'ombre double*], *Répons*
16: Varèse: *Intégrales*; Webern: Songs op. 8, 14, 13 (Bryn-Julson); Debussy:
     Danse sacrée et danse profane; Webern: Five Pieces op. 10; Boulez:
     Improvisations sur Mallarmé I–II (Bryn-Julson); Messiaen: *Oiseaux
     exotiques*
18: Stravinsky: Concertino, Eight Instrumental Miniatures, *Berceuses du
     chat*, *Pribaoutki* (Bryn-Julson); Schoenberg: Chamber Symphony no. 1;
     Le marteau sans maître (Bryn-Julson)

24 August 1992   Salzburg (Los Angeles PO)
     Bartók: Four Pieces op. 12
     Berg: Seven Early Songs (Bryn-Julson)
     Debussy: *Images*, *Trois ballades de Villon* (Bryn-Julson)

30 August/10 September 1992   Salzburg/London (Vienna PO)
     Stravinsky: *Chant du rossignol*
     Debussy: *Nocturnes*
     Boulez: *Livre pour cordes*
     Bartók: *The Miraculous Mandarin*

1–5 October 1992   Madrid/Barcelona (EIC)
(four concerts with the following repertory)
     Boulez: *Le marteau sans maître* (Bryn-Julson), *Répons*, [*Dialogue de
     l'ombre double*]; Schoenberg: Chamber Symphony no. 1; Stravinsky:
     Concertino, Eight Instrumental Miniatures, *Berceuses du chat*,
     Pribaoutki (Bryn-Julson)

17 October 1992   Paris (Châtelet: EIC)
     Webern: Op. 2, 19, 17, 16, 24, 15, 10
     Bonnet: *Les eaux étroites**
     Schoenberg: Four Pieces op. 27, Three Satires op. 28

23 October 1992   Paris (Châtelet: EIC)
     Webern: Songs op. 14, 8, 13 (Françoise Pollet), [Piano Quintet, Quartet]
     Ligeti: Cello Concerto, Piano Concerto

25 November–19 December 1992   Chicago (Chicago SO)
I: Stravinsky: *Fireworks*, Four Etudes; Carter: *Three Occasions*; Bartók:
     Concerto for Orchestra
II: Bartók: *Two Pictures*, Dance Suite; Ravel: Piano Concerto for the Left
     Hand (Fleischer); Messiaen: *Et exspecto resurrectionem mortuorum*
III: Bartók: Four Pieces op. 12; Prokofiev: Piano Concerto no. 5 (Alexeev);
     Stravinsky: *The Firebird*
IV: Bach/Stravinsky: *Vom Himmel hoch*; Stravinsky: *Agon, Zvezdoliki, The
     Rite of Spring*

7 December 1992   New York (New York PO)
(the orchestra's sesquicentenary concert, shared with Mehta and Masur)
    Debussy: *La mer*

14–27 January 1993   Birmingham/Nottingham/London (City of
                      Birmingham SO)
(five concerts with the following repertory)
    Bartók: Piano Concerto no. 1 (Zimerman); Boulez: *Notations I–IV,*
    Dérive, Mémoriale; Debussy: *Nocturnes*; Schoenberg: *Pelleas und*
    Melisande, Five Pieces op. 16, Suite op. 29; Stravinsky: *Petrushka*;
    Webern: Cantata no. 1, Variations op. 30, Cantata no. 2, Passacaglia

7/8 February 1993   London/Paris (EIC, Philharmonia)
    Messiaen: *Un vitrail et des oiseaux* (Dimitri Vassilakis)
    Boulez: *Dérive II**
    Carter: Oboe Concerto (Hadady), *Three Occasions*
    Messiaen: *Poèmes pour Mi* (Ewing)

February–March 1993   Cleveland/New York (Cleveland Orchestra)
I: Debussy: *Nocturnes*; Ravel: *Une barque sur l'océan, Alborada del*
    gracioso; Messiaen: *La Ville d'En-haut, Et exspecto resurrectionem*
    mortuorum
II: Debussy: *Jeux*; Bartók: Piano Concerto no. 1 (Schiff); Debussy: *La mer*;
    Messiaen: *Chronochromie*

17–25 March 1993   Berlin (Berlin PO)
(six concerts with the following repertory)
    Bartók: *The Miraculous Mandarin*; Debussy: *Prélude à "L'après-midi*
    d'un faune"; Ravel: *Une barque sur l'océan, Alborada del gracioso,*
    Rapsodie espagnole, Boléro, Ma mère l'oye, Le tombeau de Couperin,
    La valse; Stravinsky: *Scherzo fantastique*; Webern: Six Pieces op. 6

21–23 April 1993   Paris (Salle Pleyel: Orchestre de Paris)
    Wagner: Prelude to *Parsifal*
    Mahler: *Kindertotenlieder* (Waltraud Meier)
    Schoenberg: *Pelleas und Melisande*

5/6/8 May 1993   Paris/Anvers/London (EIC, Philharmonia)
    Schoenberg: *Incidental Music to a Motion Picture Scene* op. 34
    Birtwistle: *Antiphonies** (Joanna MacGregor)
    Stravinsky: *Pulcinella*

13 May 1993   Rome (EIC)
    Donatoni: *Tema*
    Petrassi: *Beatitudines*
    Berio: *O King*
    Stravinsky: *Pulcinella*

21–22 May 1993   Berlin (Staatsoper)
    Mahler: *Totenfeier*
    Schoenberg: *Die Jakobsleiter*

9 June 1993   Lyon (EIC)
    Schoenberg: Five Pieces op. 16
    Ligeti: Violin Concerto (Gawriloff)
    Birtwistle: *Tragoedia*
    Boulez: *Le marteau sans maître* (Laurence)

June–July 1993   London/Paris/Frankfurt/Strasbourg/ Istanbul/Ravenna
                              (London SO)
(tour with the following repertory)
    Bartók: Piano Concerto no. 1 (Barenboim); Debussy: *Jeux*; Schoenberg:
    Five Pieces op. 16, *Erwartung* (Norman); Stravinsky: *The Rite of Spring*,
    Symphonies of Wind Instruments; Webern: Six Pieces op. 6

25 September 1993   Strasbourg (Palais des Fêtes: EIC)
    Dalbavie: *Seuils*
    Boulez: . . . *explosante-fixe* . . . (new version*)

3 October 1993   London (Barbican: London SO)
    Messiaen: *L'Ascension*, *Chronochromie*, *La Ville d'En-haut*, *Poèmes
    pour Mi* (Pollet)

20/21/23 October 1993   Paris/Brussels (Orchestre de Paris)
    Stravinsky: *Scherzo fantastique*
    Berg: Violin Concerto (Mulova)
    Debussy: *Nocturnes*
    Messiaen: *Chronochromie*

11 November 1993   New York (Carnegie Hall: EIC)
    Boulez: . . . *explosante-fixe* . . .
    Manoury: *Partition du ciel et de l'enfer*

November–December 1993   Chicago (Chicago SO)
(ten concerts with the following repertory)
    Bartók: Piano Concertos nos. 1, 3 (Zimerman), *Bluebeard's Castle*,
    Divertimento, *Hungarian Sketches*; Mahler: Symphony no. 6; Rands: *Le
    tambourin*; Ravel: *Rapsodie espagnole*, *Boléro*

14 January 1994   Paris (Centre Pompidou: EIC)
    Charles Edward Lefebvre: *X* . . .

5 April 1994   Paris (Centre Pompidou: EIC)
    Varèse: *Intégrales*
    Boulez: . . . *explosante-fixe* . . .

12 April 1994   Paris (Châtelet: EIC)
Stravinsky: Symphonies of Wind Instruments
Zimmermann: *Stille und Umkehr*
Stravinsky: Two Balmont Poems, Three Japanese Lyrics
Schoenberg: Serenade

22 April–1 May 1994   Los Angeles (Los Angeles PO)
(seven concerts with the following repertory)
     Bartók: *The Miraculous Mandarin*; Boulez: *Le visage nuptial*; Debussy:
     Prélude à "L'après-midi d'un faune," La mer; Ravel: *Une barque sur*
     l'océan, Alborada del gracioso; Schoenberg: *Verklärte Nacht*; Wagner:
     Prelude to *Parsifal*

7–9 May 1994   Vienna (Vienna PO)
Berg: Seven Early Songs (Suzanne Mentzer)
Mahler: Symphony no. 6

22–24 May 1994   Berlin (Berlin PO)
Stravinsky: Symphonies of Wind Instruments, *Chant du rossignol*
Ravel: *Daphnis et Chloé*

19/21/22 June 1994   Cologne/Bologna/Milan (EIC)
(three concerts with the following repertory)
     Bonnet: *Les eaux étroites*; Boulez: *Dérive I–II, Le marteau sans maître,*
     Mémoriale; Fedeli: *Duo en résonance*; Varèse: *Intégrales, Offrandes*

7 August 1994   London (Albert Hall: BBC SO)
Stravinsky: *Symphony of Psalms*
Boulez: *Cummings ist der Dichter*

23–24 August 1994   Salzburg (EIC)
Dalbavie: *Seuils*
Boulez: *. . . explosante-fixe . . .*

27 August 1994   Salzburg (Vienna PO)
Stravinsky: Symphonies of Wind Instruments
Debussy: *Prélude à "L'après-midi d'un faune," Jet d'eau* (Norman)
Ravel: *Shéhérazade* (Norman)
Webern: Six Pieces op. 6
Berg: Three Pieces op. 6

3 September 1994   Edinburgh (EIC)
Boulez: [*Dialogue de l'ombre double*], *Improvisations sur Mallarmé*
I–II, . . . explosante-fixe . . .

27 September 1994   Berlin (EIC)
Webern: [Piano Quintet], Songs op. 17, 16 (Christiane Oelze), Concerto,
Six Songs op. 14

Boulez: *Dérive II–I*
Ligeti: Piano Concerto
Webern: *Entflieht auf leichten Kähnen*, Songs op. 19, 18, 15, Quartet op. 22, Songs op. 8, 13

28–29 September 1994   Berlin (Berlin PO)
    Webern: Cantata no. 2, *Das Augenlicht*, Variations op. 30, Cantata no. 1
    Stravinsky: *Zvezdoliki, The Rite of Spring*

8–12 October 1994   Ludwigshafen/Milan/Rome/Vienna (EIC)
    Berg: Three Pieces from the *Lyric Suite*
    Webern: Concerto, Five Pieces op. 10
    Schoenberg: *Von heute auf morgen*

3–11 November 1994   Cleveland (Cleveland Orchestra)
(six concerts with the following repertory)
    Mahler: Symphony no. 7; Messiaen: *Poèmes pour Mi*; Ravel: Piano Concerto in G (Zimerman), *Valses nobles et sentimentales* [also piano version (Zimerman)]; Stravinsky: *Scherzo fantastique, Fireworks*

November–December 1994   Chicago (Chicago SO)
(thirteen concerts with the following repertory)
    Bartók: Music for Strings, Percussion, and Celesta, *The Miraculous Mandarin*; Berio: *Sinfonia*; Boulez: *Le visage nuptial*; Debussy: *Première rapsodie*; Mahler: Symphony no. 7; Strauss: *Metamorphosen*; Webern: Passacaglia, Six Pieces op. 6, Five Movements op. 5

4 December 1994   Chicago (Civic Orchestra)
    Boulez: *Rituel*

January–May 1995   London/Paris/New York/Vienna/Linz (London SO)
(seventieth-birthday tour with the following repertory)
    Bartók: Piano Concerto no. 2 (Béroff, Pollini), Violin Concerto no. 2 (Chung), *The Miraculous Mandarin*; Berg: Seven Early Songs, *Altenberglieder* (Norman), Violin Concerto (Mutter); Boulez: *Notations I–IV, Figures-Doubles-Prismes, Messagesquisse, Livre pour cordes, Improvisation sur Mallarmé III* (Laura Aiken); Debussy: *La mer, Prélude à "L'après-midi d'un faune"*; Messiaen: *Poèmes pour Mi* (Ewing), *Chronochromie*; Ravel: *Le tombeau de Couperin, Ma mère l'oye*; Stravinsky: *Petrushka, The Rite of Spring, Chant du rossignol*; Webern: Six Pieces op. 6

24/26 February 1995   Paris (Cité de la Musique: EIC)
    Boulez: *Rituel*

30–31 March/1 April 1995   Chicago (Chicago SO)
Debussy: *Jeux, Ibéria*
Bartók: Piano Concerto no. 1 (Barenboim)
[Boulez: *Notations I–IV* (Barenboim)]

May–June 1995   Tokyo (London SO, EIC, NHK SO, Chicago SO)
(eight concerts with the following repertory)
Bach/Schoenberg: Prelude and Fugue in E-flat; Bach/Stravinsky: *Vom Himmel hoch*; Bach/Webern: Ricercare; Bartók: Piano Concertos nos. 1 (Barenboim), 2 (Pollini), *The Miraculous Mandarin*; Berg: Seven Early Songs, *Altenberglieder* (Norman), Chamber Concerto (Barenboim, Kremer); Berio: *Sinfonia*; Boulez: *Livre pour cordes, Répons, Le marteau sans maître* (Stene), [*Dialogue de l'ombre double*]; Dalbavie: *Diadèmes*; Debussy: *Prélude à "L'après-midi d'un faune," La mer*; Messiaen: *Chronochromie*; Ravel: *Le tombeau de Couperin, Daphnis et Chloé*; Schoenberg: Chamber Symphony no. 1, Three Pieces op. posth., [Phantasy (Kremer, Barenboim)]; Stockhausen: *Kontra-Punkte*; Stravinsky: *Symphony of Psalms*, Suite from *Pulcinella, The Rite of Spring*; Webern: Passacaglia, Six Pieces op. 6, Five Pieces op. 10

6 June 1995   Brussels (Monnaie: EIC)
Boulez: *Répons*, [*Dialogue de l'ombre double*]

17–18 June 1995   Berlin (Staatsoper)
Debussy: *Nocturnes*
Bartók: Piano Concerto no. 1
Boulez: *Le visage nuptial*

10–16 July 1995   Paris (Cité de la Musique: summer academy with EIC)
Carter: *Penthode*
Schoenberg: Chamber Symphony no. 1
Boulez: *Originel* from . . . *explosante-fixe* . . .
Varèse: *Déserts*

25 July 1995   London (Albert Hall: BBC SO)
Bartók: Music for Strings, Percussion, and Celesta
Debussy: *Jeux, Trois ballades de Villon, Jet d'eau*
Boulez: *Le soleil des eaux*
Messiaen: *Et exspecto resurrectionem mortuorum*

24/28 August 1995   Colmar/Edinburgh (EIC)
[Berg: Four Pieces op. 5]
Webern: Concerto, Five Pieces op. 10
Mahler/Schoenberg: *Lieder eines fahrenden Gesellen*
Schoenberg: "Lied der Waldtaube", Chamber Symphony no. 1

4 October 1995   Amsterdam (Netherlands Opera)
(nine subsequent performances)
    Schoenberg: *Moses und Aron* (Peter Stein production)

27 October 1995   Amsterdam (Concertgebouw)
    Ravel: *Ma mère l'oye*
    Debussy: *Trois ballades de Villon*
    Boulez: *Notations I–IV*
    Schoenberg: *Accompaniment to a Film Scene*
    Berg: *Altenberglieder*, Three Pieces op. 6

10 November 1995   Paris (Châtelet: EIC)
    Schoenberg: *Von heute auf morgen*

24 November–16 December 1995   Chicago (Chicago SO)
I: Boulez; Debussy: Suite from *Le martyre de Saint-Sébastien*; Strauss: *Till Eulenspiegel*
II: Schumann: Overture, Scherzo and Finale; Mahler: Symphony no. 9
III: Dukas: *La péri*; Debussy: *La mer*; Varèse: *Ionisation, Amériques*
IV   Ravel: *Le tombeau de Couperin, Pavane pour une infante défunte*, Piano Concerto for the Left Hand; Berg: Three Pieces from the *Lyric Suite*, Three Pieces op. 6

Compact Discography

Note: Recording dates are noted within parentheses.

C. P. E. Bach: Flute Concerto in D minor, Cello Concerto in A major (1964)
Harmonia Mundi HMP 390545

Bartók: Piano Concerto no. 2 (1966)   Montaigne TCE 8800
————: *The Wooden Prince* (1975), Music for Strings, Percussion, and Celesta
(1967), Dance Suite (1972)   Sony SM2K 64100
————: Concerto for Orchestra (1972)   Sony MK 37259
————: *The Miraculous Mandarin* (1971), Four Pieces op. 12 (1977), *Village
Scenes* (1977)   Sony SMK 45837
————: *Bluebeard's Castle* (1976)   Sony SMK 64110
————: *Cantata profana, The Wooden Prince* (1991)   DG 435 863
————: Four Pieces op. 12, Concerto for Orchestra (1992)   DG 437 826
————: *Dance Suite, Two Pictures, Hungarian Sketches*, Divertimento
(1992–93)   DG 445 825
————: *Bluebeard's Castle* (1993)   DG 447 040
————: *The Miraculous Mandarin*, Music for Strings, Percussion and Celesta
(1994)   DG 447 747

Berg: Three Pieces op. 6 (1966)   Montaigne TCE 8800 / Enterprise LV 915/6
————: *Wozzeck* (1966)   CBS M2K 30852
————: Suite from *Lulu, Der Wein*, Three Pieces from the *Lyric Suite* (1974–77)
SMK 45838
————: Chamber Concerto (1977)   DG 423 237
————: *Lulu* (1979)   DG 415 489
————: *Altenberglieder* (1984), Seven Early Songs (1987–88)   Sony SK
66826

Berio: *Serenata I* (1957)   Adès 14164
————: *Sinfonia* (1981), *Eindrücke*   Erato 2292 45228

————: *Ritorno degli Snovidenia, Chemins II, Chemins IV, Corale, Points on the Curve to Find . . .* (1989)   Sony SK 45862

Berlioz: *Nuits d'été* (1973)   Artists FED 041/2
————: *Symphonie fantastique, Lélio* (1968), Overture and Entr'acte from *Béatrice et Bénédict, Chasse royale et orage,* Overture to *Benvenuto Cellini,* Overture *Le carnaval romain* (1971–72), *Nuits d'été, La mort de Cléopâtre* (1976)   Sony SM3K 64103

Birtwistle: . . . *agm* . . . (1982)   Erato 2292 45410
————: *Tragoedia, Five Distances, Secret Theatre*   DG 439 910

Boulez: *Poésie pour pouvoir* (1958)   Col Legno AU 031 800
————: *Improvisations sur Mallarmé I–II* (1959)   Stradivarius 10028
————: *Le soleil des eaux* (1964)   EMI CDM 7 63948
————: *Le marteau sans maître* (1964)   Adès 14073
————: *Le soleil des eaux* (1966)   Stradivarius 10029
————: *Rituel* (1976), *Eclat/multiples* (1981)   Sony SMK 45839
————: *Pli selon pli* (1981)   Erato ECD 88074
————: *Le marteau sans maître* (1985)   CBS MK 42619
————: *Figures-Doubles-Prismes* (1985), *Le soleil des eaux, Le visage nuptial* (1989)   Erato 2292 45494
————: *Cummings ist der Dichter, Dérive, Mémoriale* (1990)   Erato 2292 45648
————: . . . *explosante-fixe* . . . (1994)   DG 445 833-2

Brahms: *Ein deutsches Requiem* (1973)   Memories HR 4493/4

Carter: Oboe Concerto, *Penthode, A Mirror on Which to Dwell* (1988)   Erato ECD 75553

Dallapiccola: *Cinque canti* (1958)   Stradivarius 10029

Debussy: *Jeux* (1966)   Montaigne TCE 8800 / Enterprise LV 915/6
————: *La mer, Prélude à "L'après-midi d'un faune," Jeux* (1966)   CBS MYK 37261
————: *Pelléas et Mélisande* (1970)   Sony SM3K 47265
————: *Prélude à "L'après-midi d'un faune," Images, Printemps* (1991)   DG 435 766
————: *Nocturnes, Première rapsodie, Jeux, La mer* (1991/93)   DG 439 896

Donatoni: *Tema* (1985), *Cadeau* (1986)   Erato 2292 45366

Dufourt: *Antiphysis* (1982)   Erato ECD 88261

Ferneyhough: *Funérailles I–II* (1981)   Erato ECD 88261

Grisey: *Modulations* (1983)   Erato 2292 45410

Kurtág: *Messages of the Late Miss R. V. Trusova* (1983)   Erato 2292 45410

Ligeti: *Aventures* (1981), *Ramifications*, Chamber Concerto (1982)   DG 423 244
————: Cello Concerto, Piano Concerto (1992), Violin Concerto (1993)   DG 439 808

Mahler: Symphony no. 5 (1968)   Enterprise LV 901/2
————: *Das klagende Lied* (1970)   Sony SK 45841
————: Symphony no. 5 (1970)   Arkadia CDGI 718 1
————: Symphony no. 9 (1972)   Memories HR 4493/4 / Enterprise LV 901/2
————: Symphony no. 2 (1973)   Enterprise LV 915/6
————: Symphony no. 6 (1973)   Artists FED 032 / Enterprise LV 995
————: Symphony no. 8 (1975)   Artists FED 041/2
————: Symphony no. 6 (1994)   DG 445 835

Messiaen: *Sept haïkaï* (1964)   Adès 14073
————: *Couleurs de la Cité Céleste, Et exspecto resurrectionem mortuorum* (1965)   Erato ECD 71587
————: *Sept haïkaï, Couleurs de la Cité Céleste, Un vitrail et des oiseaux, Oiseaux exotiques* (1988)   Montaigne WM 332
————: *Chronochromie, La Ville d'En-haut, Et exspecto resurrectionem mortuorum* (1993)   DG 445 827
————: *Poèmes pour Mi* (1994)   DG *(forthcoming)*

Ravel: *Menuet antique, La valse, Daphnis et Chloé*, Overture *Shéhérazade, Rapsodie espagnole, Valses nobles et sentimentales, Ma mère l'oye, Fanfare pour "L'éventail de Jeanne," Alborada del gracioso, Le tombeau de Couperin*, Concerto for the Left Hand, *Pavane pour une infante défunte, Une barque sur l'océan, Boléro* (1972–83)   Sony SM3K 45842
————: *Shéhérazade, Trois poèmes de Mallarmé, Chansons madécasses, Don Quichotte à Dulcinée, Cinq mélodies populaires grecques* (1972–79) Sony SMK 64107
————: *Ma mère l'oye, Une barque sur l'océan, Alborada del gracioso, Rapsodie espagnole, Boléro* (1993)   DG 439 859
————: *Daphnis et Chloé, La valse* (1994)   DG 447 057

Roussel: Symphony no. 3 (1975)   Sony SMK 64107

Schoenberg: *Pelleas und Melisande* (1970)   Arkadia CDHP 585
————: *Gurrelieder* (1974), Four Songs op. 22 (1981)   Sony SM2K 48459
————: *Moses und Aron* (1975), Chamber Symphony no. 2 (1982)   Sony SM2K 48456
————: *Die Jakobsleiter* (1977), Chamber Symphony no. 1 (1981), *Incidental Music to a Motion Picture Scene* (1977)   Sony SMK 48462

————: *Erwartung* (1977), *Pierrot lunaire* (1977), "Lied der Waldtaube" (1981)   Sony SMK 48466

————: *A Survivor from Warsaw* (1976), *Friede auf Erden*, Four Pieces op. 27, Three Satires, *Dreimal tausend Jahre, De profundis* (1982), Six Pieces op. 35, *Kol nidre, Modern Psalm* (1984), Three Folksongs op. 49, Two Goethe Canons, Three German Folksongs (1986)   Sony S2K 44571

————: *Pelleas und Melisande*, Variations op. 31 (1991)   Erato 2292 45827

Scriabin: *Le poème de l'extase* (1975)   Sony SM2K 64100

Stockhausen: *Punkte* (1963)   Col Legno AU 031 800

Stravinsky: Four Etudes, *Zvezdoliki*, Symphonies of Wind Instruments, *A Sermon, a Narrative, and a Prayer, The Rite of Spring* (1963)   Montaigne TCE 8800

————: *The Rite of Spring* (1963)   Cetra CDE 3008

————: *Elegy for J. F. K., Abraham and Isaac* (1965)   Stradivarius 10029

————: *Petrushka* (1971), *The Rite of Spring* (1969)   Sony MK 42395

————: Suite from *The Firebird* (1967), Suite from *Pulcinella* (1975), *Scherzo fantastique* (1975), Suites nos. 1 and 2 (1980)   Sony SMK 45843

————: *The Firebird, Chant du rossignol* (1976)   Sony MK 42396

————: Songs (1980)   DG 431 751

————: *Ebony Concerto*, Eight Instrumental Miniatures, "Dumbarton Oaks" (1980)   DG 2531 378

————: Three Japanese Lyrics, Concertino (1987–88)   Montaigne MO 780518

————: *Pulcinella, Chant du rossignol, The Nightingale*, Four Russian Songs, Four Etudes, *Histoire du soldat*, Concertino (1980–81)   Erato 4509 98955

————: *Petrushka, The Rite of Spring* (1991)   DG 435 769

————: *The Firebird, Fireworks*, Four Etudes (1992)   DG 437 850

Varèse: *Hyperprism, Octandre, Intégrale* (1959)   Adès 14164

————: *Ionisation, Amériques, Offrandes, Arcana, Octandre, Intégrales* (1975–83)   Sony SK 45844

————: *Ionisation* (1987–88)   Montaigne MO 780518

Wagner: *Parsifal* (1970)   DG 435 718

————: Overtures *Die Meistersinger, Tannhäuser, Faust, Tristan und Isolde, Siegfried Idyll* (1973–78)   Sony SMK 64108

————: *Der Ring des Niebelungen* (1980)   Philips 434 421/422/423/424

Webern: *Das Augenlicht*, Cantatas nos. 1 and 2 (1966)   Stradivarius 10029

————: Complete works (1967–72)   Sony SM3K 45845

————: Five Pieces op. 10 (1987–88)   Montaigne MO 780518

————: Op. 2, 8, 10, 13–19, 22, 24 (1992–94)   DG 437 786

Xenakis: *Jalons* (1990)   Erato 2292 45770

Video Discs

Wagner: *Der Ring des Niebelungen* (1980)   Philips 070 501/502/503/504

Debussy: *Pelléas et Mélisande* (1992)   DG 440 072 531

Boulez in Salzburg (concert of 30 August 1992)   DG 440 072 244

Index

This index includes principal names appearing in the interviews and notes. Page numbers beginning with 141 refer to notes.

251